NIGHTSHINING

ALSO BY JENNIFER KABAT

The Eighth Moon: A Memoir of Belonging and Rebellion

NIGHTSHINING

A Memoir in Four Floods

JENNIFER KABAT

MILKWEED EDITIONS

Published 2025 by Milkweed Editions
Printed in Canada
Cover design by Mary Austin Speaker
Author photo by CJ Harvey
25 26 27 28 29   5 4 3 2 1
First Edition

Library of Congress Cataloging-in-Publication Data

Names: Kabat, Jennifer, 1968- author.
Title: Nightshining / Jennifer Kabat.
Description: Minneapolis : Milkweed Editions, 2025. | Summary: "A braided memoir about flooding in the Catskills, the region's history regarding GE and cloud seeding, and the author's personal experiences."-- Provided by publisher.
Identifiers: LCCN 2024032923 (print) | LCCN 2024032924 (ebook) | ISBN 9781639550708 (paperback) | ISBN 9781639550715 (ebook)
Subjects: LCSH: Kabat, Jennifer, 1968- | Upstate New York--History, Local. | Floods--New York (State)--Catskill Mountains--History. | Rain-making--Research--United States--History. | Schaefer, Vincent J.--Influence. | General Electric Company. Research Laboratory--History. | Catskill Mountains Region (New York State)--Climatic changes. | Natural history--Upstate New York. | Women authors, American--Biography. | Margaretville (N.Y.)--Biography.
Classification: LCC F126.8 .K333 2025 (print) | LCC F126.8 (ebook) | DDC 974.7/38043092 [B]--dc23/eng/20241125
LC record available at https://lccn.loc.gov/2024032923
LC ebook record available at https://lccn.loc.gov/2024032924

Milkweed Editions is committed to ecological stewardship. We strive to align our book production practices with this principle, and to reduce the impact of our operations in the environment. We are a member of the Green Press Initiative, a nonprofit coalition of publishers, manufacturers, and authors working to protect the world's endangered forests and conserve natural resources. *Nightshining* was printed on acid-free 100% postconsumer-waste paper by Friesens Corporation.

For my father and for my friends

"The concept of the historical progress of mankind cannot be sundered from the concept of its progression through a homogenous, empty time. A critique of the concept of such a progression must be the basis of any criticism of the concept of progress itself."

—WALTER BENJAMIN
Theses on the Philosophy of History

NIGHTSHINING

Part I

Chapter 1

You and I are with Iris and her baby on a cliff edge in the Catksills as I tell this story. Farm fields quilt the valley below. Looking down it, other bluffs like this, long and flat, frame the view. I imagine the mountains all filled in and the land a thousand feet higher in the air, as if we are all floating, levitating together.

The sun has burned off the fog, and the sky is a cerulean so bright language fails it. Two hawks screech past, floating on thermals. Light catches in Iris's hair. Her mass of curls and corkscrews is illuminated like a halo. It is a few days after the solstice, and we wear cutoffs and masks because it is June 2020. Hers is emblazoned BLM. Mine bears the Maltese cross of my volunteer fire department. The hike to this plateau is teeming with children—so many it feels dystopian, like the world is ending, and maybe it is. It is also a pandemic, where we have been told to be scared of each other and are unsure how to be together, even outside. Sharing space feels transgressive and transcendent. Behind us people have strung hammocks between the few trees at the summit, and country music plays. The kids climb past in their shorts and high-top sneakers, flip-flops and T-shirts emblazoned with sports teams and school names, owls, unicorns, and dinosaurs.

On the trail, I love most the one little girl in an impractical lace sundress and sandals. I love, too, this

Whitmanesque sense of nature, us all together, asses and elbows, bodies sharing breath and space; that in this catastrophe we have taken en masse to the outdoors. This is not some Thoreau or Emersonlike bracing experience of the individual in the wilderness, the self against the world. I ask the girl if she likes hiking. She buries her head in her father's legs.

And, I see myself in a Snoopy sweatshirt in the photo my father takes when I am six: blond hair gold in the light and a view of Vermont several thousand feet below. He has carried me up these heights as I complain, and I stand with him on the granite ledge. Before me is some kind of a bird, a brown hen, I now know is a grouse. He takes a picture of me, and in it I shrug. Maybe at the bird and this view, as if they are nothing, or his work in delivering me to the summit, nothing.

Now Iris waves at a field a thousand feet below. Silver flares of light reflect off cars as they park. She asks if that's a U-pick farm, and I say yes, I did pick strawberries there a few days ago with my husband, David. The woman who weighed our baskets told us it's the busiest start ever. People are worried about food and supply chains. The farm just opened for the season, and already the fields are nearly picked clean.

At our feet names are carved into a long, flat boulder, so big and broad it's called the dance floor. It is sedimentary stone from a sea nearly 400 million years old, and in a time frame closer to ours it was covered in moss. Sometime a century ago, people rolled the moss up like a giant carpet and started inscribing their names into stone. "LEO" is rounded as if carved in Arial. "Frank and Lydia" came in 1985. An arrow points to Frank's name and the date. In what seems to me an act of hubris, "JA & GB" only put "86" after their initials. Is it 1886 or 1986? Or, don't they think it will one day be 2086? Maybe JA and GB just give up. Or, perhaps that year 2086 is unreachable, impossible, and we will never make it that far.

The biggest carving reads "DOW VROMAN," and this hill is called Vroman's Nose, not for the person whose name is incised in grand serifs but his forebear who steals the land from the Mohawks, who've lived here for millennia. I tell Iris that the farm below sits on the grounds of a Mohawk village. Onistagrawa. I sound out the word with the long "youh" of the first syllable and "nee-sta-grawa" as I've been taught to say it. At its margin is a river that's called a creek, the Schoharie Creek, spelled Skóhare in Mohawk. The creek runs north and gives its name to this county and region.

Onistagrawa means "the place where the corn grows by the hill," and the people whose land this is do not name themselves Mohawk. Here they are the Skóhare, part of the Kanien'kehá:ka, the people of the flint place. Their lands extend almost all the way to the Hudson River and north through the Adirondacks into Canada. At the foot of this bluff, the Skóhare Mohawks take in refugees from white colonization, Mohicans and Munsee Lenape and others, all together, even, I will learn soon, white refugees from British tyranny and greed.

On the way up, boulders are scarred with striations, glacial chatter it's called, as if we can hear the ice. And, I want the names at our feet to talk, everyone here speaking, jostling together outside—this communion of us in nature. I picture the public, a collective body that cuts across time and is impossible to pin down outside the frail two letters, U and S, of the first-person plural. I want all of it—all of us—plus the girl in her impractical dress, the people in hammocks, and the clouds. They are lazy in the sky, a blue I learn that if not for vapor, for aerosols, would be black. Those aerosols are in the news, too, now, as our breath is an aerosol that carries a virus.

Iris gestures to a wobbly 1929 in the rock. Was it before or after the crash? she wonders. The jump down is precipitous. The twang of guitar catches in the air. I imagine us all waltzing together on this dance floor. I rock the baby and have come here for a dead man. He draped the landscape in smoke. He brings floods and clouds and studies forest fires. I have been tracking him now a half dozen years, and he loved this mountain. I have come to love him too, even though a technology he develops destroys my village in a flood in 1950. It is the floods that carry me here.

This summer (and every summer is now this summer) will bring the worst fire season in the West and brush fires in my town. Greenland's ice sheet will melt beyond repair. People die in deluges around the world, and for this moment we stand here together—you and Iris and her baby and me, and the man I've come searching for. Vince—his name is Vincent Schaefer—and I learn of him after my second flood.

Chapter 2

THE FIRST FLOOD COMES MY first year in Margaretville, New York, a tiny village in the Western Catskills where at that point, the population is around 594. It is early morning, and a friend tries to rouse me.

He pounds on my bedroom door.

I've moved from London to a Victorian house with gingerbread, it's called, for the fancy details outside, like a house in a fairy tale. It also has a turret, and right now my husband, David, is away for work and I am asleep in the turret like Rapunzel, like some princess, like, wake up now, Jennifer, like hearing voices call, *Jen, Jen*, in my dreams.

Only I am drugged. Sleeping pills. Zolpidem tartrate.

And, this turret is not a turret at all, just a bulge inside the house. From the street, yes, it has that Rapunzel-let-down-your-hair look, even three inset windows. Inside, however, the walls simply curve around and are just big enough to fit the headboard of a queen-sized bed in this Queen Anne Victorian home, and me, on Ambien.

I've taken it to drown out the banging of rocks in the stream outside. The boulders in the century-old walls lining the banks pummel each other with the force of water lifting and dropping each rock as the creek rises. They strike with heavy thuds, a resounding bass that crashes through the house, through the bed, through my shoulders and neck.

Jen, Jennifer! Wake up. I smell gas.

The word gas is repeated more than once.

—

The stream is called Bull Run, and in all my years here I never learn why it has that name. My guess is that this now, today, is the reason. It is running like a bull, and I will come to know that the straighter the stream, the faster it runs. To straighten it is to try to get it to obey the laws of our world—rationality and order (or what seems like order)—and to abide by where we put our roads and houses. Walling it in only makes the water race faster, higher, with more danger in moments like this, in a wet summer when it has been raining all day and all night and into this moment now with this banging about the gas.

My friend, Free, his name is, he's staying with us while David is back in the UK. Free is 6'5", maybe taller, with the broad torso of one who lifts weights and wears muscle shirts to accentuate said weightlifting. He is also gentle and shy, too shy to barge into my bedroom even in a disaster. His Long Island accent presses down on the "g" of gas, and that gas he repeats is an immediate danger. I am finally awake, and he is amazed that I did not smell anything because I can smell cigarettes from a hundred yards off—not to mention drier sheets and perfume. I'm allergic to them all, as well as mold, mildew, and car exhaust. That sleeping pill, however, has pushed everything aside and left just fog, clouds, and blur.

Downstairs. Somehow I am in the basement in a T-shirt. It is not just gas leaking but water. It is a flood. A 2,000-gallon heating oil tank is stuck under the bridge a dozen feet from my kitchen door, and water, brown, red, and muddy, laps at the basement door. I have yet to have coffee, but a precise awareness dawns. My house is about to be inundated. I grab everything I can off the floor. A cooler, dirty laundry, a bag of birdseed. I shove them all on the washer. The water seeps in through angled metal doors in the ground that make me think of the storm cellar where Dorothy hides in the *Wizard of Oz*. An inch rises, then another. Water creeps closer. It pools in the middle where the floor slopes imperceptibly. I run back upstairs to the window to see what is happening outside. Water overtakes our yard and the neighbors'. My mouth tastes of copper—pennies and panic. Free runs after me. We peer out the window. The heating oil tank slips loose. Free and I cheer. I don't know yet that it has floated off a concrete pad where it stood behind a house, up this stream called Bull Run.

We celebrate our luck of disaster averted; only a small bit of water, easy to dry, less than an inch really. We will be fine. A year ago when David and I were buying the house, moving here to escape London's pollution that was making me sick, we asked the realtor about the foundation's ability to survive floods. We ask specifically of a historic flood that came a decade before. The real estate agent promises the building was unscathed. Back then the house was fine, and now we are fine, and it is fine. I call David and tell him we are fine. There is a flood but we are fine.

Until we are not fine.

The oil tank gets moored under the next bridge thirty feet down.

This tank, big and hulking, is wedged under that bridge. Water backs up farther, closer, higher and nearer to my door. The bridge collapses. I cannot see this collapse. A hole has opened in the roadway big enough to swallow a car, and the tank is trapped. Together with the bridge's debris, they create a dam. What I see is water. Waves rush toward my house and down again, like the ocean, like a red sea on the lawn, crashing and breaking. The swells pound up toward us and back into the neighbor's yard. The water blows out their windows.

—

By the time you read this, people in cities have witnessed such waters, but then, in every city where I've lived—New York, London, San Francisco, and Washington, DC— water is tamed, contained. In London it's hidden in a culvert under my road, the River Effra. You won't even know it exists. It is just the name of a street, and if you search for information, legend has it that King Canute sailed up it and the first Queen Elizabeth down, one escaping Danish invaders, the other the Virgin Queen, to see Walter Raleigh, her maybe lover.

That previous summer when we are buying the house, the realtor comments on the babbling brook, with its lulling dulcet sounds.

—

We move to this house with the gingerbread to be on the East Coast, closer to my elderly parents and away from London's pollution. I am sensitive not just to perfume and drier sheets but also smoke—car exhaust and cigarettes, bonfires, and diesel fumes; plus forest fires, mold and mildew—a litany of dangers carried in the air, invisible to the eye. In the UK I long tried to pretend they are not a problem, so here I think I am safe. I have to be.

Waves three feet high crest at the basement door. I watch from the stairs as the room fills slowly. Mud, sludge, and stream rise, and we are lucky. We live near the headwaters, meaning the water has yet to collect many pollutants, just the tank and its oil. And, this, too, is fortuitous, someone will say.

There is a red switch at the top of the stairs for the boiler, and I don't know I am supposed to turn it off, to protect it from the flood. The water stops less than an inch from the boiler's mechanisms. And that, too, is lucky.

Less lucky: outside there is a crash and thud. The stream wall tumbles into the current. I watch from a window at the back of the house with the best view. It's not enough though really to see. I run outside. Torrents swallow the dirt. Wall dissolves into mud. I realize I shouldn't stand here. The ground is unstable, subsiding. The stream is a foot from our foundation.

We are fine, but we are not so lucky.

Volunteer firefighters—men in high-vis florescent vests, the color of blue-collar work and road construction—close the street. Traffic is diverted. The tank fished from the stream. The water goes down—except in my basement where five inches remain, more in the middle with the sloping floor.

———

Zoom out and to see me from above; I am brittle and taut. My cheek throbs, a muscle spasms. I am on the phone with a hardware store. How do I know what I need from the store? The answer comes in a flash. A prism of light, the prism of thought, everything fragmented, urgent and pulsing because not to manage this is too frightening.

My voice sharp with panic, I say, yes, a dehumidifier and pump and Shop-Vac—wet vac. Yes.

I read out a credit card number. I hang up the phone. It is an actual telephone, a landline that hangs on the wall of the kitchen.

I exhort Free to drive me in his pickup to the hardware store seven miles away.

He says kindly, gently, that the roads are closed.

I beg. I promise: Your truck it will be fine. It's higher; it's high enough. We will go the back route. It's higher too, I say, and not flooded. How do I know this? (I do not.)

There are lines people say about driving in a flood, about crossing flooded roadways, facts about how easy it is— just a few inches of water—to sweep you away. You can see the phrases flashed on signs over the interstate in an emergency. Weather forecasters repeat these sayings on the news when a flood is expected. I do not know those lines, not yet.

On the drive back, we get turned around at a roadblock where the bridge into town is closed. I tell Free another route back over a mountain, ten miles out of our way. We descend a dirt road. A diamond-shaped sign is posted at a stream crossing. The diamond declares: Flood Zone. We cross that zone. I have no idea how dangerous it is. If Free knows, he does not say.

But we are fine.

My arms are still tight at my chest. I hold myself together, as if to loosen my grasp would be likewise to float away. In my cutoffs and now dirty T-shirt I am in the basement and up the stairs, all the journeys up the stairs, using the Shop-Vac to empty the water outside in the gutter. That gutter empties into the stream and the stream into a river and the river into a reservoir two miles away. That reservoir, the Pepacton, runs straight to New York City, to its taps and faucets; I live in the New York City watershed, from which the city gets all its water.

—

Standing on the grass watching the muddy waters recede, a small crowd gathers, neighbors I don't yet know. There's a humid blue sky, coruscating light, violent and angry. One man wears coveralls, nods, takes a drag of a cigarette.

Someone mentions the fire department will pump out the basement, but I do not believe I can ask or even know how to ask for this help. I assume this service is for older people, those in frail and poor health, those in greater need. Like the demographics of most of rural America, the village is full of the older and frailer, with greater needs. So I empty this vacuum full of red silt on the green lawn and am left with two inches of mud that dries, caked to the basement floor like clay. No one says that it will be impossible to get up.

The man in the coveralls says, "Spray the walls with bleach to stop the mold."

I nod, as if I know to do this already. I cannot admit to myself even how little I know.

I, too, will spray with bleach.

I must buy bleach.

———

There is terror I cannot admit, because we have moved here to flee the allergies, the things carried in the air—mold and its spores—and now the water will bring them into our house. We have had to begin our lives over again in the village, only to find the house itself can poison me.

We are declared a federal disaster area.

Someone says to make a FEMA claim. "For that stream wall of yours, so close to your foundation and all." I don't know how this someone knows.

———

I make calls. I speak to someone named Jennifer, ID no. 48508. Next an inspector will telephone. They promise to send a package of materials. The governor sends a trifold mailer to POSTAL CUSTOMER. On the cover in twenty-four–point type: DISASTER ASSISTANCE IS AVAILABLE.

"My fellow New Yorkers," the governor writes. Inset next to this is a portrait of this governor, a nondescript white man in black and white, with a side part and a sheen on his face from the camera's flash. "The devastating floods that recently hit New York State have clearly been a disaster of major proportions."

The phone rep Jennifer tells me because we live in a federal disaster zone, we can also qualify for IRS tax relief. We need to call the IRS for the publication about disaster tax relief. That number is 1-800-829-3676. Request publication no. 2194.

—

The FEMA claim form:

Cause of damages: Flood. Hail/Rain/Wind Driven Rain.

13a. Was your home damaged by the disaster?

13b. Personal property damaged?

13c. Was the access to your home restricted?

14. Are any of your essential utilities currently not working as a result of the disaster?

16. Do you own or lease a working farm or ranch that was affected by the disaster? (*Does not include farm home*)

17. Do you own a business or rental property that was affected by the disaster? (*Not farm damage*)

18. Has anyone in your family lost work or become unemployed due to the disaster? (*Including self-employed*)

The questions go on to ask about medical expenses and funeral expenses and if these expenses are insured and the amount of the loss.

On the back is a PAPERWORK BURDEN DISCLOSURE NOTICE.

> The public reporting burden for the application form taken by phone or in person averages 21 minutes per response. [. . .] Send comments regarding the accuracy of the burden estimate to: _____.

—

The FEMA inspector.

His name is Randy. He carries a metal clipboard. His hair is clipped, tone brisk, a lanyard with a government ID around his neck. This is the closest I've come to federal officialdom except paying taxes and voting. A tight crease runs down the front of his khakis. He is in my basement with the dried mud. He has arrived from another disaster, diverted here, he explains. He has been based in P.A., he says using the initials, and now this. "Pretty place you got. Cute town." The basement air catches; the dust from the dried mud clings to our throats.

I point to the dehumidifiers. He says, I see. I show him the sump pump and mud.

He takes photos with a digital camera that has a government barcode stuck to it.

We walk behind the house. It is a relief to be outside. I show him where the wall was, where the water is, where the foundation is, where rock and roots cling to the soil, as if trying to fight gravity. He nods. He says he will calculate the benefits. He says they usually make a decision in a couple weeks, but we're backed up—another flood, maybe a tornado. I can't remember. In his sentences, he switches pronouns between they and we. In this mix of syntax and distance, with his "they" and "we," might be a promise to hold all of us. Or, maybe that "we" just contains him and his colleagues.

He does not say that they will only approve costs inside the house, in a structure. They will only cover the dehumidifier, just one—not two. He does not explain that the government has a schedule that averages out the price for such things across the country. He does not say they will not pay for the stream wall. It is not a structure, and not even a structure protecting our structure matters. He hands me a sheaf of papers.

After the inspector leaves I look at his materials. There is a photocopied brochure about the National Flood Insurance Program (NFIP). On the cover: Hokusai's wave. In the original print from the 1820s, three tiny boats bend in the water's peaks and troughs as if we are at sea, and the waves have teeth so they look more dangerous. Now the first page of each new chapter of this brochure features this wave. The government's version is cropped to a square. There are no more fishing boats, though just this single totalizing black wave.

Introduction to the NFIP

This introduction is inundated with initials. SFHA, FIRM, LOMA, ORMS. Another pamphlet lists: IHP, IAW,

IARC, IANS, IDEA, IDNS, IDUPA, IID, IINSIVNE, and IVNR. All of those are reasons to be turned down for assistance. We are turned down with an IID, meaning "insufficient damage." When we are turned down, no mention is made of the stream wall.

A question in the Hokusai manual defines community. A community is not about affinity but officialdom. And, this community has the ability to police—that is, to adopt and enforce rules around flooding. "A community must come together," it says.

I like this foregrounding of community, of us coming together and sharing responsibility instead of its falling simply to the individual. I believe in "the public." It's a phrase my father used often, part of his vocabulary to talk about the greater good and shared resources, the collective and the communal—of us. All the things to which he devoted his life.

The brochure explains, too, that aid is only available to communities that agree, and because my community also has agreed to flood regulations, I am thus entitled to assistance.

I do not realize, though, that to accept this check the government sends for $179.00 and does not match any of the amounts we paid, we will forever need to carry flood insurance, which each year costs into the thousands of dollars.

I did not read that part of the Hokusai brochure.

———

This day as I write, eight people or more are missing in New York City. Over the next days the numbers will climb. You will know; you will have seen floods in Germany and

Tennessee this summer. Flash floods. What is a flood if it does not come in a flash?

That community in Tennessee is not a community according to the NFIP or FEMA. They did not agree to join, and they have no protection. They get no assistance.

—

My memory: the air is water, water I carry, water sticks to me. My back aches. And, still more water to carry.

Chapter 3

ON MY LAPTOP, MY FATHER leaps into the air, and I
see love. It's film of him as a toddler, this little boy Bobby,
with round eyes and round face, both too big for his body.
He clambers onto a ledge and flings himself into a lake. The
scars in the celluloid flicker, and he is three, maybe four. I
watch him fly. People stand on a pier in the distance. Other
kids play nearby. His sister must be there. She is eight or
nine. I wonder which one she is, which girl with bobbed
hair and dark wool bathing suit. His has a white belt at the
waist. The straps slip from his scrawny shoulders, and the
jumps repeat over and over a half dozen times.

As a young man he plunges off the bow of a ship into San
Francisco Bay. The boat is five stories high and he has
to leap. It's part of his training in the Merchant Marine
Academy. Others can't. They are too scared. Their class of
twelve in officer school is whittled down to five. This five
includes my father, and when I learn this, I am proud.

I wait for the splash of water on my screen, and it never
comes.

———

In the film there's a trip to Washington. Maybe it is the late
1920s. I don't know. There are no people in these scenes, just

buildings. First I recognize the Supreme Court like a marble Parthenon of DC, then the Library of Congress with its arches from which nine thinkers—all men, including Demosthenes, Emerson, Hawthorne, and Goethe—stare down. The camera lingers on the details, which I find telling too—that the family wants to record these grand institutions with their majestic staircases, temples of justice and knowledge representing our country, and that these people, my forebears, my father's people, feel it is important to capture on film, an expensive new technology. I see aspirations—assertions—of their Americanness. The family has not been long in the United States, a little more than generation, and they travel to Washington to say they belong here.

Sometime before the film is shot, my family changes their name. They become Kabat, not Kabatchnik, leaving Lithuania and its shtetels far behind. My grandfather owns a store. I picture small-town capitalism, the era of Calvin Coolidge Republicans and a dream of the middle class, of belonging to civic groups like the Rotary and the Lions Club. As Kabats, we Anglicize ourselves to fit into this world, but my grandmother was born on the ship crossing, as if to belong not to here but to the water, and there is a split in the family too. My great-grandparents and their daughters, my father's aunts, remain Kabatchnik. I don't know why. I also hear a legend growing up, too, about how the Cabots, the wealthy New England family, sue us so we don't sound even more English, or take on pretensions that are not ours.

———

Finally, the film goes to Mount Vernon, and one day I will grow up not even four miles away.

———

Before he jumps, I study this little boy's smile, his pride in climbing onto the wall, but also that someone is watching, and that in their filming, they, too, are pleased with my father, and he is pleased with himself. Whoever holds the camera does not believe this is a waste of film. I think of the money it costs to capture this child: the camera, the film, the developing, the projector, even the family vacation. This is how I know he was loved, at least for a time. Then his mother is institutionalized and his father loses his house and business in the Depression.

The sun gleams on his wet limbs. He totters up. I take a screenshot to try to capture him in the air. I want to hold onto the moment. He is just a blur. He disappears into the lake.

Chapter 4

MY SECOND FLOOD COMES FIVE years after the first. My father has been dead a year, and this deluge arrives on the wings of a storm with a woman's name, Irene; and here a woman dies. The building she is in, a tiny rental cabin attached to a motel, is swept away. Rain falls in so many inches an hour. The governor is stranded here. He was on his way to New York City after visiting a dam twenty-five miles north on the Schoharie Creek. The rain is too much for his helicopter to fly, so he and his retinue are detoured via my village in a black SUV. The fire department performs swift boat rescues on Main Street. Main Street is a river. Main Street is normally two hundred feet from the actual river, which is called the East Branch, being the eastern finger of the Delaware River.

Firefighters tie ropes around people to carry them to freedom. Someone I know is rescued in a fishing boat. A motorboat bobs on the brown waves of Main Street. Water reaches the neck of the chainsaw bear that towers ten feet high over the grocery store's parking lot. Someone films this bear. The bear doesn't fall. Everything else in the water's path does. There is a question whether the dam will hold on the New York City reservoir downstream.

Rumors swirl that the city is letting out water. There is discussion of strategic flooding, that the village downstream from the dam is being evacuated and rumors, too,

27

that our mayor has had a heart attack. Other rumors will come, about people searching the floodwaters for prescription drugs flushed down the river from the CVS, and rumors of people stealing lumber washed away from the hardware store I visited in the first flood. Though, theft is a question at this point when the wood is miles downstream and warped by the waters. Over the next few days there are rumors, too, of arson. Someone who owns a building on Main Street is accused of burning it down after sustaining flood damage because he wants the insurance payout. These insinuations all fly across social media.

It turns out the building fire is from water-damaged wiring, but people denounce the owner and extol the poor firefighters and all the work they've done for days straight.

All of this is a flood.

—

The next day we—David, you, and I—stand in the grocery store parking lot with the bear and with half the town too. We circle, stunned and silent mostly. A person touches someone on a shoulder; another says hey, or yeah, or well.

The sky is an impossible blue—also, impossibly, the parking lot has been lifted and shattered into slabs like icebergs on a distant shore.

The CVS has collapsed. One corner of its foundation is now a brown lake. There is nothing left that says this was a pharmacy. There are no signs, no aisles. The shelves are pushed into the parking lot, and the lake reflects the sky and a single cloud. At the back a couple of cinder blocks dangle on wires. At the front, the doors that once opened automatically hang on hinges where the water forced them ajar. Metal shelving wraps around a pylon, and two florescent striplights swing from wires. To see the doors and shelving and lights is to see the water.

Round bales of hay encased in white plastic have landed on the deck of the diner, the Bun 'n' Cone. They look like giant marshmallows. Another wrapped white bale stands on Main Street. An oil tank sits on the corner by the bank.

David shoves his hands in his pockets. He wears an old pair of cutoffs and muddy boots. His hair is dirty, straggly under a Husqvarna hat because we haven't showered, because the village is under a boil-water order, because we have been told the municipal well is in danger. Two days earlier was his birthday. We hiked to find black trumpets, prized chanterelles, up the mountain that shoulders the village. On the way we talk exuberantly and celebrate our lives here and the rains, the wet summer that has brought abundance to this hillside. Now he rolls in his lips and studies the scene.

Plate glass windows from the supermarket are blown out and into this parking lot. It is strewn with toppled shopping carts. Foliage and grass are braided into the metal. The grocery store's wall has collapsed in one solid piece alongside a lotto kiosk. On top are packages of paper towels—Bounty Basics and regular Bounty—as if the flood knows what we need. Two bottles of dish detergent—one shamrock green, the other a bold blue that matches the Bounty and lotto kiosk—stand upright. "Take me," they say, "You will need me." The lotto kiosk says: "Play me!" The letters are yellow and blue, that Bounty blue, the same shade as the shopping cart handles that are woven with weeds and grasses. From the broken windows you can see inside, and above what was the produce aisle, a sign declares: "Fresh Cut Prices!!!"

Everyone is silent. Everything glistens in the light, in this blue of disaster, and the sky is blue, and the woman has died. She dies at the Valkyrian Motel; it, too, is painted sky blue.

In the arms of the chainsaw bear, someone has put an American flag. In the parking lot I find an unscathed red, white, and blue votive candle. I lay it at the bear's feet. All of this would normally strike me as saccharine, but right now among the slabs of asphalt the gesture feels like hope itself. David touches my arm.

This place where we have moved keeps washing away.

———

Later I go to a sandwich shop and help people throw everything out. "Everything," the owner says. It all must go. Fancy tinned teas and cookies and biscuits from Scotland and Belgium. Even if they look fine, she insists, trash. She has cropped hair and a nasal accent from downstate, maybe the Bronx. She has fed me toasted cheese sandwiches for lunch when I need to escape my house and writing. Before most others know our names here in Margaretville, she will greet David and me on the street. She is someone who attends to all the flowers in the village, ensuring planters spill forth with blooms—brilliant reds and pinks—in our short summers, and now surrounding her are giant gray rubbish bags. Nothing in her voice gives away her emotions. We open bottles of Snapple and pour them into the gutters, the ones that drain into the river, the river to the reservoir. Meanwhile, shouldering over us—over the village—is Pakatakan Mountain, whose name means "marriage of the waters."

David is dispatched to a trailer park. Get out whatever you can, the volunteers are told. The trailer is on its side. It is full of mud. It is impossible. There is nothing. Nothing to save. His voice is quiet. He is normally quiet, but now he barely whispers.

Evacuees sleep in the fire hall. The Red Cross serves meals three times a day for volunteers and people displaced and just anyone in the town needing fellowship. The first thing that arrives after the Red Cross: clothes—bags and bags of people's old clothes. The clothes and the refugees, the evacuees, they move to the church next to the fire hall.

All of this is a flood.

—

Outside the church I'm stationed at a plastic folding table. I cannot clean basements so I am armed with a clipboard, a list, and names of volunteers. A woman from the trailer park comes to ask for help. I can still see her hands, her knuckles, thick with arthritis and held tight. I cannot remember her facial gestures. I cannot bear to. Her house is the one David is sent to first, where nothing could be saved. Please send more people, she says. Just the photos. I just want the pictures back.

The roads remain closed. The National Guard arrives and stands on my corner. The Red Cross surveys all the homes in the village. The Red Cross lists: address, gender, age, own/or rent, and if people have power, insurance, are flooded, have mud, drinking water. . . . The cells in the spreadsheet are set up to list: Y/N. The final column is reserved for notes: *Leaving area; Lost Office (trying to do anything she can); water to ceiling and mud to basement; already moving; 7th time flooded; house in foreclosure; has mold and fuel around flooded water; yellow tag.* That means the building is condemned. At ours there is No Answer.

———

Over the next month in our town, trash grows in one place. And, in another it is dispatched to the church basement where people from across the country have sent their used clothing. People think this generous. This is their trash. We will all have to sort through the trash. The generosity creates more work. I write for a news site of the flood dump, the mountain of debris—siding and refrigerators, sofas, tires, shipping pallets, and one intact round picnic table. It grows where the Water Discovery Center will soon be built to celebrate the achievements of the New York City watershed and its system of six reservoirs where we live. This is just a mile from Margaretville, in Arkville, whose name comes from its ability to survive floods in the nineteenth century. The news says we are resilient; the news moves on. In New York City people gather in a public–private park to protest wealth and inequality. And, the National Guard, in sand-colored clothing, camouflage fatigues, remains on my corner and asks for my ID to prove we live here. I feel guilty that I cannot go to the park and guilty that I cannot clean basements.

The governor is shocked when he's stranded here that there is no cell service, that he cannot make a call. This is how we get cell coverage, first in mobile units provided by the military, then in a tower over Arkville, where David helps empty the trailers, where the woman lives who folds her hands over and over before asking for help recovering her family photos.

Spiral out, zoom above, and here I am again, arms crossed as if they might hold back my feelings.

———

This summer a decade after that storm, I scroll through the governor's Flickr account (Flickr itself makes me think of extinctions). The governor is also this very day I type officially no longer the governor. He is now a predator. As he resigns, he says that the lines have changed without his knowing it. "In my mind, I've never crossed the line with anyone, but I didn't realize the extent to which the line has been redrawn."

On my screen it is the end of August 2011, and we are inside the leather interior of his SUV. In a video someone holds a camera out the window. Water overtops the car's hood. In one blurry image, the governor raises a hand to his mouth. Shock, I assume. Next the camera is inexplicably focused at an angle inside the vehicle. A wooden coat hanger stuck in the leather seatback pocket fills the screen. A man's muffled gruff voice: "It's a long way to Manhattan."

In the video, the car drives past two volunteer firefighters in their high-vis vests. They gesture at him. It looks like they're saying stop or turn around. I can imagine what they say, with what I know now. I am now the person in such disasters, in the high-vis jacket, a member of the fire department, telling people the road is closed and saying: "Don't Drown, Turn Around."

That's the phrase I don't know in the first flood when I exhort Free to drive through the waters.

—

As I write, in Tennessee they describe the flood as a tidal wave. Hokusai's wave is often mistaken as a tsunami. In Tennessee a woman in the paper says the flood smells of death—and here it smells of oil, mold, and mud, and shit. A heaviness collects at the back the throat. It stings; it crawls up your sinuses.

In Germany this summer a low front stations. This type of front has a name: Weatherman's Woe. It's a cutoff low, meaning stalled and orphaned from the weather currents that normally move across the Northern Hemisphere from west to east. One such front in Margaretville drops sixty inches of snow in forty-eight hours. In Germany the storm turns roads into sweeping canyons. Later this summer at Summit in Greenland, not the top of a mountain but an ice-bound research station where it never rains, showers fall.

I cannot stop thinking about these facts or facts like this. I collect the stories and stuff them in a folder that has FEMA written across the top and contains my claim information.

That second flood comes the year after my father's death. Sometime after that I quit working on a crime novel and then give up on fiction entirely, even though writing has held all my yearning. The climate, these floods, and those facts are too big to hold in a narrative. The only way to write is to move forward, a friend says. Crime novels come with a dream of forward momentum—progress, resolution, and stability restored. I need to ignore the news, but I cannot. I take screenshots of headlines and add them to the folder. They feel too big, too catastrophic to let go of, so instead the file bulges. In it, too, are the pictures of my dad. Pages spill out; Post-it notes decorate the sheets like strange petals on a flower.

I scrawl notes on index cards and tear articles from the local paper. Over time I begin to hang them on a wall behind my desk hoping to hold them together with all their discontinuous moments of shock. I lay them next to each other, not chronologically, but as if in proximity I will get some perspective. I read a line of the German historian and philosopher Walter Benjamin's about time cutting through millennia, and how history exists in the here and now. He writes that events are not "like the beads of a rosary," and I stare at the mass of notes.

Newsprint curls in the humidity. I tape news accounts next to quotes from scientists. They seem unconnected— or to me they are all connected, but I do not have a language to link them. How do I summarize the emotional condition of this—whatever *this* the current moment is? These current moments spread out over a decade.

———

That first flood, which inundates my basement, is a one-hundred-year flood; the next one that destroys my village is five hundred years—time in biblical numbers. Then there are floods here 380 million years ago. What is now my town sits on the floodplains of a Devonian sea. On its shores the first trees appear. Not trees at all, they're giant ferns and fix oxygen for life on earth. Meanwhile, other kinds of life—which then are fish—collapse in the wake of those trees. It is a great extinction: 96 percent of all species die and nearly all the corals disappear. This is all time beyond my conception. Lived time and geological time defy the time frame of a novel. As I have been in Margaretville, the two times come to seem inseparable. Those statistics for a flood's occurrence are not about how often they come but the odds of a flood of that magnitude in any single year. Now biblical years come every year. We are all experiencing the acceleration of catastrophic time.

———

This morning the birds fly. It's late summer, and they have stopped singing. Rainwater glistens on leaves. They shimmer and shake with disco ball striations. Spiderwebs too are silvered with light. Droplets line the filaments woven in wheels and orbs.

David and I visit the fossils of the first trees. They are found near Vroman's Nose after a flood in 1869 and are used to repair a wall. More are uncovered as a dam is constructed in Gilboa, a town a half hour north of me, for one of New York City's first reservoirs, in 1920. Ninety-one years later, the governor visits this dam in Irene, just before being stranded in my town.

We park on a road that skirts the submerged village. The stumps of roots sit on a bed of gravel outside the town hall. The roots of these primeval trees are all that remain of the species. Some scientists say they look like a parasol. That sounds elegant, but they don't actually look like much. The ones here are big—three feet or more across—and seem like something forged in an old industrial shop, maybe made of iron to run a mill or factory in the nineteenth century. The trunks and leaves have long since decomposed, and all that is left are these stumps, in this town that is gone, marking time in another age of disappearances.

—

I read about the scientist Vince Schaefer, the one who floods my town. I study his experiments with ice, how dew freezes on a web when the air is just above freezing. There's a line in one of his reports from the 1960s about how, at 2 degrees Celsius, when the relative humidity is one hundred percent, "If we examine spiders' threads [. . .] ice particles may be seen through the multitude of dew drops. [. . .] This lead to an unforeseeable discovery: all the residues of ice particles contained a black nucleus"—the word is underlined in the report—"composed entirely of carbon black."

The beauty of that sentence about spiderwebs and carbon black, one that sounds as if it's blacker than any other, stops me. The ice is threaded through like beads on the web. From this research, he and his colleagues learn ways of extrapolating how drops freeze even above freezing, and this understanding applies to clouds, to aerosols, to the settling of layers in clouds.

I think about this as I see a milkweed pod after the rain. Water clings to the fibers, themselves like a web or cocoon. I text Iris about how just the idea of scientists studying spiderwebs and dew, the interconnection between them all, makes me happy.

Chapter 5

IN THE BRIGHT LIGHT OF afternoon atop the bluff, Iris adjusts her ball cap. She hands me the baby, her son. She has a heart-shaped face and curly brown hair, a small dash of freckles. The hat is from Pepacton Bait & Tackle, named for the New York City reservoir in our town. To make way for it in 1955, four villages in our community are destroyed. They are submerged in the waters.

We're on this dance floor with its names incised into rock, and she takes a picture of the view. I tell her about Vince Schaefer. He camps here as a child and hikes here as an adult. He loves this place. I tell her that he makes a fog for war here in the early forties, and afterward works with Kurt Vonnegut's brother, Bernard. Bernie, I call him. I use their first names. I've been trailing them so long I feel like I know them, and they're both so alive to me they exist in the present tense. Together at GE, the two make snow as a Cold War weapon, to make that war even colder. They figure out how to seed clouds with flaming-hot silver iodide and tiny grains of dry ice.

We're here on the anniversary of the day, to the day in June, that Vince bathes this mountain in smoke. It is the first of an accumulation of coincidences that string this story together. I tell Iris about the flood, the Rainmaker's Flood, it's called, that his technology causes. I don't mention my own floods or my father, or how he and those floods have carried us to the mountain together. I don't think I even realize yet.

Like ice-nine? she asks, in *Cats Cradle?* Isn't that the story, the end of the world, everything freezes, catastrophe, like nuclear war?

Yeah, yeah, I say quickly. Kurt Vonnegut's book is published in the early sixties with a plot that seems like he is holding a mirror up to his brother's work at GE. I tell her how, just before Thanksgiving in 1950, Bernie and Vince's cloud seeding inundates Margaretville. There's not enough water for New York City. In 1949 drought threatens California, the East Coast, and Europe. New York's reservoirs are at less than fifty percent capacity. By early 1950, the city is desperate. Its largest reservoirs—the two in our county—are yet to be built. So, it undertakes this experiment with planes spraying silver iodide to make particles condense, to make ice crystals, to make it rain, to fill the reservoirs. The storms spread across the Catskills and our town is destroyed.

For years I've been obsessed with these men and their snow and rain. Vince, I say, drops out of high school to support his family. He doesn't even finish correspondence school as an arborist, but he spends much of his life outside in forests. And Bernie, he's the favorite son. His family sacrifices and saves so he can follow his father and grandfather to MIT. The way I say it rhymes the PhD and MIT, and in that, too, you can hear my judgment.

The two men start snowmaking, and both become consumed by the weather. We have unleaded fuel because of Vince, I say, and Bernie works on war, on Reagan's Star Wars, trying to blow holes in clouds with lasers. Their rainmaking is used in Vietnam too, bombing Laos and North Vietnam with rain and storms to cause floods, I tell her.

—

Iris adjusts the baby's sun hat, and I take a picture of the two of them. Behind her are the sky and fields, and now on my laptop, too, I see her and the baby and the valley below.

—

In his photos Schaefer is loose and open collared, Vonnegut buttoned up, hat on, wearing tweed and ties. From their appearances I divine insights into their personalities, but you could also read my biases, holding each man up as the other's opposite. In the Adirondacks Vince follows how fir trees transpire like exhalation, like breath. He finds in the breathing trees that they cause the blue of distance and discovers a simple test for ozone.

Iris talks about learning of redwoods and clouds from the poet Mary Norbert Korte, on whom she's writing her dissertation. It's on the friendship between Korte and the Beat poet Diane di Prima, and their unlikely collaboration: di Prima wrote an autobiography of her sexual liberation; Korte was a nun. In the sixties she left her religious order for poetry and then left the poetry scene in San Francisco for the redwoods. She teaches Iris how *Sequoia semper-virens* make their own weather and clouds. From coastal fog, she tells me. It condenses on the needles to produce rain.

Iris visits her often, but the first time, Korte tells her that her house can't be found on GPS and so gives Iris detailed directions which lead her down a long, unpaved road deep in the redwood forest. Then she finds her smoking roll-up cigarettes and pot.

Iris and I talk of the air and virus, writing and the environment. The music wafts on the breeze behind us, and cars continue to pull in below. Light mirrors off windshields. Between us is our exuberant conversation and a swelling joy. It is a surge of oxytocin, the hormone that doctors say is the chemical that bonds women as we speak, as if it were held in the air between us. Clouds scudder past overhead. They're the cotton ball kind that kids draw, and I don't know their names, not yet. But I am here for the clouds, of which Schaefer writes, and the smoke and fog he makes for war. Like our breath, all are aerosols.

———

On June 24, 1942, Vince Schaefer comes here to test his fog. Nearly a year before Pearl Harbor, the Pentagon gives his boss at GE orders to create a smokescreen for the war to come. Schaefer starts by heating an oilcan so the smoke emerges at what he calls "sonic speed," that is, at the speed of sound, the highest speed at which a gas will travel. Soon as it hits the air, the oil, now a hot vapor, condenses, like exhaling warm breath on a cold day. Schaefer's full-sized prototype looks like a Victorian steam engine, and he uses these glacial hills as a wind tunnel ten miles long. At dawn the air warms and lifts as it hits the rocks. The smoke rises on the thermals like the hawks this afternoon. Dozens of officials from the armed forces come to watch.

On the day of the test he writes, "The dawn is cloudless and the air calm . . . Arriving at the summit everyone had a light breakfast." He is thirty-five.

I picture that morning, nearly the longest day of

the year. They leave Schenectady at three to arrive before sunrise. As I try to imagine what happens, I get stuck on the light breakfast. Somehow that there is food bothers me. I see these men in their military uniforms, greens and grays, and imagine flasks of coffee, a table spread with hard-boiled eggs, donuts, and cold toast. The officers speak and jostle. Someone waves at the view and clutches a Danish. He gestures at the fields below. The air is warm, there's the sweet scent of humidity and dew. Someone says you can't beat a sunrise like that. You won't get that in Gazala, or El Adem, or Bir Hakeim, or anywhere else in North Africa, where battles rage that month. Meanwhile Vince and his team set up the smoke machine on the valley floor, where there is once a Mohawk village and now people pick strawberries.

"As soon as the flats of Vroomansland"—Vince uses the name of the white colonizer—"were visible, we gave the order to start. [. . .] Within ten minutes a spectacular screen fog forms, hiding the apple orchards, barns, houses and everything else across the flats. [. . .] Our visitors were quite elated."

More than 50,000 of his machines are built, and during the Second World War they hide troops fighting at Ainzo Beach and crossing the Rhine. The smoke is only 0.6 microns. In the news I've been reading about our breath and the virus—exhalations of one or three or five microns—and just how long those molecules remain in the air. The smaller the size, the longer they linger.

Iris talks about how Korte weaves the redwoods into her writing and explains the poet's belief in the "Long Time." It's not linear time, not human time, not at the scale that we can understand, and it is definitely not progress.

It happens in the time frame of the redwoods, 1,500 years or more. Here on this mountain is glacial time, the rocks speaking and names carved into stone over the last two hundred years, the blink of an eye.

Not long before he dies, Schaefer writes a history of this mountain beginning in the ice age. During his life he writes, too, of trees and of forest fires, with "an extremely high concentration of very fine particles. Most of them smaller than a half micron [. . .] The visible smoke often appears blue by scattered light."

Blue smoke, fog, the speed of sound, the sound of country music over my shoulder, the view of the valley. The virus comes in microns. Sunlight glints off the line of cars at the farm below. I hold my breath and hold the baby. I exhale, and time here collapses. History circles around: May 19, 1780.

———

Night descends at noon. The whip-poor-wills start singing. Bats take to the sky. No one knows why dusk falls so early. Scientists decide centuries later that smoke brings the darkness. It's delivered by forest fires raging so far away no one has any idea they are burning. Across New England and New York it feels like an apocalypse. The United States is in the midst of the long slog of the War for Independence.

Stationed in New Jersey, George Washington writes in his diary, "Dark & at the same time a bright and reddish kind of light [. . .] brightning & darkning alternately." Yale's president, theologian Timothy Dwight, records, "A very general opinion prevailed that the day of judgment was at hand." Attributing the darkness to the sins of war, one anonymous New England farmer believes, "Some singular judgment will follow [. . .] the very beginning of sorrow." They call it the Dark Day.

Two days later Mohawk warriors burn houses in this glacial valley with its chattering rocks and ice's retreat. The fire is a reckoning. The fighters are aligned with the British and return to their lands that have been stolen. Here the Revolution isn't some great battle for Enlightenment ideals and the "rights of men." The year before, in 1779, George Washington ordered Sullivan's Campaign, attacking five of the six Haudenosaunee nations: the Mohawk, Seneca, Tuscarora, Onondaga, and Cayuga. He called for their "total destruction and devastation [. . . so] the country may not be merely overrun, but destroyed." Sullivan's Campaign is genocide: the most expedient way to claim the fertile territory from here to the Ohio Valley. Below me, this river-flat land and its village once named "the place where corn grows" become known as the "breadbasket of the Revolution." The Mohawk name for George Washington is still "Ranatakaras, Town Destroyer."

All that smoke and war here. It feels like a portent, or a palimpsest whose traces you can read in this place. There's Vince Schaefer, and the aerosols in our breath, the dangers in our laughing and talking and singing, this mountain and valley and its people shaped by war, and the technologies of war that have harnessed clouds and weather. There's global warming and a global pandemic, plus the microns of pollution—aerosols and diesel particulates—that lead me here.

Even the blue, blue sky this day foreshadows darkness. Vince Schaefer wrote that its deep azure comes from "the air molecules themselves." They scatter light like those molecules of smoke and fog. "If there were no light scattering, the sky would be black except for the sun, stars and [. . .] planets."

Chapter 6

IN ANOTHER FILM FROM MY father's childhood maybe it's early 1930s, maybe the late twenties. People mill in a backyard. My dad's brother has left for Annapolis, one of the only Jewish boys admitted to the Naval Academy and *what an honor too*, I will be told. In the garden women wear cloche hats; children chase a white rabbit. They pick it up. It wiggles away. In one scene, my dad and his sister and their parents stand together as if posing for a photograph. My dad has on a suit with shorts. His mother a white sleeveless blouse; his father's arm is around her, and his hand rests on his daughter, my aunt's, shoulder. My dad breaks the moment. He touches his hair, his brow. They freeze again.

Seconds pass on the progress bar on my screen. The group separates. I study their coming together and splitting apart.

My grandfather strides forward. My aunt reaches out to him. Her mother still holds her hand, and my grandfather—my father's father, a man I'll never know—starts to run. Maybe it's a game, maybe chase. In the background everyone smiles: my grandmother, aunt, and father. My grandfather sprints toward the camera, his arm swinging. It looks like he's about to strike someone. His face fills the screen, his mouth open in a gash. It looks like terror—or rage. Framed in the background little Bobby in his suit watches.

My father is born not long before the Depression. He grows up in a small town, Somerset, Pennsylvania, in one of only two Jewish families there. His has money enough for the film camera, which costs a little less than a Model T, and with those kinds of resources, his parents must have

a car too. His childhood though is a mystery. All I have are
these fragments. He barely talks of it. He has two siblings, an older brother and sister,
Herbert and Dorothy. Herb is maybe a decade older. I am
never clear exactly on his age. I hear occasionally a story of
the two brothers walking together through old rail tun-
nels that will one day become the Pennsylvania Turnpike.
Their mother worries, and my dad loves these times with
Herb in the outdoors. I can imagine it only happens once
or twice, and the experience being so powerful it's polished
into his memory. Dorothy is always protective of my dad
for reasons I don't comprehend at first. The three of them
all go on to serve in World War II. She will be a nurse;
she will be at Normandy just after D-Day. Later in life she
gets an award from the French government for her service.
After his career in the Navy ends, Herb becomes a physicist at Cal Poly in 1952, but I never meet him.

———

Once, I glimpse their childhood home. We're driving to my
mother's parents in Akron and detour to see it on the way.
I'm eight. It's the day before Thanksgiving. The air in the car
is heavy with my mom's anxiety about visiting her folks. I
remember an unremarkable two-story home. Now in pictures on Zillow there's an apple tree in the backyard and a
cramped child's bedroom—all pink. Could that be my father's, with the narrow bed shoved up against the window?

———

He is part of why I move to the Catskills. He has a rare
blood disorder, aplastic anemia where his marrow will not
make new blood cells, and he is dying.

———

I cannot say what I am looking for here, or what I hope to find in him. He devotes his life to co-operatives in rural places, mostly rural electric co-ops, and travels throughout my childhood, visiting them. I grow up hearing how they are the product of FDR's New Deal and how important this is, but not why.

Early in their marriage he and my mother run a co-operative too, not far from where I end up living in up-state New York. A few years later they move to Washington, DC, where he works for a trade association serving all the rural electric co-operatives. At first my father is a lobby-ist—his title: legislative assistant. This position doesn't last long. Soon he dedicates himself to co-op management.

He becomes a management consultant, and in my childhood two decades later, the job sounds ethereal, even as it gains some currency for an abstract kind of work in the Reagan eighties. I do not understand it, and I will not, not really, not until nearly the end of his life. He explains then that he had wanted to build lasting institutions in ru-ral America as an alternative to capitalism. He tells me he worried about the boards and managers, all volunteers and farmers, dairy farmers, he says, and schoolteachers, with no training for running a co-operative, so—. He sips his tea; his voice rumbles deeply in the way it does when he speaks of his work. He has gray hair thinned almost to tonsures, always unruly. He wears a cardigan even in summer and says that the co-ops are not an ordinary business, not a corporate util-ity, not a power company, not like your NYSEG, he says, re-ferring to my utility. But, the money stays in the community, and, I wanted to make sure they could succeed.

—

When I'm little, I believe he's a statue in the middle of my hometown. Every Sunday we take him to the airport. He's traveling to places like Broken Bow and Bison, Kalispell, Grand Forks, and Pahrump. He flies in crop dusters and sleeps in people's dens because these towns are so small they have no motels. Sometimes he will fly overseas and be gone for weeks. As he leaves, we drive past this tall, bronze man—a soldier who is so important traffic has to swerve around him. High on a pedestal, he looks down at the road, at me. I am convinced this man is my dad. I have this strange kind of magic, an associative logic I still haven't quite lost.

He returns from these trips, and I flock around his suitcase flapping like a crow. What did you bring, I demand, what did you get me? My mom shushes me away and tells me not to be greedy. But, he always brings something: a batik blouse or a doll or a tiny giraffe sewn from swirling pink paisley. Once he produces a model of the very plane on which he's flown. For him, I think, these gifts have special powers too. They try to embody his love and cover the distance between us.

There are conversations I overhear and do not follow. My father's voice drops an octave, and he talks of public utilities and what the word *public* means, *for all*, he'll say. He says words about boards and navigating and does not mean ships. Or, he tells my mom that he's worried about a project in one of the countries he's visited and how the government there wants a piece of the co-ops. His voice rises in disbelief. Or, there's corruption. He'll shake his head.

Don't they realize that co-operatives lift up a community by keeping money in it?

This is something he tells me about co-ops: they are owned and operated by the people they serve. He says this to explain to me where he's going, and he adopts his deep work voice so I understand the trips are important. He talks with my mother about this place with the corruption and kickbacks, and I glean this is bad, that it means he can't build his rural electric co-operatives.

Don't they see—? He shakes his head, his hair is graying and his growing potbelly presses against his blue dress shirt. He stands in the kitchen with my mom. He is pouring her a drink, bourbon with water, and he says, don't they know, birth rates go down and education goes up. All from just one light bulb?

And that is magic too.

———

And, my father is his work and his work voice, that baritone with its burr that, now thinking of it, I feel deep in my body.

One of the reasons I stop writing fiction is that it requires me to reduce these elements to what suits a narrative. Details are shaped and bent to create a sense of character and their motivations and actions. What doesn't fit, what isn't necessary, what doesn't elucidate or explain or further the plot gets cut. This idea of everything working in one direction stifles the nuance I hope to find. And I do not want to construct a story of anger at my father, to support my mother's resentments. I also cannot bear to turn those incidents into scenes, which means reinhabiting them here on the page and keeping them alive. Instead, come with me on a Sunday in Washington, DC, to my father's office. It is on the seventh floor. I rummage through the stationary cupboard. There is the smell of pencil lead and a slightly acid hint of the ink from ballpoint pens, and yes, I am bored but also thrilled.

I pick up phones and push buttons to transfer calls to a pretend friend on another floor. I write on a slip that has printed "While You Were Out" across the top and make up stories of the people who come to see my father. The best parts of the day are when we go out to lunch together where I feel special, adult, in the restaurant with its white tablecloths, and then on the drive home in his yellow Karmann Ghia. I get to eat a candy bar. My seat is covered with a beach towel so the upholstery won't be too hot. The chocolate melts in my fingers, and my father is next to me. He pats my knee and says, Jenny, I am so glad you came in with me.

There are things, too, that sound banal: my parents' mid-century marriage, the couple in the suburbs with three kids, the shoals of identity, and rules about who is home and who is not, who raises the children and who has a career. There is also who is angry and sad—who *gets* to be angry and sad. I wonder too, as I write, about my father's sadness. Is his devotion to work what exiles him from us, or how he copes with the separation? Or, is it his childhood and all that loss, so he has no idea how to be in a family? Or, is it that with his childhood and all that loss, he needs to save others from capitalism, so that is what he devotes his life to?

I stare at him in pictures, and he is impossibly handsome, skinny and suntanned, black hair with a wave at the side and a movie star's smile, the way I never see him when I'm a child. He is at the beach with my mom and sisters before I'm born. My sisters wear bikinis and have tans. They are teenagers and sit on a wall before some dunes.

For me, as I look at the images, it is the middle of autumn. Leaves flutter; reds and yellows stain the sky and roads. One sister mails a textbook of his from the Merchant Marine Academy. In *Knight's Modern Seamanship*, tenth edition, a gold anchor is embossed on the spine, and I study the syllabus he pastes in the front. I realize on his birthday he reads about clouds and storms. For him it is December. He is nineteen.

On page 762, four plates, photos, show a sailor struggling to hoist a man in civilian clothes. The caption: REVIVING THE APPARENTLY DEAD.

Chapter 7

I CAN'T CONCENTRATE AT MY desk. It is a shaggy summer, hot and sweltering, the season of my first flood. I walk up the road beyond our house. Cleft between two ridges, it's steep and narrow. The stream Bull Run courses alongside, and a few houses cling to the flats. One man I pass sets his chair by the water and says it's his air conditioning. He's always friendly, tells jokes, and wonders where I'm wandering. What is there to see up that hill— he asks—in this heat?

Just before I reach him is a house with red siding like iron, like blood. It's where the tank came loose. Now two grown men, both stocky, one with gray hair, fill a dumpster and load boxes into a pickup. They are Robert E. Gray, father and son, senior and junior. I rush past and try not to watch or stare or show too much curiosity because I don't know them, and each time, too, I want to say something. But there is nothing that feels like enough. Or, to say enough would be to risk saying something too personal. So, I just say *hi*, or *hey*, or *nice weather*. Or, *that rain* . . . They are nothing words because "sorry" is too much and too little.

Then the men are gone. Then the house is gone. It disappears, and grass is seeded, hay strewn where the foundation was. The Gray House is the ghost house. Someone tells me it's bought out by New York City for the water. I don't know where the men go, and don't really know yet what it means to disappear for water and for a city or both. Over time there are more disappearances, and I start to connect them: the city, my house, water, and my father. Not quite in that order and not quite with those exact links—or rather, they are the connections I make. Or, the connections I search for, because I need them to make some sense. Because, how do you make sense when things are disappearing, when the losses weigh so heavily, simply because they are loss?

—

Vince is never my project—not at first. I find him as I'm searching for local histories and information about floods. It's for a collaboration with my friend Kate, an artist. I read about the rainmakers in *The New York Times*, then follow the man, Wallace Howell, who makes the rain in my town, and trace the technology he uses, cloudseeding. There, I find, General Electric and the Cold War as weather, as snow, and also Vince and Bernie. Because it is before Kurt is famous or a novelist, perhaps even before he knows he is a novelist; connecting the brothers takes some time. In 1946, none of the articles identifies Bernie as Kurt's older sibling.

—

A friend, Sarah Miller, who's a hydrologist for New York City, comes to look at the stream with its collapsing walls. She has long russet hair and sings in a bluegrass band and on weekends helps her father Steve on his farm nearby. He is one of the first people I meet here, and he and his wife, Jane, welcome David and me into their lives.

Sarah and I walk the banks behind my house. It is a late spring day. The air smells damp, of mud and soil. She reminds me of the women detectives in crime dramas, not that she is that misanthropic genius-type, the one so absorbed in a case she ignores people, not at all. But, she has this quality of seeing something beyond what normal people notice, what I can't see, and I will turn her into a protagonist in the novel I start and quit. Today she steps past the hostas someone planted in the shade by the foundation and bends down as if the stream is speaking to her.

She nods; she shakes her head. The stream burbles. Well, she says finally, and turns to me. Look, it's a head cut. It's undermining the walls from the bridge. A head cut, a knickpoint, it runs up. You don't know it's there; you can't see it, but somehow someone disturbed the streambed. Maybe when they put in the culvert below? Who knows, they dug down. See those trees there? She points to trunks lying lengthwise under the stone walls. Those old hemlocks, the walls are built on them, and as long as the wood's underwater, it won't rot, but now? It's like receding gums but then you lose all your teeth. She tells me this head cut, it's a law of hydrology, and it will migrate upstream. It deepens the stream floor to match the water's flow.

She adds to this other disturbing news—erosion up the road where the hill is collapsing, just beyond where the house disappears. The land there is sliding into the water. This, too, needs fixing if the stream near our house is to stabilize. But, she says, there are no fixes, not really, not for any of this. Any fix will only be temporary; the water will find its way. Water always does. Her voice is somber.

So, the retaining wall is eroding; the stream will keep getting closer to our foundation, and there is nothing we can do. She says it is nearly impossible to repair; and, me, I stare at her and down at the rocks in the creek, rocks that had once been wall. The water burbles like the realtor said it would, and panic again grips my chest.

———

I ask her to teach me about hydrology because I need the water to speak to me too. If I cannot master it one way, I must another. And, I need to understand the stream, the waters, the floods, so I can grasp all these disappearances.

———

In Vince's story, I am moved by his leaving school so young and his love of trees, and that snow—this substance that melts and disappears, that is water—becomes the thing to which he devotes himself. In photos I find him bundled in plaid wool shirts and parkas, knit hats and heavy boots. These images are beside a campfire, or a tent, or at the top of peaks. His hair is always brushed back from his forehead, and he has a broad, open face and eyes that squeeze shut when he smiles.

In high school Vince dreams of being an archeologist. He digs for arrowheads and ruins and ancient Indigenous villages. He is fifteen and writes letters to Arthur C. Parker, a Seneca chief and the New York State Archeologist. Vince describes both his finds and himself. "Well," he adds at the end of one letter that's gone on for pages, "undoubtedly you're getting weary of this talk, so I'll close with a short description of myself." The description is not short. He includes his height and age and weight and says, "I love to collect and study relics better than to eat."

Then he has to drop out at sixteen, just after his sophomore year. His mother tells him the family needs him to work. They need the money. He enrolls as an apprentice machinist at GE in 1922 and is paid eighteen cents an hour. When he graduates to journeyman, he gets the worst jobs, the dirtiest ones, the tasks no one else wants, like machining slabs of graphite and steel. Frustrated, he quits to train as a tree surgeon where, at least, he can be outside in nature, with the trees.

Vince's letters to Parker might well have bored him, but they end up in the New York State Museum, and later the two become friends. They hike together, even plan on starting a hiking club. Over the years Vince also studies plants and fossils and ferns. He is a birder and builds ski trails and hiking trails, including one, the Long Path, that goes from the George Washington Bridge at the far north of Manhattan, all the way up over Vroman's Nose to the Adirondacks. It's not blazed but supposed to follow a path of curiosity with a low impact on the land.

He returns to GE in 1929 somehow convinced that being a machinist working in the shop at the company is a better path than working with trees. Who would he be if he had stayed with the forest?

———

A few years before he dies, I start interviewing my father. I need to know where he was all those years of my childhood. What was he doing, who was he being, and what was so important to him? At first the question comes with a demand. Because he was away all that time, he owes me answers. Then our relationship softens. Then, he is gone. We are maybe two years into this new relationship, and the doctors never say he is dying, not like that, not at all.

———

The Gray House and its quarter-acre plot are bought out by New York City. I start to comprehend what this means. The city is the biggest landowner here with holdings spanning nearly 1,600 square miles and six reservoirs, the biggest of which is in my town. New York is also the largest employer and taxpayer and is voracious. It must always acquire more land for the water, and it is nearly impossible to build or farm on, because the land exists solely as a buffer for the water. The parcels are to fulfill a mandate from the EPA, so the city doesn't have to build an even more expensive filtration plant, because here land is cheap—or cheap compared to the multiple billions of dollars the plant would cost. There's also an entire police force to protect the water, as well as a cadre of surveyors, hydrologists like Sarah, chemists, land managers, and foresters to map, guard, and monitor the water. Once a month, two people in waders clamber into Bull Run through the neighbor's yard behind us and dip in jars to monitor the stream. They repeat this in streams across the watershed, and on many streets in New York City you can find silver boxes that connect here to there. They are Water Quality Sampling Stations, and they look like a time machine, as if they could transport across distances.

———

Sarah tells me to read Luna Leopold. His book *A View of the River* is a classic of hydrology and one of her favorites. He establishes the discipline as we understand it now. In the book, equations set out laws of how water flows in rivers and creeks and ocean currents, even. I read about riffles and meanders, and the very language is beautiful, with *a meander* meaning not to amble but a stream's course, the path of energy in the water.

———

Before I even meet Sarah, her father Steve tells me about the reservoir in our town. We have just come in from boiling sap to get water because it's so hot in the sugarhouse. It's one of the first times we hang out. We stand in his kitchen. He lifts his glass. His voice is gruff, gravely, and his hair shorn. He wears a plaid wool jacket and says, addressing me and the glass in his hand: The city needed the water and we had the water, so of course, we gave it to them. It's what is right.

He tells me this is what his father Ivan said, "We have it they need it, of course, we share. The water is a public good." The statement stands out to me not just because in Margaretville most people resent the reservoir and the city, but for the name *Ivan*. I hold it to myself like a sign and create connections where maybe there are none. My dad is Robert Ivan Kabat.

———

One winter between the floods, after the Gray House is gone and Sarah has told me that the stream will keep encroaching on my house, blizzard after blizzard hits my parents' home in Virginia. I am away and my father dies. I fly back. Two days later in a rented SUV, I drive to the funeral home to see him with my mom and sister and David, who hovers quietly in the background. A man in a black suit holds his hands behind his back. He leads us down corridors to a small, dark room. I want something to happen in that small and dark room. I can't say what.

In the coffin a sheet is pulled up to his neck. This is not his coffin, not his sheet; he's going to be cremated. They all leave me alone with him. Whatever I want to happen does not materialize. I touch him and feel nothing and apologize and nothing, and all this nothingness engulfs me.

—

Outside clouds hang heavy and gray, and dirty snow is piled in mounds.

—

A month later just before my birthday, I am in the woods approaching a ridge. A nor'easter has brought several feet of heavy snow, damp and dense as concrete. The temperatures plummet, and the water in the crystals freeze. The surface is littered with hemlock needles brought down by the wind, and I am angry, rushing to something or away from something.

Walking is loud; each step resounds. I struggle up the hill in snowshoes, following an old logging road. I'm sweaty. My jacket is off, my hat stuffed into a pocket, and I don't know what I'm trying to find.

Hemlocks tower above, and I reach a battered barbed wire fence. A posted sign declares that what lies on the other side belongs to New York City. It is land for water, though there is no water here, just the snow. I step into this metropolis that is represented in the woods. It feels forbidden. I see the land as the city, a bit like how any embassy in whatever country is still considered sovereign territory no matter how far from its homeland. Here in this New York City, my ragged breath echoes against the hard snow. A crow caws. A hundred feet away, in a clearing at the top, my father appears. He wears old army pants and a faded red turtleneck he always had on hiking in Vermont when I was little, when he would carry me up mountains.

Everywhere here feels like a landscape of displacement. The snow belongs to New York City. It will melt and run into the streams. On this parcel, stone walls mark out fields that are now forest; my father is a ghost; a city exists in towering hemlocks.

———

And my dad's hair is wiry and gray and brushed to the side. There is the same closed-mouth smile, which in my lifetime with him is crooked like my own. His grin and mine both push up higher on the left.

Chapter 8

IT IS EARLY AUTUMN, AND I visit Sarah's father Steve as a stand-in for my own. We are in his kitchen again. Sit, he says, gesturing at the round oak table. It is early afternoon, mid-September, the day still hot—too hot for what is supposed to be a week shy of our first frost date. He wears a plaid flannel shirt. His voice is gruff, low and gravely, and his hair is shorn. He pushes his wire-frame glasses high on his nose. The windows look onto the hill where I originally met him my first winter here. He asks about David, and my writing. I say David is good; the other, I shrug. I tell him instead about the porcini we've been finding in the hemlock forest even though it's so dry. We talk about butterflies and the weather. He's been mowing the fields this morning, trying to avoid goldenrod so there's enough food for the monarchs' migration. He says, It's come late this year.

He tells me about moving to this hill and this house. Steve grew up in Union Grove, a place that no longer exists, that is now underwater. Their village is flooded for the Pepacton Reservoir, and his parents lose their home because of eminent domain. For months before the new house is finished his family camps in a tent outside. He is eleven, twelve. . . . He tells me it was fun for him as a kid, an adventure. But, they had no other place to go. This house is nearly an exact copy of that other inundated house. He sweeps his hand across the table. The gesture is like a gambler folding his cards. He brushes aside all in his wake. Everything, he says, everything was gone.

His family is the last to leave. It is April 1954. They have the longest reprieve because his mother is the postmaster, and the post office is inside their home and has to stay open. His parents get a letter from the city in November 1953. "Effective December 31, 1953, you are directed to remove yourself and your belongings from said parcel on or before that date."

"Very truly yours," it is signed.

"Only a month," Steve says. I have never seen him bitter before. I've heard him frustrated with Republicans in Washington, and administrative decisions in our town, and how the city governs the watershed, but never anything like this. He is the one who said that we have a moral obligation to share the water. Now his mouth tightens; the words shorten. "A month and you're out. For most people that's not enough time."

Because of his mother's job, his family has more time, more months than their neighbors to plan for the future, and still it is not enough. He looks aside as if collecting his breath. Still he starts school that fall doing homework in the tent, living cooped up with his brother and parents. His mother, Agnes, is exhausted and exasperated at trying to hold a family together there.

He talks of his old village, Union Grove. You'd see these gnarled stumps, giant trees, houses—entire houses—all of it, all of them, everything bulldozed together and swept up below the high water line.

This is when he sweeps his hands across the table, again and again, once, twice, five times. The gesture and its repetition are haunting, involuntary, like the repetition of a trauma. The land swept free.

You could bulldoze your own house, but who would? These are poor people, poor houses. He shakes his head. Or you could move it. And the city, they cut down the trees, giant trunks, and move them to the pile and then grub out the stumps, and all of this is heaped together in mountains of trash. Remember like after Irene? he asks. The linens and belongings and abandoned homes, all of it. Then, they burn it.

—

We talk of the flood dump and the Water Discovery Center in its place.

—

In building that reservoir, work crews find a fossil of a tree, another of those giant ferns, from the edge of the Devonian sea. Now it's on display in a museum near the cliff where Iris and I stood—on that hill, that "nose" where the rock is made of the sediments of that sea.

—

I want to touch time. Maybe it is in moss or maybe in rocks. I ask a friend, a roadside geologist for the state's Department of Transportation, to recommend books on geology. I take David to a spot he tells me about. It's along a highway that bisects the Catskills. We stand on a median strip. Here continents rip apart. We search for the tear. It is called a plumose structure. Africa splits from North America; neither is Africa or North America yet. They are part of a single continent, Pangea: The

Americas, Europe, and Africa united together. It is 300 million years ago.

The break happens at the speed of sound, not far from where Vince makes his vapor at sonic speed, cloaking the cliff in mist. The fracture is supposed to look like a feather or the imprint of a bird's wing in snow. I walk along the shoulder searching for feathers and wings in the rock face. David is on the other side. Cars speed by; the grasses shimmy.

I worry about ticks and stare at the rock face for any clue. In a puddle, fat tadpoles flee my shadow and fight for space. I catch a tractor-trailer in my peripheral vision. Hubcaps, beer cans, and empty plastic bottles of Sprite decorate the gravel. The air is dry and hot, and grit catches in my throat. I take pictures of anything that looks vaguely like a feather. I think if I find time frozen in this moment in rock, I'll understand something of our moment and its chaos, or maybe some sense of causality. Maybe, I will simply understand something about here, about what is held here, how place holds time.

—

In New York City, sidewalks are made of bluestone, slate from the Catskills, and in these sedimentary rocks you can sometimes see ripples of that ancient sea.

—

Just before creating the reservoir, in the drought of 1949 and 1950, the city decides to cut down all the trees lining the streams and rivers in the watershed. The trees absorb water. Each trunk holds hundreds of gallons, and the leaves breathe. They transpire, sharing the water. Without trees, the stream banks become more flood prone, and water runs faster, a bit like what happens behind my house. The city believes the trees are stealing water.

———

Steve's wife Jane comes in. "Hello dearest." Her voice enfolds me. She puts down her groceries and gives me a hug.

———

This is also a stand-in: on his porch a sign reads "Union Grove Post Office." It hung, too, on his parents' porch. Steve tells me his kitchen cabinets are built from the pews in the Union Grove church. I read that at an auction his parents buy back the scraps of their original home to put into this one. This house is a replica of the first, and he becomes an engineer because he is fascinated as a child by the work he sees on the reservoir. He works on the state's last big interstate project, the route I take to Albany. His daughter is the hydrologist, and there is also all this anger and loss. None of this is lost on me.

A highway sign by the reservoir declares: "Former Site of Union Grove."

One afternoon Sarah tells me about a horse that kept returning to its home long after the place had been flooded for the reservoir. Over and over, she says, the mare kept coming back, and how sad is that? Her long hair is tied back in a braid that reaches to her waist. She wears an old knit hat, jeans, and a fleece. We stand together looking out at a sand-brown landscape where the snow has melted and willows send red tips throbbing for the sky.

—

In the novel I write and abandon, Sarah is Laura—the names ridiculously similar—and her character is both a hydrologist and detective. Because of money to fight terrorism after 9/11, in the manuscript the city has resources for cops, not scientists. A warm winter storm rolls in, and Laura is more interested in the snowpack and the possibility of flooding than the murder she is supposed to investigate. The story comes out in her police reports as an EPO, environmental patrol officer. She records the snow's density and whether the ground is frozen, whether the water will run off or be absorbed into the soil. The murder makes her nervous, not for the grisly details, but having to solve it—that solving it might disrupt the community.

In the book's opening, municipal workers use a front loader to dump old snow into the East Branch, the river that feeds the Pepacton. She watches in silence, and I write of flooding because that is what grips me, not crime; or rather, the water is the mystery I must solve. The crime novel smuggles into its very form the fantasy of closure and answers, ones I don't believe in, which might be why I keep staring at the wall. Also, those kinds of stories revolve around a main character, one singular individual who can solve the mystery instead of solutions coming from us enmeshed together. I want the book, though, to take in water and place and loss, but how to frame that into a story?

—

After my dad dies, I don't realize what I experience is grief. I can't name the feeling attached to the pain in my chest. It hurts so much I'm sure my bones will break, and I can't do anything, can't shake off the anger that starts to grow each day because I can't focus, can't concentrate, can't work, because everything feels like sludge, and sludge is impossible to move through. So every day at lunchtime when I can no longer sit still, David makes me a sandwich, and I must flee. Because I have no way to explain what is happening to me. Because all I have is rage, because I can't admit this is grief, because the emotion feels out of proportion with my relationship with my father, which only exists in fragments. This is when I find him in the woods. It is three days short of my birthday.

———

Today in this New York City in the trees, I find club moss. It forms a miniature fir forest at my feet and is a living fossil, one of those first plants that arose from the Devonian sea. This one is called a princess pine, and its green needles emerge in a semicircle just above the snowpack. I imagine the plant's exhaling and producing oxygen, and my breathing, and its leaves absorbing my carbon dioxide and us connected across time.

A single spike of faded yellow spores sticks straight up. Snow crunches underfoot. The sound is like my scratch of pen on paper as I write. The day I find him, the wind shakes the hemlocks.

———

Club moss, not a moss at all, is a vascular plant related to ferns. It once towered a hundred feet high. What happens in all those intervening millennia? How does it survive and shrink, witnessing the extinctions of the world?

Even in the snow, the princess pine's spores catch in the wind. They have been used for explosives and to spark the flash in photography. To capture a moment and hold it forever.

—

Hiking with my father when I was little, he'd rush ahead. My mom complains that he's too fast, that he never actually sees anything; that he doesn't notice the ferns. This she adds to the litany of his faults, and I wonder, was he running away from us or *to* something?

—

In Pittsburgh when he is a teenager and has been wrenched from the two-story house with the apple tree and the rabbit, he spends his days identifying trees in a park nearby. Like Vince, he dreams of growing up to become a forest ranger.

Now I think when we were hiking and my father was hurrying off, it was to greet the trees, his friends, who have held him all this time. In the woods he touches the hemlocks he meets and inhales the needles' crisp scent.

—

In the novel with Sarah as Laura, I use the word *meander* and pore over articles like "Dimensioning the Sine Wave," where this wave is "an idealized description of river meander form." I love that phrase with the idealizing. The day I read it, there is an oil spill in the Yellowstone River, and Obama delivers his state of the union, "Will we allow ourselves to be sorted into factions"—I hear the word as fractions—"and turned against one another?"

I read about Wallace Howell, a scientist and meteorologist at MIT and Harvard making rain for New York City. "City Allays Fears," one headline declares of his work, saying the only impacts might be in the Catskills. The story blossoms out in its strangeness: silver to make snow to make rain as a war and to fight a drought. A week later, I find in the paper, too, that this war and weather extend to Vietnam.

Here under the hemlocks, the deer bed down, and the heat from their bodies melts the snow. The air is warmer and protected by the tree boughs.

—

I read in Luna Leopold's book: "A reach of river is a transporting machine."

—

In another kitchen, another rebuilt home, I sit at another round table, with Gary Atkin this time. He is trim and talks with a smoker's chalky voice. He wears a red golf shirt and pressed pants; his gray hair, too, is neatly pressed to the side. I've come to hear about the reservoir. He tells me he was ten, and as he speaks he seems as if he is still ten. This man is thin and small, and I can see him as a little boy, even with the wrinkles on his brow and cheeks. In 1954 he lives in Shavertown just downriver from Steve Miller's home. Gary will tell me about how he and his brother have this plan, he says, for this life that would continue forever here. We were going to do our version of Shavertown. But, he's the only one who stays in the area. Now his brothers are gone; everyone is gone. The few friends who would meet up and tell the old stories—gone.

When his family has to move, they go from having money, it seems, Gary says, to little money, to desperation. He has to change schools. He is terrified and has no idea what is going on. Seeing my town destroyed, it's emotional. I didn't—I don't—understand. His tenses change too. He fails school that year and has to repeat a grade.

Like Steve's mother Agnes, his grandmother is the town's postmaster. She ran the general store and never works again. His dad doesn't work either, not at first. Finally he gets a job in construction, finishing the dam that displaces them.

———

Now it is an August day, and I sit next to him in a church that's no longer a church after its congregation is gone. The air is musty; the building only opens a day a year, and Gary smells faintly of cologne and cigarettes. It feels like the church exists just for this moment when people gather again who were forced from their homes by the reservoir.

Someone shows a 16 mm film. It begins with news footage. There are bonfires, and a man in coveralls says to the off-screen reporter, "No one likes to lose his home, but we can't stand in the way of progress." Auctions interrupt scenes of haying and church picnics.

Someone drives a tractor. A man stands atop a towering hay wagon. People gather outside a general store. On the soundtrack a woman's voice intones, "An auction. That is so-and-so's store."

Gary rides a tricycle and his brother runs alongside him. He is maybe five. A young woman in a white dress walks through a field with her mother. These are the last days of a community. The somber voice says, "Another auction." A crowd gathers below a front porch. People mill, spilling into the road. Thousands, Gary tells me. There are thousands here. He doesn't say this particular auction, of the dozens shown, is his family's store. Dogs cavort. Children turn to the camera, and adults look down or away as if ashamed.

So many auctions and fires are intercut with bucolic scenes, the movie seems like an experimental film—like something from Godard, maybe on capitalism. The girl in the white dress walks her bike. A dog is in the basket. Gary tells me she is the woman at the front of the church before us. It is her solemn voice on the soundtrack. She is stooped and wears khaki trousers; her thin white hair is cut into a bob. Gary says she is given a movie camera when she graduates high school, and this is what she films, the end of her town.

At his kitchen table Gary gets up. He reaches for something off a shelf. It's a handstamp to cancel mail, and the date on it is the final day the post leaves his grandmother's store: March 31, 1954.

In the film, the final building in the town burns. Flames spread from a barn to a shed to a house's white siding. The deck is engorged, the roof collapses. The shock steals my breath as I realize what is disappearing. Heavy smoke hangs over the valley. Then the iron bridge that crosses the river at his town collapses into the rising reservoir. The metal is supposed to be sold for scrap. The woman's voice says, "Even the bridge doesn't want to leave."

Outside the church someone tells me of the lost farms, the rich river-flat land, bottomland, he says, prone to floods. But, the water brings nutrients.

What happens when the river is gone and disappears, what becomes of that transporting machine?

———

In Gary's kitchen, he studies his hands. His wedding ring is simple, and he says about the reservoir, All this time, fifty, sixty years? It's just a body of water now. Everything is forgotten. I can never go home. I have no home. No place that I belong to.

Chapter 9

NOT JUST OUR LAND, BUT also our house begins to disappear. Between the floods, the town replaces the bridge, and I write as if these two facts are connected, but we do not understand the facts or their connections, not at first. The steps outside the kitchen door start to separate, pulling apart at the base. A gap grows. I think it's chipmunks digging holes. The basement stairs, the ones that lead to the Oz-like slanting doors, have always had a small crack. It widens, and the change happens so imperceptibly we cannot measure it, not at first, not for years. Then the steel doors themselves no longer quite close. We have to jam them shut, until finally we stop opening them at all. In the crawl space below, the window starts to pull from its frame. Red squirrels move into the basement.

———

Crime novels exist to make sense of disappearances, to turn them into story and plot.

Our friend Rudd comes to examine the basement. It's a dry July, and in the stream the water is low. With his brother he fished out the oil tank in the first flood and patched the road and bridge, but I didn't know him then. We meet a few years later, and last night I mentioned the hole growing in our foundation. David and I were hanging out with him and his girlfriend, Barb, in their backyard: sunset, fireflies, fire pit from whose smoke I must keep moving. Two dogs nuzzle close. There is cold pizza and warm beer. Now he and Barb materialize outside our kitchen door, staring at the water. She's in a tie-dye T-shirt with the logo of his family's farm. He is in the same khaki work pants and hunting boots he always wears, that he wore last night, with the same olive-colored hat to hide his thinning hair. Yesterday as we were leaving, he nodded and said he'd swing by some time, check out that creek of yours, a word that sounds like *crick*, like my father said it.

David didn't want me to ask. He says that Rudd's too busy. It's true he is—building roads, digging out foundations, and doing stream restoration for a private fishing club that owns an entire length of waterway that feeds into the reservoir, as well as for the Rockefellers that own another stream further away. This not wanting me to ask, however, says something more of David. He wants to research the foundation and its cracks, to figure them out himself. He tries to solve problems, to hold them close, as if that will protect us and keep the squirrels and fear at bay.

Rudd balances on a stream wall rebuilt by the village. The concrete is shaped to look like rocks. David and I are outside, and Barb waves. The bangles at her wrist jingle. Rudd says howdy, in the way he has where he swallows the syllables. He walks to the end of the new wall. It stops ten feet from the kitchen, where the old retaining wall rolls into the water.

He studies the stoop and pokes a toe at a chink of grout coming loose. Behind the house he walks along the eroding bank. In our friendship we talk about our fathers and how the two men would have liked each other, my dad with his belief in family farms and farm co-ops, and Rudd's father keeping their farm going and how many generations it has been going.

He hops into the streambed and wanders down. The ground is red and jagged where stones have fallen loose. Apparently we can't even move a rock in the water without a permit from the city, even if that rock was once part of a wall on the bank. He pronounces it fine. I am smiling; we are all together and now it is fine. He grabs onto tree roots to pull himself out and says something about brookies, that there must be trout in there. He wipes his hands on his thighs and there are more words, and it is clear this is not fine, not at all. His "fine" is not an adjective but a noun: "fines." David hears these words, and I hear a blur. David's face tightens almost imperceptibly, a cleft of worry in his brow. His hand clenches, and there is Barb in the pink-orange blaze of her T-shirt like a sunset, and her strawberry blond hair catching the light, and these fines, which are not okay, are also not fees or penalties but soil, ground, the earth. I begin to comprehend that these are the fine soils from under our house, beneath the foundation, the first I've ever heard of such things. They are being sucked out by water every time there is a high-water event. The house is disappearing into the stream.

—

I decide to think of hydrology as a governing principle for my writing like the way I have turned to the thinker and theorist Walter Benjamin trying to understand time and history, or how other writers employ the ideas of Roland Barthes or Simone Weil. I want to use water like theory and apply its ideals broadly.

In this house, with its gingerbread and basement doors like Oz, I'm trying to hold onto something, water and soils so small and important that they have their own names. I want to hold on to things that wash away, things the rain brings and takes. In this escalation of disappearances, I write about water. Because I am a writer, I turn the water into writing. I start to hang notes about it on the wall, collecting them as if holding them will provide the stability I need in this new and now disappearing home.

Luna Leopold writes about how water strives to reach a state of equilibrium, as he puts it. I strive for equilibrium too.

———

In her book *the weather*, poet Lisa Robertson describes clouds and interleaves women who are lost: "Where is Ti Grace," she writes, "Where is Shulamith."

In the next poem:

> My purpose here is to advance into
> the sense of the weather, the lesson of
> the weather. Forever I'm the age 37
> to calm my mind. I'm writing sentences here
> of an unborrowed kind. The sky is
> mauve lucite. [. . .]
> You can anticipate the wind.

———

I tape these lines to my wall.

After my mother dies, I find in her house my dad's faded turtleneck he wears as I see him. It is now in my closet. You might call the color mauve.

Now he is another disappearance to make sense of.

—

A crime novel searches for causality, constructing a sense of order from a constellation of events. But I cannot write to the connections a novel like that requires with everything working in one direction. It is too simple here with my family. Or, maybe it requires too much self-exposure. There is also a need to name who is wrong, who to blame, who did or did not do something, who is the victim. Instead, here we are in the hemlocks, with this species that is dying, and around me are all these other plants—lichen, moss, and ferns—outside the time frame of my narrative. They create their own connections that defy a single causality, the way, say, algae and the fungi join together to form lichen and how runners of club moss reach out to propagate themselves, each arm a new being, borne of itself. In the face of grief I cannot name they also hold my emotions. They become my dad. The plants feel like they give some kind of care, but I don't have a language for that either, so I just feel them as my father.

—

I find a letter he sends on his ninth birthday to his father. It is just before Christmas and just after my dad moves in with his grandparents. His mother is in a mental hospital and will eventually die in the county home. I learn these facts from my aunt. Years before that I hear rumors that my grandmother has a breakdown maybe because my grandfather runs around with other women. Or, maybe my grandmother has a breakdown because of a botched surgery, a tonsillectomy, or maybe my grandfather has her committed so he can have affairs. I do not know the truth of these things or who says them, or even how I absorb them. In the Depression, though, my grandfather loses everything, his store and the family home. My father and his sister are going to be sent to an orphanage if his grandparents, my great-grandparents, don't take them in.

But they do, they did.

My dad and his sister move to Pittsburgh the week before he writes. The two of them sleep in the unheated attic. "It is lonsome hear without you." He spells it "lonsome" without the "e," and I see him struggle with the word. He lists the presents his aunts give him—a game, a dollar—and asks, "When are you leaving? Do you know where you're going?" His father has to go somewhere, anywhere. He can't stay where he is, wherever that is. "Please write. Please. Kisses, Bobby." Below, my father, Bobby, makes fifty-four cross marks, X's for the kisses, and writes: "A hundred more kisses too."

A head cut, it comes from the smallest thing and migrates upstream. Undermining from the base.

—

One morning at dawn, a winter day: lines of contrails blaze like writing across the sky. Another day I wake up and pink fingers extend in the clouds. I take pictures of them and hang them on my wall too.

—

Passing the Gray House today, the ghost house, all that remains is green; green grass and a red 911 number for the address. The plot is so narrow bordering this Bull Run of no bulls but floods that you'd never know a house had been there. It just looks like a spot where the neighbor mows and occasionally parks his car.

——

At home the notes on my wall spread from one room to another, crossing the white expanse over the bed in the guest room. A decade after that second flood, they billow out toward Vince. There's the smoke, clouds, and war; floods, and his black-blue sky. They are a portrait of him or me, or both. There's a Goethe poem dedicated to Luke Howard, who came up with the first taxonomy for clouds. Howard is in the *Peterson's Field Guide to the Atmosphere*, which Vince Schaefer co-authored. In a 1953 *New York Times* article about nuclear war he is mentioned in a line, and there are lines of a Natalie Diaz poem where the clouds are American imperialism. She writes on love and longing and looking for love in white people, who have stolen land and so much more. This poem comes with a refrain by the Yeah Yeah Yeahs, followed by the question:

> What is America if not a clot
> Of clouds? If not spilled milk? Or blood?

Another poem of hers from an earlier book is a single sentence, both title and poem, which looks like a cloud. "The Clouds Are Buffalo Limping Toward Jesus," reads

> weeping   blooms
> 　　　　of　　　　white
> 　　　　smoke

These clouds I see extend to something larger about our country and its values and politics. Each fragment feels irreducible to me, as if it holds some 1:1 correspondence to an unfolding catastrophe. Or, maybe it's just the craziness of my craving clarity and connection.

How to talk of the grief that goes onto my wall? Is it the feeling of rough paper or the cool touch of the paint on drywall? This mass grows across it as I don't feel what is held tight inside me, what me—the character me—is trying to avoid or approach, or can only approach in this sidelong way.

These are things I want to convey: The loss of writing fiction, something that has felt like it holds my deepest self, and a father I have lost who I barely know and my village that I now love, and a house that feels like it can float away or sprout blooming clouds of spores naked to the eye but that might make me sick, might make me have to move again. I run my hands over his faded turtleneck and stand in this room and stare. What is there to tell you so you can see with me? There is David at his desk across from me in our shared office. He watches me and doesn't ask any questions, just allows this to be me in this space with these cards, which in itself feels like love.

On the wall there are notes, too, about the Shakers, the celibate socialists who get their start not far from me on the outskirts of Albany during the Revolution. At first the few believers crowd together in in one log cabin. They follow a woman named Ann Lee who believes she is the second coming of Christ. They call her Ann the Word and Mother Ann (though all her children die). Her adherents straighten the streams and drain swamps and build a new society, heaven on earth, where everyone, men and women, Black and white, are equal. They live and toil communally in "families," but the members all leave their biological families behind. Instead they adopt any child in need. When the smoke comes on the Dark Day in 1780, the Shakers don't see a premonition but a promise. They decide to start preaching the word.

I tape up lyrics about a cloud and sadness from a musical one Shaker sister sees during the Depression. Another Shaker, an eldress, one of the few Black Shaker eldresses, Rebecca Cox Jackson, reports visions of the atmosphere in the 1830s and 1840s. She writes a hundred years before Vince Schaefer and Bernard Vonnegut discover their snowmaking techniques, and she lives not far from GE, where they work. A vision was a "gift," as the Shakers call it, a communication with the spirit realm. Her dead brother later appears in one: "His heavenly love falling in bright sparks like rain."

The GE press release announcing snowmaking with silver iodide is titled "Rain by Fire." It comes in hot, violent sparks. The eldress testifies about the atmosphere. "Nothing can live above it. [. . .] It is always calm and serene between its face and the starry heaven." In another dream rain falls like cotton.

The headline of that 1953 *Times* article:

BOMBS AND WEATHER

—

Clouds of an Atomic Explosion Are
Not Thunder Clouds

The unnamed, anonymous reporter (as if the voice of God) describes one nuclear test followed by "bolts of lightning flashing and darting all around it." Everyone expected disaster. The article is meant to be reassuring. It says these storms have nothing in common with Schaefer's cloud seeding, and insists: "There is no evidence that the explosion of an atomic bomb has been followed by anything more than a passing local downpour."

A headline this week in the paper asks: "How Much Will the Planet Warm if the Carbon Dioxide Levels Double?" I take a screenshot and tape it up. A survivor of Hiroshima says in a news report on the seventy-fifth anniversary: "It happened in the morning, it was dark like twilight." Another Dark Day. War, weather, technology, and climate change all run together across my wall. There are also the storms my father learns about in the Merchant Marine. He joins because of the war but for decades won't be acknowledged as a veteran even though more die on these ships than in any other branch of the service. He is there because he is poor, because the Merchant Marine pays more than any other part of the military—and because he idolizes his brother, a Navy lieutenant.

In the very middle I hang a photo of a snowflake. It glows like an X-ray, a white vibration against a black background. The picture runs on the cover of *Science* magazine in 1966, and Vince Schaefer shoots it. The snow is made with lead from gasoline, from the exhaust. He's discovered our cars were making clouds and ice. At that moment they are killing us.

—

I want to lay all of these moments next to each other, as if to hold time itself, as if I could run my fingers over its grooves, like something incised in stone. Set side-by-side, epochs, eras, millennia, days, and years are not distant but held in a place, together on my wall.

———

I return over and over to the woods, up the steep hill. Before the ridge, the stone walls peter out, and then on the other side is a field. It's on a five hundred–acre plot owned by New York City. As child in the summer, I'd visit meadows like this alone. We would spend our two-week vacation each year at a defunct ski resort in Vermont. There was no one else around, no other kids, no families. My sisters had left for college and adulthood, and people often assumed my parents were my grandparents. I was lonely and desperate for someone, anyone, my age to play with.

I nag. I whine. I circle the table where my dad is working. See him writing in a yellow legal pad, feel the table shake with his notes. (I, too, now use a yellow legal pad for my drafts.) He says, We'll go out in a bit, Jenny, and take a swim. Go read. My mom will send me out to pick and identify wildflowers, just to give me something to do.

I walk up the dirt road. It clings to the side of the mountain, doubling back on itself as it follows the slope. I study the ground and stare at the ditches, collecting buttercups and daisies. They are flowers of spring but still in bloom here this far north, this high up. My favorite is bladder campion. It looks like little white bonnets. They dry and keep their shape as if made of tissue paper. I cut through someone's yard, past their empty, maybe-abandoned chalet, and sit on a boulder on the ski slope. The world feels green.

The flowers in my hand, their stems grow limp with my sweat. Strawberry runners cross the rock. It's dotted with red lichen. Surrounding me is goldenrod yet to bloom and milkweed and bracken ferns. Enveloped in the grasses and leaves, the plants hold my longing.

———

Now in the woods with the club moss, I am sure it has built the world that we can inhabit. Once it created forests, and here I run my fingers over the needles. They are soft and gentle. I read in a geology textbook from my friend how those ancient forests where I live are the first place to have the sound of wind or insects. I love that fact because, of course, you need trees and plants to hear the breeze.

Club moss often takes longer to reach reproductive age than us—fifteen years. They were part of changing oxygen on earth. Touching them, with their tender needles, feels like touching time, like reaching Pangea.

Part II

Chapter 10

IT IS AUGUST, AND I drive across an inland sand sea, searching for Vince Schaefer and Bernard Vonnegut. The sea is created in a moment of climate collapse 13,000 years ago, a period of warming. The glaciers are melting, and water rushes down what will become in our times the Mohawk and Hudson Rivers. The torrent rages with more force than Niagara Falls and leaves sand in its wake, spreading across forty square miles from what's now called Schenectady to Albany, the state capital.

Twenty minutes from the mountain where Vince makes smoke and Iris and I climb, the remnants of the sand sea are a landscape of two interstates. Their on-ramps and off-ramps curve and circle. Traffic merges and accelerates, speeding past the glacial terrain. You can still see the traces of that older landscape if you focus. Pitch pines sway as trucks pass. Here, too, is where the Shakers get their start; so does General Electric, cofounded by Thomas Edison, ushering in the electrical age and producing the first halogen bulb. Now the area is home to the strip mall where I buy running shoes, two municipal airports, the landfill, and a state university campus.

On the phone I talk to a Mohawk elder, Tom Porter. His voice is soft and deliberate. The edges sound buffed, as if he were speaking from somewhere far away. He grew up speaking Mohawk first, then English, and living on the US/Canadian border, near Malone, New York. In the early nineties Tom creates a community in the Mohawk Valley as a way to return to his ancestral home. He tells me Schenectady means "the far side of the pines," but pine itself is not quite the word. It is gum for the pine tar. He spells it out "s-k-a-n-e-t-a-t-i," and pronounces it. The *T* a *D*, the *I* an *E*, and the *E* a short *A*. It actually means the place we now call Albany, which was and is to the Mohawk people the other side of the pines. Like the place where the ice speaks and Vince Schaefer makes smoke, this is all Mohawk land.

I talk, too, to Paul Gorgen, a historian who is also friends with Tom and on the board of the Mohawk community. Paul's parents worked at GE and so did he for a year before joining IBM. His family is Palatine German and Dutch with Mohawk relatives on both sides. He grows up near the Mohawk Valley. He has a rumbling, laconic voice and tells me that in the early eighteenth century the British put the Germans into labor camps making turpentine for the British Navy. They're forced to gather pitch from pine trees in the Hudson Valley, but they're the wrong kinds of pines, and the Germans are starving to death and abandoned by the British. So, they take off for a place they've heard about called Schoharie.

The name, he says, means "driftwood bridge." It's the creek that runs north from the dam the governor inspects the day of my second flood. Paul explains that on their way there, the Germans cut through the forest near Schenectady, where ironically there is the right kind of pine tree for turpentine, and they meet the Mohawk people. The Germans are taken in as refugees. He says too,

Any place names that didn't get replaced by white settlers still tell about the importance of the location.

———

Here on one side of the pines, I pull up to the GE campus. Overhead, a neon General Electric sign towers above, a beacon from another age. Behind an iron fence, the grass is verdant. Twinned red brick buildings stand seven stories high. One is the corporate headquarters, the other the lab where Vince and Bernie worked. Its research is so important to the company that the buildings are connected by an aerial bridge, as if crossing between them means walking on air, in the sky.

There's a picture of the two men standing in a long line of scientists, each in their office doorways, down a hallway that seems to continue forever into infinity. Everyone smiles and all but one is male. Vince is in his shirtsleeves; Bernie a suit slouched open. With everyone grinning, it looks like the set of a Broadway musical, if one were set in a lab, and I expect them to break out in song, dancing down the hall.

Staring at the buildings protected by a gate and guard, I wonder, too, how Vince gets to be at the front of that long line of researchers in the hallway. How far is the distance emotionally and otherwise from being a machinist? The people in that hall, the GE Research Lab, are not just any engineers in any corporate lab but the apex of achievement at the company, and the best scientists in the country. They are so lofty you have to reach them from a bridge in the sky.

———

Bernie and Vince are white men of a certain era. They believe in the twin promises of progress and science, that they will unfurl into the future, leading to the perfection of humanity. They also believe in serendipity, Vince calls it. In the GE Research Lab, he learns that science is pure and that their research benefits from following their curiosity. Nothing should stand in the way. It is a theory of joy, and one where nothing can really go wrong. Even if an experiment doesn't pan out, there are no consequences, as if the men are above such things.

———

What does it take to become this man, no longer a machinist, but a scientist? It's the same question I have about my dad. He leaves his grandparents' for Oberlin on a scholarship and is so poor his cousins take a collection so he can have clothes for college.

———

Nothing and Nothing.

February 1940. Vince walks to the bus after work. A snowflake falls on his sleeve, and then another and another. Snow is bewitching. He knows these flakes are rare and dreams of possessing one forever. They are six-sided crystals, the product of a specific temperature and humidity. Walking home from the bus stop, he gets an idea how to capture a single flake. He's been practicing making surface films, plastic films, and calculates how long the plastic solution will remain liquid below freezing. Just long enough, maybe, to preserve the snow. First he tries in the freezer. The solution evaporates, leaving a single perfect crystal of ice. In his backyard, he repeats the process again and again on glass slides. There's a photo of him in the snow: knit cap and gloves, wool jacket, microscope and vials. Later he uses the technique to improve TV tubes and preserve leaf structures and dragonfly eyes, which strikes me as impossibly cruel. The insects have five different eyes and thousands of lenses as well as the ability to see hues that we can't even imagine, like ultraviolet and polarized lights bouncing off water.

"I thought," he says of the snow, "as I saw this evanescent beauty that it would be wonderful if such crystals could be preserved."

A quarter century later he photographs those flakes I have on my wall, the ones made of lead exhaust.

———

In 1610 another scientist, Johannes Kepler, crosses a bridge in Prague, and snow falls on his sleeve. He needs a New Year's gift, and this is it, he thinks: this single flake. It descends from the heavens and looks like a star. Instead of trying to encapsulate forever the crystal on his sleeve as Schaefer will do centuries later, Kepler creates a meditation on nothing and nothingness—and poverty. He writes a slim fifteen-page treatise on this six-sided snowflake.

Somewhere between poetry and philosophy, his study is a play on language, meaning, and evanescence. He works in Latin, whose word for snow is *nix*, which in Kepler's German sounds like *nichts*, or "nothing." Kepler gets at snow's fleeting nature, but that "nothing" has another meaning too. Kepler is poor; the emperor avoids paying him, so the essay, the snowflake—nothing—is all Kepler can give his friend. "Here was something smaller than a drop, yet endowed with a shape. Here, indeed, was a most desirable New Year's gift for the lover of Nothing, and one worthy as well of a mathematician (who has Nothing, and receives Nothing). [. . .] Let us then go back to our patron while the little gift lasts before the warmth of my body dissolves it into nothing."

He searches to understand how and why a flake is formed, and his quest becomes the foundations of crystallography, a discipline so important to our world that a decade ago the UN declares 2014 the Year of Crystallography. The word comes from the Greek crystallon, "cold frozen drop," and grapho, "I write." Here I write of cold, frozen drops.

———

Kepler asks too: "From this almost Nothing I have very nearly recreated the entire universe, which contains everything! [. . .] Am I now to present [. . .] the orb of the earth in a tiny atom of snow?"

It's in the snow that I first find my dad. A Victorian nature writer, John Burroughs, from my neighboring town, writes of snow in 1866: "All sounds are sharper in winter; the air transmits better. [. . .] The world lies about me in a 'trance of snow.' The clouds are [. . .] the ghosts of clouds," and here I am with my dad, the ghost. There is Kepler, too, and his tiny atoms holding the world. My father feels like a presence, an enveloping kindness in the air surrounding me, and I don't want to explain more or scrutinize his appearance. It lasts for six years until my mother's death.

In this time we have a single fight. It's just after my cousin dies of a heart attack at fifty-two. That same weekend my sister undergoes surgery. The operation lasts far longer than anyone predicts, and the doctors discover cancer. Her odds extend to months, and in my mind I yell at him. I think at my dad that, if nothing else, he must protect her. This makes no sense, or makes as much sense as any. She is the one closest to him in life, and she is with him as he is dying, and he better do something, I think. Now in this moment as I write, she has lived for nine years and is still alive.

Kepler returns to his mother's home not long after giving his friend the essay on snow. He goes to defend her from forty-nine charges of witchcraft. He is a scientist who straddles faith, magic, math, astronomy, and astrology, and while there the only other work he does is on his *Harmonices Mundi*, where he posits that on one day all the planets will align and sing.

—

I stand outside GE with its lush grass, with the skybridge no one crosses to a lab that is no longer there, in a glacial landscape that is a shopping mall, and I am searching for snow in August. Here I write of nothing, of these men who have nothing, Vince and my father, men who lose things, who have longing, who dream of snow, or trees, or hiking. Who believe they can forge better worlds. Idealism always comes laced with innocence and hope, bearing the seeds of its failures.

Chapter 11

AFTER THE WAR, BERNARD VONNEGUT joins GE. Like Vince, he has studied aerosols to make better gas masks in the war and then works on ice, on deicing planes for the military. Bernie wears his brown hair in a quiff and has a penchant for tweed. He is both imperious and goofy with an inclination to scatological jokes, I read, fart jokes in particular. Decades later, in the hospital as he is dying of cancer, one colleague tells me, he's still joking. "No need to buy green bananas," Bernie says drily. He will also quit his office in that hallway at GE in a huff. Someone deigns to clean his desk while he's on vacation; and later at another job, he holds a simmering standoff, a resentment that builds for weeks when an assistant makes the same mistake.

I feel like I should be more sensitive or charitable. The family loses all their money before the Depression and sacrifices to send Bernie to college. In the 1940s, he survives his mother's suicide, and at GE secures his brother Kurt a job in the company's PR division, as Kurt struggles to be a writer, as he tries to find his place after the war, after being firebombed and declared dead and mourned and lost by his family. Visiting General Electric's labs in the sky, Kurt Vonnegut will help make Bernie a star too.

At the end of World War II Bernie comes to GE for a job interview. He meets Vince, and the men talk intently about ice. They are fascinated with the weather. In the late 1930s Vince experiments with ice cube trays, with getting ice out of the aluminum trays, and in World War II, the experiments become how water freezes on metal sheets—the same deicing problems Bernie tries to solve. Vince takes his research to Mt. Washington, the highest peak in the Northeast, with temperatures below zero and winds over 100 mph. He hikes up to the observatory at the top and skis down afterward. There, Vince finds clouds where water remains as drops even as temperatures plunge below freezing. The water is so pure, there's no snow. There's a term for these clouds, "supercooled," and they're why planes get coated in ice as they fly, passing through them.

———

What is snow, Kepler asks. "There must be some definite cause why, whenever snow begins to fall, its initial formations invariably display the shape of a six-cornered starlet." He argues, too, in his essay that dust has more substance than a drop of water.

But snow is dust and dirt. That water in the supercooled cloud is pure, too pure to make a crystal. It needs a seed, an ice nucleus, it is called, and the drops cohere to it. The snow falls from the particles of forest fires and emissions of diesel trucks and sand blown across the planet. Snow can come from something called black carbon, soot, which resembles carbon black. Flakes even form around the debris of dead stars.

Finding a seed they can use in the lab becomes Vince and Bernie's quest. After the war they want to make snow, which is to make rain. That's freedom at GE: to make weather, to shape it and control it.

It is 1946, the year my father is diving off boats into the bay and studying clouds. Alone, he steers ships to shore because these ships must return to harbor, because the war is over, because he needs the money, because for him there is no GI Bill for college tuition.

———

I find his union cards and the logbook that details what ships he's on, the hours he works, and his overtime, written carefully in pen.

In the lab that same summer Vince plans to make snow in an icebox. He's obsessed with those supercooled clouds, with getting the drops of water to transform into flakes—crystals. He takes a GE chest freezer like the kind in my basement and lines it in black velvet. In one photo he's bent over it, and you can see the velvet nailed to plywood, frost gathering at the edges. The idea is he will breathe into the freezer, and exhaling will make a cloud just like seeing our breath on a winter's day. That, too, is a cloud, a fog—the vapor, our breath, condensing.

The freezer is so cold, the cloud of breath won't dissipate. It weighs more than the warm air above in the lab. He shakes in dust, soils, ash, chemical dusts . . . anything to precipitate snow. He gets nothing, nothing, and nothing, not until one sweltering day. It is too humid for the freezer to stay cold. He finds some dry ice to cool it and exhales. Instantly his breath sparkles in a blue haze. Snow. He makes snow. He just needed dry ice as a precipitate for the moist air in his breath to cling to.

Picture the celebration that must follow: the haze and humidity of Schenectady outside, and here the long hallway lined with doors crowded now with people. I imagine their cheering and jostling Vince. Someone will find a seven-inch copy of "A White Christmas." They serve ice cream and sing along, *I'm dreaming of . . .*

———

GE releases a photo of a cloud, this fog, he makes. It looks like a bright smudge, the kind of image a paranormal might advertise as the photo of a ghost.

THIS IS WHAT INSIDE OF A CLOUD LOOKS LIKE. BEAM OF LIGHT SHINING THROUGH CLOUD RE-VEALS FOGGY ATMOSPHERE, WHICH ACTUALLY IS MILLIONS OF TINY WATER DROPLETS WHICH ARE REFERRED TO AS "SUPERCOOLED" BECAUSE EVEN THOUGH THEY HAVE A TEMPERATURE BELOW FREEZING, THEY REMAIN LIQUID.

In another picture, Vince, Bernie, and the scientist for whom they both work bend over the freezer. Bernie watches intently as Vince breathes into the velvet. A mysterious glow emerges like in a 1950s sci-fi movie. The freezer's lid is propped open and taped to it are photos of snowflakes Vince has made by freezing them and affixing them to plastic film.

Crystallized water, ice and snow, has a hexagonal structure, and comes in more forms than any other material. At different temperatures, it creates different solids: plates, dendrites, needles, and columns. At 23 degrees Fahrenheit, snow falls as hollow columns, and Kepler's six-sided star is found at both 5 and 28 degrees. What temperature is it on the bridge that day in Prague?

Kepler searches to understand the hexagonal structure of snow. He examines beehives and pomegranate seeds, even stacking cannonballs on boats. These drops, these flakes, these men, this need to control, to understand. (And me, I need to understand too. I want to preserve the ephemeral, the melting and dissolving.)

———

A few months later in November 1946 Vince flies east from Schenectady in a plane all the way to Mount Greylock in Massachusetts to see if he can recreate his experiment and make snow, real snow, in the sky. He's been waiting months for the right weather. Now he and the pilot fly into the cloud, and I feel like I'm reading the Shaker eldress Rebecca Cox Jackson. "I looked toward the sun and observed a beautiful colored corona and saw it gradually disappear as a sharply outlined disc [. . .] I also noticed brilliant iridescent colors in portions of the cloud edges." Then he drops six pounds of dry ice from the airplane door.

The New York Times reports the plane reaches 14,000 feet, and the flakes evaporate before many of them reach the ground. GE estimates that one pea-sized pellet of dry ice will produce enough precipitation to develop several tons of snow. Vince is elated. The plane passes "through a mass of glinting snow crystals," he writes. Then just as quickly the snow dries up.

Bernie is sure he can make something better, that lasts longer, that doesn't evaporate. He will use silver iodide. Its structure is similar to an ice crystal's, close enough to trick water molecules into forming snowflakes around it. No longer dust or dirt or ash as the seed, it will be this compound.

He needs to make smoke with the silver iodide to get it into the air. First he experiments using the generators Vince developed in World War II that cloaked the mountain in fog. Soon as Bernie tries them, the lab fills with crystals. On cold nights he strolls through his suburb, holding aloft a burning newspaper dipped in silver iodide to make smoke. The crystal fog follows him, I read, as he wanders the streets.

Later will come the PR shots of snowmaking at GE. Bernie is often in the center. He'll hold a balloon or a toy popgun, even a bottle of soda into a freezer. Each of these will make snow. In one image he stands at the icebox with a circle of military officials.

The *New York Times* calls snowmaking "a powerful weapon." As a weapon, it is impossible to ignore. The silver iodide, though, remains in the atmosphere longer than other precipitates. *Time* magazine reports, "Here apparently was a tool of almost miraculous potency." In the magazine's pages the head of GE's Research Lab, Irving Langmuir, calculates that "pure silver iodide was so powerful that only 200 pounds would be enough to seed the planet's entire atmosphere." Imagine a world covered in ice and snow from two hundred pounds of anything. That's less than the weight of two people. That is ice-nine, or something close. Soon the US Army takes over the seeding and snowmaking. They call it Project Cirrus. There's something enchanting about turning ice into a weapon, this nothing and nothing with its dazzling prisms, daggers of light that can hold a rainbow, or in the woods can muffle sound and make the world quiet. It is the same thing Sarah-as-Laura in my novel likes. She writes in her reports about the snow, how over the time of her investigation, the surface hardens to amplify every tiny noise.

———

The GE press release declaring in all caps RAIN BY FIRE hangs on my wall. Vonnegut's technique, "uses fire [. . .] to dispense tiny silver iodide particles into the atmosphere." They need to be hot. "Fiercely burning," GE explains, "charcoal impregnated with silver iodide solution emits thousands of sparks, each of which produce millions of silver iodide particles." I think of Bernie's younger brother Kurt firebombed in Dresden, and how not far from where I stand at GE the Shaker eldress lived with her visions of the atmosphere. In one her brother returns from the dead in sparks of fire.

———

Bernie needs to keep his brother close, safe; that's why he gets him the job. I imagine after all the losses he can't bear another. In my mind, too, these reasons are impossible for Bernie to express—because of the era, because he is not good with his feelings, because he must deflect them in a joke, because he didn't fight in the war, because he feels guilty that he did not fight in the war, because he was a scientist and not in danger, because it is a time men do not speak of their love.

Chapter 12

BEHIND THE IRON FENCE, I watch the guard in his booth at GE and wonder how long until he tells me to move. A shadow of his form shifts. His arm lifts, and overhead the clouds are cirrus. High above, somewhere, it is snowing and evaporating. Trees cast shadows on the perfect lawn, and beyond the gate, the road passes under the brick bridge between the buildings. Through its windows you can see the blue skies of forever, or darkness, as Vince put it. The gate opens. A black Volvo drives out. The guard comes out too, and I hop in my car before he can say anything.

I drive east, past other GE entrances. One is now a concrete barrier blocking the road, another a gray metal gate made of cyclone fencing. Barbed wire tops it, along with two stop signs. Which gate does Vince pass through that night in 1940 as snow falls on his shirt and shoulder? Back then Schenectady was called the Electric City. I wonder at this company that has made land mines and wind turbines, microwaves and military turbojets, light bulbs and the first TV broadcast in a house a couple miles from here. All of these things General Electric has produced—TVs, too, and TV shows and TV stations and things to advertise on TV and radio, refrigerators and stoves and ovens, and things to see inside our bodies, using sound waves with frequencies so high we can't hear them, but they see our soft tissues, our breasts and babies and lungs. With magnetic fields and radio waves, the company tracks the hydrogen atoms in our bodies. It scans our bones and their densities, our cells and their cancers. General Electric has marshaled the world to make it better or destroy it or illuminate it. And before you read this, in 2021, the company itself begins to vanish. It is "broken up," the news announces, a disappearance for capitalism, in an attempt to protect shareholders' interests.

Ice once covers this land. Twenty thousand years ago, the glaciers here are two miles thick. It licks down in lobes, and those very words, the Ls, the "lick" and "lobe," loll on my tongue. They sound so gentle. They can't match the ice's violence. The earth's mantle bows and breaks under the burden. Lake beds are carved; layers of rock sheered off, ground into sand and debris.

Then a few thousand years of warming, the debris— boulders and gravel—held by the ice is moved hundreds of miles. A chain of frozen lakes is left in its wake. The ice retreats; the earth rebounds. It still is rebounding, and I imagine the sheer weight of those crystals—snow compacted over centuries—and how one night, maybe it's 5:30 p.m. or 6:23, under the glow of streetlights Vince leaves through the same iron railings where I stand. They swing open for him and he gets snow on his sleeve.

All those floods and that melting ice, that cold water, spills into the ocean, shutting its currents down and starting a new ice age. What is that in the face of our melting glaciers, polar ice caps, desalinization, currents destabilizing and slowing?

I drive east toward Albany. The land is flat and green. I pass farm stands and suburban tract homes, the Open

Arms Church, self-storage units, squat office buildings, hair salons with punned names, and Lasting Memories Taxidermy. Over millennia here the sands settle and species arrive. They depend on the sand and fire. People, the Haudenosaunee and their predecessors, burn the land to manage it.

Then white people come and the sands come to be called a "barren," a pine barren. The barrenness of this place also leads it to be termed a waste and a wasteland, because nothing of value seems to grow here, no crops at least.

I reach the land of the strip mall and Starbucks, Speedway gas stations and the airport. The area is called Colonie, the *ie* some holdover of Dutch colonization. Over the years the name has changed. It's been Niskayuna for "where the corn grows," like Onistagrawa, and also Watervliet, which means "water flood."

I drive to Whole Foods and at the mall wonder about other more recent extinctions: the Regal Cinemas and Sears. I pull out from the Colonie Center with an expensive bottle of probiotics, and across the street is an empty beige building. A shadow of its past adorns the front: Barnes & Noble.

I think of what Paul Gorgen, the historian, tells me about the irony of the wrong pine trees and how somewhere near here, too, the Palatine Germans meet the Mohawk people.

The Shakers come in 1776, and Nabokov comes as well 153 years later. In 1959 he writes of the sand: "People go there on Sundays to picnic, shedding papers and beer cans." In a letter he says, "Nothing else of popular or scientific interest is to be found in that neighborhood." Except butterflies, that is. He comes for them. He discovers here one little blue butterfly, the Karner blue. It flits on tiny azure wings and lives for a couple days then dies around the Fourth of July. It, too, is dependent on the fires. It feeds and lays its eggs on one specific lupine that only grows here, and the Karner blue is now nearly extinct.

His novel *Pnin* describes how they rise from "a damp patch of sand [. . . and] revealing the celestial hue of their upper surface, they fluttered around like blue snowflakes before settling again."

—

My father also comes here. He travels these roads. It is the early 1950s; my sisters aren't born yet. My parents are just married. They live ninety miles away, and still he arrives. He comes for a dream of something held communally, a dream of the "public."

—

The first time I come is in the year of my flood. I take David to the airport. A sign with a silhouette of a plane points left, so does another that says SHAKER SITE. I follow the Shakers and the plane. I turn onto Albany Shaker Road. I drop him at departures and decide to find those radical socialists, thrilled they are nearby.

After the airport, the Shaker signs disappear. Time and space spreads out. I get lost. Marsh grasses wave at an angry sky hazed with heat. A sign says I'm driving to Schenectady. A blue sign implores drivers looking for "Old Albany Shaker Road Businesses" to turn right. I turn right. There are no Shakers here, no history, no sites, nothing picturesque, just Hertz, the Comfort Inn, and rusting chain-link fences. The road dead-ends at the county jail, another fence, and the runway. I have no idea this is all the Shaker site.

Another day I find a glacier. I am here to meet Neil Gifford, a conservation biologist in the Pine Bush Preserve whose job is to protect the tiny slivers of sand that are left and the species that depend on it. We stand at a fence guarding a dirt track. It faces what looks like a meadow, a prairie, at the base of a mountain. Asters and goldenrod bob their heads. There is a stream and a pond. Neil wears hiking boots and trekking gear. He waves around us and says a few years before this was a subdivision: streets, houses, septic systems, driveways . . . The county bought it up to transform back to sands that it will burn regularly.

Just beyond us, the mountain is fenced in, and the top is flat like a smaller version of Vroman's Nose to our west. On it a tanker spews water. The truck is so high and distant it looks like a toy. This bluff, though, is not a mountain—it is the Albany landfill, a hundred acres of trash, 360,000 tons deposited a year. Neil first arrived here for the fires twenty-five years ago to volunteer on prescribed burns set each summer to preserve the sand and butterflies, scrub oak and pines. He met his wife on one of the burns.

We cross a sandy track so fine and golden we could be at the beach. A few feet away, the ground goes gray. A tire tread is hardened into it. Neil tells me it's clay, like glaciers deposit today. They melt, leaving areas that pond and pool where the clay filters out. Same here, he says, just millennia ago. He is showing me a glacier in this shadow of the dump, a shadow of trash filled with what we've discarded.

The dump will disappear soon too. It is supposed to close in 2026 to be returned to sand and scrub and hopefully harbor Nabokov's butterflies, those blue clouds of snow.

—

This is where the Black Shaker eldress Rebecca Cox Jackson records her visions of the weather, the ones that hang on my wall. She dreams of clouds and the atmosphere. She also becomes celibate, leaves her husband, and travels the East Coast preaching a vision of salvation before joining the Shakers. She is illiterate but discovers she can read. It is a blessing. It is God. She picks up a Bible and the words are alive. Via the title, "eldress," she becomes a leader, and in 1843, just after her first visit to Watervliet, the water flood, she dreams of rain and flowers.

The day I see the glacier, I ask Neil, in his beige safari pants and boots, why the tanker sprays water on top of the mountain.

Water? he says, puzzled.

Up there, I point, for the grasses, right?

I assume native grasses have been planted on the dump's plateau.

He laughs. It's not water. It's air freshener—Febreze.

Indeed, the smell wafts over us. It has a green chemical scent like drier sheets. He and I stand on these spectral streets, the air filled with clouds of water, of rain—and of chemicals sprayed to mask the smell of trash. Jackson's flowers fall in bunches after the rain. "I put some in my bosom, but I am not able to tell what they smelt like. The whole air was perfumed with their odor, yea, with their heavenly smell."

The Shakers call this the gift. If you're a true believer, you can see the spirit world clear as day. I stand with Neil and his red pickup where a suburb was, and a glacier is now exposed. At home later I zoom in on this spot with Google Earth. Shadowy lines appear on-screen over the sand and scrub. These shadows are roads. Hovering over them with my mouse, their names appear: Fox Run Lane, Brier Fox Boulevard, Tally Ho Drive, Fox Hound Avenue, Hunters Glen Avenue. They conjure British landed gentry, the sort who wear red tailcoats and jodhpurs and ride to hounds, as if that could ever exist behind the landfill. I find a paneled home with an SUV outside, next door a sedan, and yellow siding on the house. Some lots just appear as grass and foundation, and I think this might be my gift.

Chapter 13

I GET ON THE HIGHWAY, following two lanes of traffic that funnel onto the interstate Steve Miller built. On the horizon floats a single cloud that looks like a Titian—fulsome and creamy, edged in pink and gold. It's so gorgeous I feel like I could die for having seen it. Schaefer loved clouds. He takes pictures of them all his life and is nearly eighty when he co-authors *Petersen's Field Guide to the Atmosphere*. On its opening page: an Olmec petroglyph of maize, the sun, and cumulus clouds thousands of years old. Circles blow like winds.

He returns to GE as a machinist in 1929, the same year my father leaps into the lake and the Albany Shaker community is closing. Their fields and pastures are being sold off. People come in trucks to pick up the furniture, those chairs that, in their simplicity, come to seem a harbinger of modernism. One of the buildings becomes a TB sanatorium and another a "preventorium" for children at risk of tuberculosis. One of the last sisters left, Lucy Bowers, keeps a diary that year. She writes of visiting kids in the "pre," she calls it, and going to the airport and flying in planes. I'm fascinated by how this woman who is supposed to live an abstinent simple life is also one of the first people in the United States to fly.

On Thanksgiving the sisters have a chicken dinner and go to a movie, *The Gold Diggers of Broadway*. It's a play within a play where showgirls search for men and money. There's drinking and dancing on tables. Girls sleep with married men. The story hinges on one dancer's failure to say: "I am the spirit of the ages and the progress of civilization." Its hit song is "Painting the Clouds with Sunshine."

The Shakers and their socialist dreams are nearly extinct, and the movie is lost, all but the last twenty minutes. Now there are only two practicing Shakers left. They live in Maine. I don't know what Sister Lucy thinks of the film. I can't imagine with all that sex and money. Her last diary entry is Thanksgiving Day.

"Painting the blue, beautiful hues," the song goes, "Colored with gold and old rose . . . Trying to drown all of my woes . . . If I keep painting the clouds with sunshine . . ."

Eldress Rebecca writes: "And in my heart," she says of the snow and silver and ice, "the sight was magnificent."

———

A signboard over the interstate flashes: ONE SMALL ASK WEAR A MASK.

———

In the 1820s Welsh industrialist-turned-socialist reformer Robert Owen also comes to Watervliet. He's realized capitalism is impossible—or impossible to fix. It will never empower the workers, however many schools he starts or how much childcare he provides, so he comes to learn from the Shakers. The Victorian reformer Jeremy Bentham, who pioneers prisons and the panopticon and dedicates himself to progress, engineering, and determinism, says of Owen: "He begins in vapor and ends in smoke."

When my father arrives, his words begin in water and air and end in us. He comes for floods, dams, and electricity. I will add this to the wall too.

———

I pass an Amazon distribution plant, rolling hills, and dairy farms, all in the blur of sixty-five mph that's really eighty as I speed. My dad, he travels the two-lane highway that runs parallel to the interstate. The interstate does not yet exist. He comes here to harangue anyone who will listen about the state's planned hydroelectric projects to ensure they are not privatized. He believes that resources belong to all of us, rather than corporations and shareholders. That is in 1951, the same year Vince and Bernie testify about their rainmaking to Congress.

At home on my desk a manila envelope is stained with age. Square in the center, a sticker bears my father's name. Inside, the pages are dusty, the paper decaying. It hurts my throat. My sinuses swell, and touching the sheets my fingers grow sore. The file contains the testimony he drives here to deliver, and he invokes an "air of humbleness" as he opens. The water he speaks of is not connected to the ships or the ports and harbors he visits, or his overtime at sea that I find in another folder. This water concerns public policy, and he lists all the papers he's written on the subject in college and his single year of graduate school as if to give himself some standing before this board. He is in his early twenties, and he and my mother run a tiny rural electric co-op an hour from where I live now. He is lobbying, we'd call it, though no one pays him. He's driven here on his own time, in an old run-down used car.

Whatever else the testimony contains, I grasp onto

the last lines. He declares, "One resource doesn't outweigh another, but we believe these resources belong to all the people, therefore should be developed by some agency of the people, so that they shall be available to all on an equal basis." It is this "all equal," that "we believe," this faith, this "us" I hold close.

It's six years after his death, the year my mother dies, the year a man with yellow hair, orange skin, and red rage splits us into factions. His "us" is not everyone but aggrieved white people, and however sick reading my father's pages makes me, I can't put them away. The typed letters on the sheets rise like braille. I run my fingers over them, as if to feel through time, and I am desperate for an all to believe in, so I make these words what I need and use up their charms. I keep the folder on my desk.

In a crime novel time moves forward and promises progress. In the world around me, though, people claim to make America great again, extolling a past where power over people and land was the norm.

———

Overhead, the Titian cloud has disappeared, but I want to speak its language.

A truck slows uphill with its flashers on, and I follow the sinews of the Mohawk River with its catastrophic flood thousands of years ago. Luna Leopold's equations about rivers and streams come with a beauty I can't comprehend. He also works as a meteorologist in the war. His father, the environmentalist Aldo Leopold, dies before he can complete his *Sand County Almanac*. The book describes a year in another glacial landscape. Luna finishes his father's masterpiece, one of the earliest books on conservation.

I find a picture of Luna in the field with surveying equipment in 1953. He stands on a rolling prairie. It looks like a movie set. Under Technicolor skies, he is swarthy and tan, and dressed all in sand in his Stetson and khakis.

I imagine the conversations Luna Leopold might have with Vince and Bernie talking about war, water, and weather. The three of them speak earnestly, urgently of rain and snow. In my imagination, they talk of rivers, but mean atmospheric ones, dense and saturated storms that travel from Hawaii, where Luna Leopold is stationed, to the continental United States.

—

In writing on rivers and streams and their laws, he says they come with "caveats [. . .] that do not dictate one and only one solution. [. . .] Thus random chance plays a major role in local changes."

Random chance. I underline that and add the quote to my wall.

Chapter 14

ON THANKSGIVING WEEKEND IN 1950 a group of hunters in Arkville, named for weathering floods, report a "soft substance" falling from the sky. They think it is silver iodide. My local weekly, the *Catskill Mountain News*, reports that one of the six, "Mrs. Lyman Todd"—Esther is her name. It takes me hours of searching genealogy websites and obituaries to discover it, but I want her not to be simply identified by her husband's details—"was so saturated with the substance that she had great difficulty after reaching home to wash it out of her hair." It says, too, that the hunters hear a plane but can't see it. Simultaneously nearby, "the home of Hiram Fairbairn [. . .] was also sprinkled with a foreign substance." Then come the rains and floods.

Not even six months afterward, the GE executive in charge of the research lab testifies before Congress. He describes silver iodide as a "very fine mist."

It is also insoluble—part of why it's good for rainmaking. Silver iodide won't dissipate or dissolve in the pure water of a supercooled cloud. That, too, makes it hard to get out of your hair.

Bernard Vonnegut tells the senators that a "tiny generator fed with burning gas and silver iodide sends up one quadrillion particles of silver iodide per second. Each particle is enough under proper conditions to make one snowflake or raindrop."

It isn't a plane the hunters hear that day, but a generator with its one quadrillion particles, a number so large I can't even parse it.

—

Before the city starts rainmaking, it introduces "Shaveless Fridays," and it outlaws car washing to save water. Cardinal Spellman seeks prayers for rain. The five boroughs are pitted against each other in the fight to cut water use. Headlines publish water statistics: how much has been conserved, how many days of water are left, and how many millions of gallons a day the city needs to restore its reservoirs. The reservoir that swallows four villages, including Steve and Gary's, comes five years later in 1954.

Life magazine prints photos of the barren banks of another city reservoir about twenty minutes from my house. Officials consult foresters. They are the ones who recommend cutting all the trees. The city meets with Vince and Bernie's boss Irving Langmuir, searching for solutions. He suggests they hire a "cloud physicist," a rainmaker. The phrase, with clouds and physics together, sounds beautiful, ephemeral, but also as if trying to bring the physics of the nuclear age to the sky.

GE won't take the job. The company worries about liability. Instead GE puts forward Dr. Wallace E. Howell. That day Vince calls him and so does the head of the American Meteorology Association, telling him to ask "for a top fee, $100 a day would benefit the profession." That's more than $1,200 a day now, a sum guaranteed to garner attention for rainmaking. It is still nascent. The army is trying it, but this will be the biggest trial yet, and it will spread across the Catskills' 6,000 square miles. My county alone is the size of Rhode Island.

—

Howell is thirty-five and handsome. Photos show him climbing the steps of planes or else at his desk, hair Brylcreemed into submission, maps spread before him, phone clutched under his shoulder, ashtray pushed aside. He looks like a man who can remake himself and tackle anything; even make the weather.

On April 8, *The New Yorker* runs a Talk of the Town story about him in the jocular voice the section still uses. "We've had a pleasant talk with Dr. Wallace E Howell, the city's rainmaking consultant, and can report," it reads. "His father was a real estate man," Howell, the writer, states, "climbed many an Alp during summers in his teens." I learn, too, he lives in a glass Gropius house where a plastic cloud mobile he made dangles from the living room ceiling.

My own parents' house is built with walls of glass and dreams of a better world, one that can be engineered into existence through modern design—open plan, open lives. Even as he resides with us between his trips, my dad lives in exile. My mom keeps him at bay. What does it feels like to have a family who is held from you, as if our home's glass walls were constructed to allow him to see in but not be part of the family?

—

The New Yorker follows Howell on TV and radio interviews. Leaving one, Howell spots a sign in the elevator that says, "You can't make rain, but you can save water." There is a laugh at this.

At the end of the piece, he explains to the magazine, "We won't be able to distinguish positively between man-made rain and natural rain," but "the possibilities are good," simply because of the geography of the Catskills with its mountains. "Regardless," he says, "we'll never be able to make the desert bloom."

The reason the Catskills are so good: orographic lift. As storms move from west to east, clouds draft up a peak, hit the ridge, and drop their precipitation.

—

Every week, Howell's every movement is tracked in *The New York Times*. As he searches the Catskills for a suitable base for his operation, five cars of reporters follow him. They hike after him up Overlook Mountain in Woodstock in the snow on St. Patrick's Day, and the *Times* reports, "[Water] Commissioner Carney looked ruefully at the natty suit and coat he had planned to wear in the St. Patrick's Day Parade on Fifth Avenue at about that moment. 'When I planned to parade today I didn't have any intention of parading up here,' he said."

Two days later there is another hike up Slide Mountain, the Catskills' tallest peak, and then a climb up Balsam Mountain, near where the six hunters will be on Thanksgiving. Finally he settles on Walton as his base. It's the site of my county fair. (Think kids in 4-H with their rabbits and prized vegetables and the demolition derby on Friday nights.) The choice makes sense. West of the mountains, it's relatively flat, so with prevailing weather patterns, when the clouds reach the peaks, the rain will fall on the ridges and run into the reservoirs.

—

Howell's first attempt is on April 13. It snows from the Catskills to New York City. Howell's snow, it's called, and the *Times* headline asks "Is It His? Or Nature's?" A photo in the paper has him in profile downtown in front of City Hall, looking aside deep in thought.

—

Seven months into his experiments and thirty-some seeding attempts later, the rains that Thanksgiving are epic. They are part of a much bigger storm system, an extratropical cyclone, a nor'easter, and it stations like a cutoff low. It is a front so big it's called the "storm of the century." It is also deemed the "Great Appalachian Storm," and stretches from the Carolinas to Canada. It drops more than five feet of snow in the Ohio Valley. Frigid temps in the single digits reach down to Florida. Further north, it is warmer with wind and rains. In New York City, LaGuardia Airport floods and so does the Lower East Side. The storm's biggest gust—140 mph—is recorded at Bear Mountain, not far from the city. And here, I read in the *Catskill Mountain News*, is "the highest flood and most damaging flood this valley ever experienced since first settlers." The worst devastation is along the path that is seeded, to make rain, to make water to run down the mountains and into the streams and into the rivers and into the reservoirs.

—

I search for coverage of the flood in the village library, two bungalows joined together. It's a block from my house with the gingerbread and turret. The librarian, Doris, sends me to the attic after the bound volumes of the paper. She is in a mask—we are still wearing them—and it muffles her voice. I can still hear the squeak, an uptick of warmth, that comes with her words. You know where they are. Just mind the stairs. Be careful.

They're steep and dark. I search for the issues in the eaves and poke around. There are kids' games, a *Star Wars* board game, books marked "Do Not Sell—Thank you, The Board." Finally behind one oak paneled door and another, copies of the paper are stacked to the ceiling.

I carry the heavy volume covering 1950–51 downstairs. It has a red marbleized cover and pages running to dust. In my mask, the smell hardly bothers me. I flick through the weeks until I reach the flood. On the front page: Roads washed out, houses and barns collapse; a dozen bridges are carried off their foundations including one covered bridge. It is moved 1,000 feet, "never to be replaced," the paper reports mournfully. (It doesn't say the structure won't be rebuilt because the reservoir is coming.) Another bridge gives way with a car still on it. The passengers fight their way out to safety. Five thousand-gallon oil tanks are washed away, and another gas tank weighing over seventy-five tons is carried downriver and dropped onto the state highway.

The photo is hard to make sense of. The tank is upright, the size of a house, and in the middle of the highway. I don't understand how something so huge gets into a road.

Cows drown. Arkville, I read, loses seven hundred fifty chickens, and a cabin is picked up off its foundation and moved six hundred feet. The paper reports, "Its lumber can be saved." Another headline on the front page: "Flood's Best Joke." The brief piece reads in its entirety: "New York rainmakers went out in the Ashokan section Saturday morning with a generator crew to make rain. Shortly after 5 p.m., the department hurriedly called the gang back to help in the flood emergency."

In one photo a farmhouse is tipped on its side. The caption states: "The O'Briens who have three children have lost everything." There's a picture of a gas station, and I recognize the site. It's right across from the CVS and grocery store where I stood after Hurricane Irene when the pavement landed in icebergs and grass was woven though the carts. Here gas pumps are pulled out, and I read that oilcans and tires have been swept downstream. Inside, the destruction is so total, it's impossible to know what I'm looking at in the pictures other than hay or grass and brush and floor, and I remember the pressure of sadness on my chest and the impossibility of finding words for it.

—

I track down people I think might have lived through the flood. I ask the town historian's help and go on a tour of living rooms and parlors and kitchens. There is Mabel West whose eyesight is nearly gone. She looks at the air to collect her memories—as if the air might hold them. Len Utter sits in the living room of his farmhouse, the Weather Channel on mute, the police scanner on loud. He is in his nineties and still volunteers in the fire department. He tells me proudly that he passes all the department physicals. Betty Baker is eighty-seven and has Peter Pan–style pixie cut hair. She is tiny and spry and swears with abandon. Her language is equally divided between damn and God.

—

Mabel lives in subsidized housing in a town forty-five minutes away. She tells me about the drought. "That year it was dry and not unlike now. It was very dry and there had been some minor forest fires, if you call any of them minor." Her voice has its own dry, sharpness. A slight vibration hangs in the air. As she speaks, I wish you could hear her, the way the words are also soft, reverberating as I lean in.

She sits in her recliner. She tells me that that year she has one child just turned five, and says, "Of course, I was pregnant." This line is delivered with a swallowed laugh about the facts of her life. Maybe it is irony or humor, or maybe it is conspiratorial as she recognizes that these are not the conditions of my life, that I will not have five children, though we are both women together.

She says, "I was engaged at sixteen, married at seventeen, and pushing a baby carriage at eighteen. Well, naturally, I was supposed to be pregnant." So, now in this story in the deluge, she is six months pregnant again. She is also now in her nineties and wearing a red Christmas sweater decorated with holly leaves in August, and we talk, too, of the flood with a woman's name—Irene—my second flood. We are a few days shy of its anniversary, and Mabel's nails are painted a sparkling gold, as if actual gold. In 1950, this Saturday after Thanksgiving, she is over at her Uncle Bunny's house. "It was his birthday. He lives next door, and it's raining like blazes. We don't realize how much, and the train was a-coming. The railroad were just a few hundred yards below us, and it starts honking and pulling their whistle to get our attention. We rush home, and the dirt road that was our driveway was washing down the road."

The way she says *wash* it also has an *R* in it, *warsh* like my dad, growing up in rural Pennsylvania, pronounces it. Back home, she says, the phone is ringing. The culvert is out and the train is stuck. "The way the stones sounded spraying"—she pauses, focuses on space—"so loud with the banging and banging. The stones were banging."

I say I know that sound. I remember it with Bull Run and that first flood, a minor flood, and how after that anytime there is high water the stones crack and slam, and I don't sleep.

She says, "Bits and pieces, they come back to me not in any order."

—

Len Utter is eighteen that fall. He sits in his recliner too, and gestures to a chair I should pull up close. We are in his living room on the farm a great-great- bought with his Civil War pension. We talk about his daughter who is my insurance agent and his son-in-law who is a nurse, and farmer, and ski patroller, and firefighter. It is a world where everyone has several jobs, volunteer or otherwise. Len talks of his time serving in local government. This was when we first met at a town board meeting. I am sure he won't remember.

This afternoon Len wears jeans and plaid flannel and a fire department fleece even though it is summer. He is a man accorded much respect in the department and as a former town supervisor and as someone who holds oral histories. These I hear when our departments are called out together and told to standby in the station. He will sit in the coms room and share these stories of earlier times and farming.

His voice is raspy, punctuated by deep inhalations. He nods at my phone, wondering about the recording. Does he have to speak in any special way? He says, "I look back"—pause, breath, broken sentence—"and try to remember, but it was during hunting season. I was out that afternoon" [pause, inhalation] "and probably the only really two things" [pause] "I remember well about it was the fact that it started raining and I never in my life have I felt such rain. Of course, and I had been in thundershowers" [pause, breath] "I was just a young fellow then, but it literally rained so hard it took your breath right away from you." He says too, "The worst damage was up the Dry Brook Road, the Dry Brook Valley."

It is still an isolated valley, framed by mountains and a brook and a single road in and out that tries to cling to the water's path. The route crosses the stream in many places before dead-ending at a mountain where the paved road turns to dirt. In my second flood it is a week before people there can get out.

—

Betty Baker lives in Dry Brook. She leads me to her kitchen table. More Weather Channel playing. Or, Fox News. She has on jeans and a rose-colored sweatshirt. She is funny and devoted to cussing and her late husband. An entire room in her house is a museum to him. She doesn't call it that, but it's full of artifacts from his life, from his time as a fire spotter on the ridge. She says, "That day it was raining from hell to Harlem."

Her irreverence defies what I expect from a woman her age, with a tartness that also takes in faith and God. We sit in her kitchen, and she says, "That damn flood it tore this place apart, just tore it apart. It took out all the bridges and abutments. I don't think there was a bridge left in the damn valley."

—

Mabel, with her soft, dry voice, recalls trying to get out the next day. There is no road, no driveway, no culvert, she says. Her face squints in pain.

I see her now, the cropped silver hair, her skin still smooth and dewy. The gilt nail polish, her tidy room, the clothes piled neatly on her bed, and I know how poor her sight is. She tells me, even before I come, that she can never call me back. She can't see the numbers on the handset. She doesn't apologize for this or sound sorry for herself. They are just facts. She shows me around her apartment, holding to the wall to navigate, and I realize that she sleeps in her chair. That's why the clothes are in neat piles across the bedspread. It serves as her bureau so she can find them easily. I want to hang on to her every word, like how she tells me her husband loses his hearing in the South Pacific, and that what she's really saying is how much she loves him. She picks up a photo of him made from one of the banners hung in town for Memorial Day. A friend made her this copy, big enough so she can see him. She misses him; she misses the wild strawberries and huckleberries from her place on the mountain.

"That next morning we surveyed the damage. The culvert was out completely so we were isolated up there. My husband comes home and says get everything you need for a few days."

I picture her with a young child, Mabel's pregnant belly, and trying to navigate the steep slope, trying to carry enough, all the things she does not recount but that I try to fill in in my mind.

"The stream was loud, and you had to holler because we couldn't understand each other for nothing. We went along our edge of the mountain and down in that stream. We had an old 1934 Chevy truck that was just about hanging together. Getting down the driveway was a bit of a hairy thing. There was no driveway at that point. We're in the middle of the stream, right? They were trying to build up the culvert, but it was not possible. It was just too steep. And, my uncle Bunny he's trying to guide us and he says, You'll just have to sort of slide down and jump it. My uncle says, 'If you're coming, come on.'"

Basically he means, it's now or never, and she waves her hand almost airily, at the memory, because she is doing the driving, she is having to jump the culvert, she is at the wheel as a man on either side is trying to heave the truck up one side of the tracks and down the other, while she is six months pregnant and has a five year-old daughter with her. It is not air that she waves at but the old fear.

She says, "The mountain was just reeking with water. And, this, this is twenty hours after." The men lifted and pushed as she steered over the railroad tracks. "The next part was very, very steep. It was like going through a crick bed, but there wasn't any gullies in it because it was so steep. I'm re-living this," she says. "We get down to Route 28"—(the state highway that cuts through our town)—"it's been washed out. The car"—the one I see in the paper plunged nose-first into a river—she says, "that car my friend Rosie and Paul Bunker Green"—she pauses, looks in the distance and down again—"were in the car. But, they were okay. Rosie lost her teeth. That was . . ."—her voice slows, catches on a word. She looks for what to say, because Rosie is okay. But also not. She says, "That was quite painful . . . Sad—she was the one, we were the ones—used to sing in school. Loved singing."

———

In the paper, there's a tiny notice of goings-on in Union Grove, where Steve grows up. It's written by his mother, Agnes, and she reports that the flood losses include someone's pigpens.

———

And, I am back in his kitchen, in the house that is a replica, clutching a mug of tea. Jane has set out a plate of cookies. The kitchen is his parents', and the table is round, and the round gold frames of his wire-rimmed glasses accentuate his deep eyes. They suggest a patient presence, warm and wise. He tells me about being nine and how they've just gotten electricity. He tells me about the hogs. These are not just a neighbor's pigpens. His dad has a spare lot for his garden and then a shed with two pigs. "Now this being autumn," he says, "the pigs were full-grown animals, and it's the middle of the night and the power is out and the brook is up, and within two hours there's this flood, and it's nine, ten p.m. and dark and night, and guys are yelling for my dad to bring a lantern. The pig, the pigs are getting flooded. People are banging on the door.

"Now," Steve says, "pigs, they can't swim." He's told to stay in bed, but he doesn't. He didn't. He goes to watch.

There's a lot of swearing and these men are no match for this struggling pig. The pig's terrified and going crazy. One guy has a rope around himself and a rope around the pig, and three guys are holding the rope.

I imagine this full-sized pig, four hundred pounds, struggling and scared. I think about what they say about trying to save a drowning person, how their flailing can drag you under with them, and I picture the pigs and the danger they'd pose.

Steve says, "They get a rope around the pig's neck, but it gets loose, and the pig's downstream and gone forever." He flips open his hands as if to show that it is lost and gone. The other is on its hind legs in the corner.

Steve interrupts himself. "And, I was told not come outside during any of this but I did." His eyes sparkle with trouble. "And, this pig, I am fascinated." He smiles and I see him as a child, the terror, the excitement, all of this going off in his yard, his house, his garage. The flood and the dark water glinting and the pig's pink skin and its head, and Steve's curiosity sparked with awe. He gestures at his chest and neck. "You can't just put one rope around the pig's neck." He makes the shape of the animal's sloped head and how the rope will slip off. "So they get two ropes around and three men pulled it to shore. Then it's living in our garage. Our car is under two feet of water, but the pig," he says, "the pig is fine."

———

I visit Gary again, sit in his dining room again, and he is young again in this moment, maybe six at the time. I think he might remember the flood, but maybe not. He is wearing a pale-blue shirt and he focuses on me. He says, "I'm setting in the house and the flood is coming into the house. Then, of course, we're living on the river in Shavertown. I could see the whole valley below. It was all flooded, yeah. That would have been the first major flood I've ever seen, and then hearing the rumors that Shavertown is no longer going to be here, so emotionally that has got to do something to your mind."

What sticks with me is how Gary and Steve and Len all talk about not just the flood but the reservoir. It is visceral, the auctions, the burning up of the properties, the loss. Len says, "The village that has been central to your life . . . to see it disappear. But then they do, what they called the grubbing. You see all the vegetation" [pause, sigh, inhalation] "is taken off from the land. It was clean, bulldozed up in piles and burned. We'd spend days and days with smoke."

Chapter 15

IN THE LIBRARY I GO through a month's worth of issues of the *Catskill Mountain News*, searching for stories of the Rainmaker's Flood. Reading them, I'm struck by all the other accidents and ways to die: two little children take their grandfather's pills; the egg truck crashes, killing both occupants; the milk truck overturns; a wife survives her husband's murder-suicide attempt; a hunter finds an airplane with all the passengers dead, nearly six months after it took off in New Jersey. And, someone else dies in a flood—not this flood, not the Rainmaker's one—but another that comes a week later. This one isn't made with smoke or silver. It is just rain, normal rain, and high water that cannot be absorbed into the saturated soil.

"The partially frozen, half-clad body found Saturday morning at the edge of the Delaware [. . .]" the account reads. For days no one realizes the man is missing. He lives with his father and someone else. He'll just take off sometimes, and the story details all the attempts to identify him. There's something in his life, liminal and unmissed, and I think that is the story—what the paper doesn't write.

There's also all the crime I find: a stolen Buick and a stolen eight-point buck off a friend of mine's grandfather's porch. Money is stolen, there are two separate hit and runs, and warnings to hunters of drunk bears. Together they shatter whatever pastoral-rural image I have of the place I live. So, too, all of the businesses here. Ads trumpet new-model cars and trucks. (The local Chevy dealer has four firemen climbing a pole. They're on their way: "To see the hottest thing in town—the NEW 1951 Chevrolet!") The feed store has two branches; there's a department store and clothing stores, dry cleaners, two cinemas and restaurants, bars and hotels to go out dancing on a Saturday night. None of these exist now. They all disappear in the wake of the reservoir, the Pepacton.

That same week of the flood, there's a story about a local lawyer who wins an unprecedented ruling against New York City. His clients—"business and professional men," the paper calls the insurance agents, veterinarians, and local co-operative creamery behind the case—win the right to sue for loss of revenue before the losses even occur, before the reservoir is even built over the next few years. The farmers though, are ineligible. All they will get is the price of their land, which is undervalued even as it is the best farmland around, rich bottomland near the river. The rest of the soil up on the hills is poor land, rocky land, land we call here "two rocks for every dirt."

I find, too, an editorial about water "as such," it's put. It's hard to parse exactly what the newspaper is saying with this "as such." It's legalese, I think, and translates to the land here is being bought for the water. No one, however, is paying the true value of the water rights, just for the land that is, in the city's estimate, nearly worthless.

———

After the storm Steve is told not to go down to the river. "Then zoom"—his eyes flash with mischief—"right down I go." He smiles and shrugs, and I see him as a little kid, troublesome and curious. His voice is still gravely but the enthusiasm of a child flashes. He remembers the Gulf station in town being wiped away, everything washed out. He says he's not sure which flood this was. There were two, and the floods come in many different years. I am sure though that this is the Rainmaker's Flood. I have seen the pictures of the Gulf station. Afterward he finds cans of oil and tires washed down the river. The men in the paper who find the body are picking through debris too.

Saturday morning Peter Eder, 21, and Cyrus Wright, 54, of Denver were hunting for tires and other flotsam lost during the flood when Eder saw a body, lying face down [. . .] No papers of any kind were found on the body, which was clad in a plaid hunting shirt, khaki underwear, socks and calf-length hunting boots with rubber bottoms and leather tops. [. . .] Early Sunday afternoon [. . .] the body was taken to the Old Arena Cemetery and buried in the potter's field. Trooper Knapp of the Margaretville state police, who was in charge of the investigation, sent out a 14-state request for identification [. . .] Many local folks viewed the body.

According to Faulkner, [who lived with the victim], the last time he saw the victim was Saturday evening December. 2 at his cottage. At that time [they . . .] were enjoying "some beer." [. . .] When he awoke Sunday morning, the victim Slauson, was gone. "I didn't think anything of it. [. . .] I've known him since he was knee-high. I think there's something funny about all this."

[. . .] The question remains of why the man drowned and why was the body frozen almost solid when found where the temperature of the water was above freezing? [. . .] Through the week local rumor mills ground on.

Reading the piece, I get the sense that there is little left to tell who the drowned man was. His aunt picks him out in a photo after he's been buried in the potter's field, which, too, has since disappeared to make way for the reservoir.

The week before, on the front page there's a story how another town in the path of the cloud seeding fares.

Angry water surged towards the village. A minute later it crumbled a bridge, undermining the road. It carried part of a shed away and half the bridge. Men soon were shouting warnings of "Another wave coming!" They began waving flags to warn any stray traffic away from the new danger. Rocks still flew from the bridgework. Then the main bridge caved in. It was now a black gash across the road.

It sounds melodramatic, the angry water and a black gash, but how to capture these things? How to convey the terror? On the same front page where the drowning is reported, New York City declares that its water supply is now "comfortably adequate." The water commissioner thanks God for the results. "We are where we are today," he says, "because of the goodness of God and the cooperation of the people."

———

Just above *The New Yorker* profile of Howell, there's a cartoon. It isn't meant to illustrate the story. It looks prescient though. It's a flooded suburb; each house has water to the eaves. In the foreground a couple sits on a pitched roof in fancy evening dress. "Of course you realize," the woman says in her fur, arms crossed, legs crossed. "Mr. Masters, you can't stay here all night."

———

In the interviews I hold onto each breath and pause; beyond the flood I am moved by the frailty of these older people. They make me think of my own parents.

Someone tries to conceal the heartbreak of a spouse's death earlier that year. There's an echo behind the words, and you could call it loneliness, but it is more than that. I want to convey all of these details, because these are old people and getting older, which means they are inevitably soon to disappear.

In one person's house I see their struggle to retain autonomy, how proud they are, how fiercely independent and how much they refuse to admit that things are slipping. Someone has a calendar for a long-forgotten political candidate hanging by the door. On a table are crumbs and old packets of cookies I pretend not to notice when I put my phone down to record. I recognize a life of self-sufficiency impossible to sacrifice. These people don't want to impose or ask for help or be needy, so lunch might just be these crackers or cookies, and there is no one to clean up afterward. Mabel shows me her bedroom, and I try not to let on that I realize she sleeps in the recliner, and of course she does. It is easier. I see my father and how he swears he's okay and does not need help. How he slips and falls in the bathroom in the middle of the night. How he breaks his neck and will never return home from the hospital. Later my mother will not eat in the evening because she can't carry her food from the kitchen to the table. She is too unstable, and she refuses to have anyone else come help because she doesn't want anyone else intruding in the house, on her space. She refuses, too, to tell us, and we, her children, are the last to know that she is starving.

One man, when we first met a decade and a half earlier, was stout and strong, his brush cut hair bristling and alive. Now he is diminished, having reached the age of the body's shrinking into itself. I want to hold everything, each element, to capture the people and their presence. I hear, too, Gary's words about the reservoir when we first meet: *All this time, it's just a body of water now. Everything is forgotten.*

———

I visit the reservoir, and the water is low. It is before the summer solstice, and the winter hasn't produced enough snow. Spring brings a drought and a season of brush fires. The reservoir holds the river's path. The East Branch is still there, beneath the surface, still following the river's memory and the laws of hydrology.

I stand on the shore, and most people just see how bucolic it is: boats on the water and people fishing. I see the river beneath the reservoir, but I cannot see the town, not the three churches or train station or rooming houses, not the post office in the general store, not the next village up—Steve's village that you could see from the bridge—not the bridge itself that collapses as the water rises because the bridge is too sad to leave.

I study maps, trying to make the edges hold, and Gary has also told me there was once an acid factory at the water's edge, making acetate for weapons and explosives and commercial dyes. In dry years, the old roads rise from the water, and I imagine Gary that child in the film on his tricycle.

Below here was a place called Pepacton. Originally pronounced *paw-pachton*, it was a Munsee community, then the name is said as *pee-packton* by white settlers, with the accent on the "pee." Now the village is gone but it is still the reservoir's name, said with a sigh, *puh*, like a puff of air. It means "the place where calamus flowers—sweet flag—grow," and it makes me think of Walt Whitman and his poem cycle in *Leaves of Grass*, where the plant's erect spadix becomes a stand-in for his quest for "the manly love of comrades."

Even being so dry, the light flashes through the trees, glistening as if lit with life itself and a taste in the air of late spring. Most of the flowers here are weeds, marginal plants of marginal places—fields turning to forests, plants of disturbances and ditches, plants for the overlooked. They hold this place. Poison hemlock (the flower, not the tree) spills its loose umbels, and golden Alexanders grow in tight explosions. While Iris was pregnant, she told me that umbel means sustenance delivered to nodes—like Queen Anne's lace or the placenta and the umbilical cord.

Low-hugging violets with heart-shaped leaves clutch the ground. There is clover and agrimony, motherwort (calming, good for the heart), mugwort (bringer of dreams). I tally the names and hold them close: honeysuckle takes over old farm fields and forest edges, creating a haven for birds; wild lettuce (pain relief to rival opium); mint; dandelion; strawberry; sedge; plantain (good for cuts); Saint-John's Wort (depression); dock and common nettle (both iron and mineral rich); daylily; daisy; dame's rocket; herb Robert (the Robert of its name unclear, but it repels mosquitos and fights infections. One of my sisters tells me that this tiny pink cranesbill always reminds her of our dad, and he, too, is with me here right now). There is touch-me-not and goldenrod, months from blooming. I'm sure the plants know something of the ground and what it needs.

At water's edge a thick steel chain encircles an ash tree. The bark grows around the metal. The trunk absorbs the lock into its flesh as if to say You will not have private property here. Or, to insist that this is a shared space. I find no calamus, though. Instead garlic mustard thrusts its long green seed heads into the air. Walt Whitman writes:

(For I must change the strain—these are not to be pensive leaves, but leaves of joy)

There is something else in this reservoir built for the greater good. In the parched ground, by broken glass and a beer can's pull tab, slender, nodding heads emerge. They peer just above the soil. I have stumbled on a secret, and the whole place feels like one, the promises of a river and its currents, and here is this flower. It has no leaves, no green, no chlorophyll, no way to get nutrients from the soil. How it survives is a mystery. The tea-pink stem is the shade of my inner arm. Its petals are veined, with a slim purple outline on the edges, and they beg hello. There is this tiny flower's nodding head, and the golden hairs in its mouth, yellow tongues as if to speak, and what would they say? This relation of beauty from dry, cracking earth.

Each stem bears a single bloom, and the ones yet to open look like periscopes, trying to learn something of this world. I picture Gary. He tells me of visiting in another drought. He comes in his good sneakers when the water is low. And, I come over and over to visit this tiny plant.

Look closely at its downy hairs like tender skin. The flower has had multiple names. Sometimes they include ghost. Sometimes its name is given as *orobanche uniflora*, sometimes aphyllon. The original name, the *orobanche*, comes from the Greek for strangling. Sometimes it is introduced as single flower cancer root, not because it cures or causes cancer but because it gets its nutrients from other plants. It is an "obligate parasite," or a "benign" one. This ghost flower spends most of its life underground, possibly years, waiting to sense a chemical from the goldenrod. Scientists know little of this single flower. It is chemotropic, growing toward something in goldenrod's miniscule rootlets, thinner than a single hair. I return over and over to visit these pale pink flowers. Maybe they self-fertilize? Maybe a bee does? Maybe both? One person records a honeybee on the flower in 1929. Maybe it is an annual, maybe a semiperennial taking years to emerge, only to flower fleetingly and go to seed. I see its shared existence in the tiny hairs and knotted roots of the goldenrod. I see the public, I see us. And, I see Gary, and I hear Steve talk about the reservoir and its water. *We have it they need it.* Of course we share.

This flower is endangered in seventeen states. I visit it until I can no longer find it. The blooms don't seem to die. They are just gone. I read about this cancer root, "It appears unexpectedly, only to disappear and reappear in the same habitat." Gary returns searching for his lost home and finds his toys from his childhood in the mud one summer of drought. He walks on a road that is right now water. Next to his garage where there had been a dirt cellar, he finds a truck, a tractor, and a toy monkey. I hear him say, *all this time . . . it's just a body of water.* And, he tells me, I've only been twice. The bridge, of course, is still there. You know, he says, you know.

Chapter 16

SOMETIME AFTER MY FLOODS, AFTER my dad's death, after I start reading of Vince, I put it together, my dad and the Rainmaker's Flood. I reread an interview with my father. There he is in the same storm. We sit in the dining room with the teak table and chairs, their backs supporting a slender curve of black leather. There is a sloped cathedral ceiling, lush green houseplants, Navajo rugs, and stacks of the Sunday *New York Times* waiting to be recycled, his mug of tea cooling.

He says it is late fall, 1950, his first months at the co-op he and my mom run, and a hurricane tracks 250 miles inland. It's an ice storm, and he talks of having to get poles and power lines back up. He's out standing in marshes. All the other co-operatives lend help; they all work together. That's the point of the story—co-ops helping co-ops. This is, he tells me, one of the co-operative principles. I am raised on these principles.

Now his story is tangential, but it feels like a connection. We are together in the disasters, in the floods. And, he is joyous in the moment, the mutual aid, the shared resources and care, and in sharing it with me now. He grins broadly.

I tape those words about mutual aid to my wall.

In all those conversations everyone mentions the flood with a woman's name, Irene; my second flood. People will say, Like in Irene, or, Do you remember Irene? It is the most recent flood of such magnitude against which to calculate that earlier disaster.

Even though it comes a year after my father dies, he's not with me in it. I don't know why. The times he appears are private and alone. Maybe there are just too many people around, too much crisis in the chaos of disaster for him to appear.

———

Cloud Interlude

The clouds are pewter and gold, lit from the top by the rising sun. I stare at my notes and my phone. The heavy gray and gold, the sheer beauty of the cumuli stuns me. Can they speak the losses?

———

It is spring 2016. The line between the days and months is thin. My mom starts hospice. The doctors don't know how long she will live, six months, more? they say. I am in California on a residency on the coast writing about my parents' home and modernism, trying to understand the values in which I've been raised. David calls their neighborhood my third parent. Now it is March 31, April 1. The hour is eleven and then midnight. My oldest sister picks me up at the airport where my mom and I dropped my father off when I was little. My mother is dying. She is dying this day.

At home, she is in my father's old bedroom. The

curtains are drawn, the walls of glass hidden against the night and its reflections. I was away trying to uncover something that explains the house and my parents' beliefs in modernism and progress, but also its hold on me.

At the residency on the ocean, it feels like I am with her as I write, the distance, the geography, collapsing on the page. I write of home in the waves, swells of rains, of El Niño, flood watches, dangerous tides, and swells of grief. The writing feels supernatural; it feels like sorcery. Each day I summon my father to help. We hold hands and walk up the side of a mountain, the one where we stay in Vermont when I am little. We pass steep switchbacks. Views of green-veiled vistas open at each twist in the route. Up and up and up we go, higher and higher and higher.

My writing and my mom's decline are enmeshed and as close as breath. I text her photos of the flowers I find on walks above the Pacific. I am alive in her shadows, in the roll of waves circling in and out to sea. The day I finish my manuscript, she stops eating and speaking. I change my ticket, fly home.

Now I am scared to enter the room, nervous that I will disturb her. The hospice worker, whose job is to be with us for one day and one night and then leave, tells me to come in. My mother lies in a hospital bed. Her right arm floats overhead as if she is reaching for something—or brushing away spiderwebs. Sometimes she touches her forehead to make sure she is still here, it looks like. Her attention is focused somewhere unreachable.

I take her hand. Her gaze lands on me. Her eyes soften in a way I recognize immediately and have never considered, not in isolation. The look has always been part of a chain of responses: a slight turn of her lips into a smile, her mouth softening, a dip in her voice as she'd say my name. All I have left is in her eyes. Then, they move far, far away.

I tell my mother I'm here and that I'm going to bed. It's been a long day of travel, but tomorrow we have all day.

Downstairs in my old bathroom I brush my teeth. My sister has already gone to sleep. I hear someone on the steps. The hospice nurse calls out: Come! Come now. Now. Her voice is urgent. I wake my sister.

We stand together by our mom. A white sea gurgles in her mouth. The nurse says she no longer has the ability to swallow. Should we wet her mouth, we ask. No. It's too late for that. Foam like the crash of waves gathers at her lips. She chokes at air.

Her eyes are dull but we hold her hands. My sister asks if she sees her best friend who died more than a decade ago. I name the flowers I found in California: wild lupines and irises, pussytoes and foxgloves and the field of phlox and poppies I saw that morning before I left.

The nurse says, It's over.

I don't believe it. My palm is sweaty because my mom's hand is so warm. I have her hand and her damp palm, and I am telling her about blue-eyed grass bigger than any I have ever seen. I ask if she is with Dad. Then she is gone. Then he is gone too. He disappears that night.

———

He doesn't return. In Margaretville I wander the woods trying to conjure him from the moss and the trees, from the winds, anything—the crows—all of the things that were present when I first find him, as if they might hold him.

That summer in the election my dad's beloved co-operatives endorse an angry man because he supports coal and cheap energy. Signs emblazoned with his name appear on my road and up Bull Run, and I study my father's papers and slides looking for where he travels so I can go with him.

The days are long; dusk lingers into night. I load a slide projector with his carousels from his trips. He takes hundreds of photos when he is away, and I want to see through his eyes. What I discover: airplanes. He is flying away.

Outside, voices spark and flare as kids ride bikes. A pickup without a muffler roars up the hill. Dust motes catch in the projector's light. I pore over carousel after carousel. The projector has the sweet, warm smell I remember.

The slides start a decade before I'm born. It's the dawn of the jet age, and so many of the images are shot from planes. The oval windows attenuate the landscape like a mannerist painting. There's a blue sky and billowing clouds. A coastline spreads out. In others the ground below is braided by a river delta, and you can follow its sinews, with their rules and formulas Luna Leopold lays out. For a second I think of Sarah and hydrology and my father and me held together in the waters as I watch him fly. The airplane wing appears in the corner of the shot. The carrier's name peeks into the frame, and these silvers and blues, they look like hope. I imagine him angling his camera as the plane takes off. I try to conjure that sense of being aloft. The breath lifts in his chest. He sits over the wing. The world shrinks into the distance, as if he is always saying goodbye.

Occasionally there are images of him, and me as a child. These shots are rare because he takes nearly all the pictures, but there is one in a brook in Vermont my mother must shoot. Here, give me the camera, Bob, she says, her voice sharp. Then he reaches for me in the water, his arms out to catch me as I stumble across the rocky pool. He holds me so I do not fall, and I can feel that memory in my body, the warm grip of his hand and his protection.

I project the slides on an empty wall. I am seven or eight on a dirt road studying weeds and wildflowers, framed by mountains with the hazed blue of distance. I wear a blue T-shirt. My hair is dirty and pulled back from my face. In the picture of us in the stream, he has on the mauve turtleneck, the one in my closet.

—

That fall, I drive north on the days I am not teaching in New York City. I'm going to the State University of New York at Albany's archives. It's part of a project for the university art museum, writing on the sands and dust and modernism. It is a lustrous fall day. Along the roadside asters bloom in neon colors impossible to conjure. The summer has been dry, and that makes the fall foliage even brighter, and we—you and I—are in the car, a Subaru named forest, Forester, and for a second it holds the memory of my dad and Vince's dream to be in the trees. There is dust on the dash; in grief, time is permeable. You are with me and not, and around me time spreads out in a glacial landscape on this two-lane highway, at the bottom of a ravine. The road runs along what was once a frozen lake and now is mudflats, the headwaters of the Delaware River. It looks barely remarkable, not even a stream—just a chain of beaver ponds threatening to flood the road. In this election, there is a man and a woman and a threat of violence, and it feels like everything my parents once stood for is gone.

We pass a dairy and the turn to Mabel's town. She is for this moment in the car too, in her Christmas sweater. Time bends and we are traveling together and the flowers wave in this narrow cleft that was a lake, that was a glacier. I think roads are the gift, and they contain this experience.

I turn onto Steve Miller's interstate and pass a verge where, one day years ago in April, the grass blazed gold with the blooms of dandelions. A truck stop beams the price of gas. The air is cool on my face, and I cross this land that was ice and then sand. Outside are the wavering lines of the road and cars. Nearing the university, I pass under overpasses, through traffic circles, slip roads, and side roads. A narrow snaking access road encircles the campus, which is set behind a moat of green.

The school parking lots are full. High cumulus clouds rise like castles. They swell with warmed air rising. The university is built on the sands that fed Nabokov's butterfly. In 1962 Governor Nelson Rockefeller breaks ground on the campus and throws a shovel of sand over his shoulder. It rises in a cloud. Nabokov's butterflies flutter their blue wings like snow. They depend entirely on one specific lupine and its blue flowers that depend on the sand that depends on fire. Not even three years before, Nabokov visits and says there is nothing worthwhile here, and now this school opens as a dream of universal education.

Rockefeller, a man whose name will soon appear on drug laws penalizing Black and brown New Yorkers, creates a dream of equality here. Across the state, he takes ag colleges and this, what was a teacher's college downtown, and conjures a statewide university system believing it will build a meritocracy. He wants it to be a place where the firsts in their families can go to school.

—

On the campus everything looks the same. All the buildings are gleaming and white and identical—indistinguishable. Walls of glass, arches, slender columns. I quickly get disoriented. The paths are crowded with students in dark T-shirts and shorts and backpacks. They rush past me. I do not ask for directions. I find a map with a red dot that says "you are here," but that *here* does not track to the world around me. I try a staircase—white and gleaming too. I am looking for a library and end up at *the* library but it's not the right one. I need the science library. I go outside and try again. I have a dizzying sense of vertigo. I reach the university art museum, though it doesn't look like the one I remember. I think of going in to ask for help but don't want to admit that I need help, or to be a problem for the curator who asked me to do this project.

I stumble upon a grand plaza the map says is a "podium."

It is set out in a grid that makes me think of the Renaissance and single-point perspective, that device that sets man (it's always man then) as the center of the landscape like God. I definitely do not feel centered in this landscape. My breath tightens. I try one monumental staircase and another. They seem to float in the air. Along a building, my reflection beams back to me in the glass: nervousness against a turquoise sky.

—

I grow up in the belief that stark and simple designs can change the world. It is the last gasp of the Enlightenment, and the faith is secular and positivist. This is what I was writing about in California. In my family our credo, like the school's here, is a meritocracy—but in it, too, is architecture and furniture; that our house itself, can actualize this dream of a more-just world.

The Shakers believe something similar. "Simple Gifts," their hymn preaches, and the group espouses pared-back designs so there is nothing between you and God. There's a line that the mystic monk Thomas Merton writes about how "The peculiar grace of a Shaker chair is due to the fact that it was made by someone capable of believing that an angel might come and sit on it." With modernism it's the same kind of divine grace or faith, just minus the God part. The chair still has godlike powers. The form itself will improve lives. That seems like a fairy tale, this dream of progress, that better futures can be engineered. In the architecture and furniture the human is abstracted. The buildings, the homes, are a "machine for living," as Corbusier put it, as if the people can be mechanized, or their lives and relationships can. I think about how David calls my parents' house my third parent. Maybe literally it was. If a house can be a machine to shape its occupants and their lives, this allows my father to believe that he can travel and be away, that he is no longer necessary and his absences won't hurt us. Or, that the architecture can make up for his absences, as well as for all the losses in his own life.

—

I only realize later how amazing the campus is, built from sands, and the governor flinging sand, and his dream of a university to create equality, here at the home of the Shakers with their dreams of a better world. I realize, too, that I can get lost because everything here is meant to look alike, whether it's math or science or humanities. The very idea of equality is designed into the buildings as if they themselves could engender egalitarianism. It's also funny getting lost somewhere meant to be so rational and ordered.

—

Finally, I find the science library and am swallowed in its hush. Cool air insulates everything as if to hold it apart. Two students sit at desks fifteen feet away from each other, and one librarian looks at a monitor. In a small room on the third floor, I fill in forms to see records of the school's architecture competition and others on protests and Vietnam. I read the campus paper from the sixties, and see that a Black studies program begins in 1969, making it one of the first in the country.

Boxes and boxes of files are wheeled in before me. I study an article that says on a clear day students can see the Catskill Mountains and talks of how the school will be a center for atmospheric sciences. It's published in early

1967. The author mentions sands and Siberia and the Sahara for all the dust and sand and snow that blow across the campus. He mentions, too, studies of pollution and that salaries of $30,000, which is nearly $300,000, nearly an unheard of salary for professors today, and I think of the near–minimum wage salary I am paid as an adjunct.

Then, in the finding aid I see Vince. Vincent J. Schaefer. He is here too. Of course he is, but I had no idea. He starts the school's Atmospheric Research Center, and all his papers are in this archive. The air thrums, and my heart too. You can feel the pause, the skip, the beat as I realize what I have stumbled upon. I am at a desk with its laminate surface and now stand before a nondescript white man in a blue sweatshirt. He looks up. Is something wrong? he asks. Do you need something else regarding the architecture competition?

I stammer and say, Vince, Vincent, he's here; Vince Schaefer, snow, GE?

The man frowns and nods like I might be crazy. Or, maybe the gesture is to say, Of course Schaefer is here. Doesn't everyone know? He tells me there are 135 linear feet of boxes. This is twenty-five of me stacked end to end, and I do not have enough days to go through them all. I want him to bring everything, though I am limited to three boxes at a time. He starts wheeling in cartons. There are pictures of clouds and snowflakes and airplanes—so many airplanes. I find series and subseries of boxes and folders, ones for "environmentalism," another for "silver snow." I rush to scan pages on my phone so I can look at them later. My heart races, and in my hurry I drop one file on the ground and hope the librarian doesn't get angry. It is a folder for Wallace Howell, who floods my town.

In my hand is the rough feel of manila folders, the edge of a page rusted where there was once a staple. There is the tiny pencil I'm allowed to use in the archive, and I touch Vince's handwriting and typed notes and search for answers to questions I don't even realize I have. The veneer table gleams and on it sits the yellow legal pad like my father used on which I take notes. I study old pictures from GE. There are files of Vince's typed autobiography in no real order. I find him writing about leaving school at sixteen, and hear my father tell me about his cousins and being poor.

Howell signs his letter "Wally" and says he doesn't think his work in the Catskills had much impact.

I read Vince's notes about the view from an airplane window and the clear air he finds there. He writes about "our air" and how we "are able to see that the sun can shine crystal clear, that the clean sky is a dark blue and that unlimited visibility is not a rare occurrence at 35,000 feet." The voice I hear is my father's, the one he uses for work that lowers to a bass. In another folder I read of another blue, the blue of distance.

Vince leaves GE in the mid-fifties. I don't yet know the reasons. He goes to a company spelled Munitalp and studies the atmosphere. It is ages before someone at the school explains that the word is platinum spelled backward. I find him working for the platinum corporation aloft in a jet, the Boeing 707, when it is still in testing. The British company BOAC is competing with Boeing to develop the first transcontinental jetliner, but their jet the Comet has crashed, and Vince writes to the head of Boeing about the accident.

Vince flies across the country in the 707 before it ever

makes a commercial flight. It is the same plane my dad is on. Vince is there in the corporate test runs. The jet's very name, that seven-oh-seven, conjures heaven. In the middle the buoyant "oh" has a breath, a rise, like flight itself. He is studying the jet stream. There is film from the window and pictures of the clouds, and he writes of it like a love story.

"Trace of dawn light," reads one entry in his flight log. Another: "slight lift," and the next line: "slight tremble quite a bit more," and "tremble surge again," as if this were a romance. He is tracking the jet stream. He films the clouds. The sun reflects off the top of the cirrus clouds, and further east are ground haze, meanders of the Missouri River, and snow virga falling, evaporating before it hits the ground.

There's something about Vince and my dad both looking out windows of planes at the land and clouds and sky. I think how far they've come and the distances they've traveled.

Chapter 17

THAT FALL MY STUDENTS ARE distracted, and so am I. I am teaching contemporary art and theory, and I print out scans from the archive on the back of my lecture notes and tape them up too. I return over and over to Albany. Now it is October. It is 2016 for me, and in the file I find it is 1966. That year the Albany landfill opens, and that fall students move into their dorms. Dust and sandstorms rage across the university.

The school sends out an untitled press release about Vince Schaefer's latest discovery. It is November 15.

That night he stands in Mont Pleasant High School, just over a mile from GE on the western side of the pines. He addresses a group of engineers. His talk is called "Challenging Problems in the Atmospheric Sciences," and it's not about hurricanes or tornadoes but pollution. Car exhaust from leaded fuel is making clouds and changing the weather. The lead combines with trace amounts of iodine in the air to create lead iodide. Condensation adheres to it, just like when Bernie seeds snow with silver iodide exactly twenty years earlier and walks through his suburb with the burning paper and uses the smoke generator in the lab at GE.

With cars the process is "so sensitive," Vince says, "it is difficult to visualize its effectiveness." The iodine can simply come from the soil or trees or smoke. A car idling for five seconds will produce 100 million ice crystals.

———

I imagine the high school where he gives this talk: the polished cafeteria tiles and institutional beige walls. He wears a suit and tie, his hair brushed back from the brow. In the air the smell of school lunches, the peas, the potatoes, the stale dishwater and the projector's hum, the squeak of a chair against the tile floor. He shows slides of snow. What astounds me is that he announces his discovery here.

The images of ice crystals are beautiful, like a vibrating X-ray of snow, but there is also his panic. There must be. Why else would he be here? The audience is full of local scientists and engineers. In Schenectady these are not just any scientists, not hobbyists, but some of the country's best. Still what I witness is his alarm. He is so worried about what he's learned that he won't—or can't—wait for a peer-reviewed journal. This is the fastest way to get the news out about cars and lead pollution and smog, lecturing after work in a local high school.

A month and a half later *Science* magazine publishes an issue with Schaefer's ice crystals on the cover. In his article he describes experiments in fields around Schenectady, and as I read it, sitting in the archive, Rebecca the elder is with me, and her visions of the atmosphere. I hear the distant ding of an elevator and a muffled conversation in the hall. Rebecca Cox Jackson is a woman I cannot even picture because there are no photos of her. She describes looking up at "a large body of stars in the heavens [. . . that] began to shower down out of themselves sparks of light. These sparks were like silver." In another dream "storms came in streams of light in the form of hoops white as snow bright as silver. [. . .] They went like the lightning."

Vince Schaefer writes of the massive glaciation of cumulus clouds. It sounds beautiful, metaphysical, with his one hundred million ice crystals and "undersuns," he calls them, where the crystals mirror the sun in the sky. The "smooth-surfaced plates [. . .] float horizontal to the ground [. . .] as many tiny mirrors," he puts it, in 1967. They are "spectacular," he says, and a sure sign of disaster. This vision is not a gift, not from the spirit realm. He sees them from airplane windows.

The undersuns come from pollution, jet travel, and the contrails that create cirrus clouds. The press release about his discovery demands, "Congress must act immediately."

In the boxes and files are countless papers from this time. He writes "Something in the Air," "Sewer in the Sky," "Ice Nuclei from Auto Exhaust and Organic Vapors," and "The Inadvertent Modification of the Atmosphere by Air Pollution." He contributes to the *Bulletin of the Atomic Scientists*, *Bioscience*, the *Journal of Applied Meteorology*, and the *American Meteorological Society*. The *New York Times* visits him at the Schenectady airport where the ASRC has a lab. He writes the cover story for *Science* and articles for the *Saturday Review* as well as the academic tome *Global Effects of Environmental Pollution*, whose other contributors voice early warnings about fossil fuels and carbon dioxide that seem painfully prescient.

Everywhere he goes, he measures pollution, even on the fourteenth floor of the Summit Hotel at Lexington Avenue and Fifty-First Street in New York City when he is in Manhattan overnight. The place has an undulating sea-green façade and looks like it belongs in Miami, on South Beach. I imagine him carrying a second suitcase just for his equipment. It would be the size of the case holding my dad's slide carousel and projector that he often travels with to take to meetings at distant co-ops. Vince flies on planes where he will sample the air. He also tests it in his own backyard and inside vehicles on the thruway, as well as near idling cars.

"Air is inhaled," he writes in the passive voice, describing the way he'll collect exhaust in a bag. Someone then breathes in that air and exhales into another bag. He finds that 66 percent of the small exhaust particles stay in our lungs. The passive voice makes me wonder: who is doing the inhaling and exhaling? Instead of a singular subject, the way it reads makes me think no one person is breathing but all of us collectively, together.

In my dad's slides he is in Africa. He is in front a building that says Department of Cooperation North-West Area Office Port Loko. In other images a giraffe stands on a savanna, and two monkeys sit on the hood of a car. Or, its bumper conceals a lion in the grass. I love these poorly framed shots the most. I print them out and hang them up. The car pokes into the frame and I can imagine my father taking them. I get to see with his eyes. I picture him stopping in the middle of his journey and how he wants to hold this moment forever.

One morning in the archive I'm reading notes from the ASRC and realize Bernie is Vince's first hire. I ask the person at the desk if they have any files for him. In the catalogue, I find he goes to meetings at NASA and Los Alamos where he attends a workshop on Solar Activity, Atmospheric Conductivity and Clouds. He addresses the Geophysical Union and the Electrostatics Society of America. I find an image of him looking like Dr. Strangelove. It's from Project Cirrus, when the army takes over GE's snowmaking. He is shot from below, like he's standing on a platform. There's a girder in the foreground and sparks fly around him. They are so bright, his face is overexposed and any detail is lost, but the light creates a halo around his hair.

In his records, three, four boxes cover something called Project Themis. They hold dozens of folders, correspondence,

budgets, and quarterly reports, proposals, and annual sum-
maries. They begin in 1967 and go through 1974. In them
are letters from the Defense Department. They are emblazoned THEMIS in all caps and dimensional type. Below
this, an eagle clutches arrows in a heraldic seal. It is November
1968's "Annual Summary Report No. 3." I read statements
from Robert McNamara, former president of Ford Motor
Company, now the Secretary of Defense. Themis is funding
fifty research programs. On the list SUNY Albany will "modify the environment." In the proposal, Principal Investigator is
underlined with a space above for someone to sign, and that
person is Bernard Vonnegut. The school gets $900,000 for
three years to modify the weather.

I turn these pages. It is a Thursday. It is late October.
I have come straight from teaching in the city. I am tired.
On the news on TV there are debates and rage, and here
on the drive to the school the radio crackled, and overhead
is the hum of florescent lights. Another man is bringing me
files, and a woman, too, this time.

There is the gritty feel of the papers—pulp and card-
board. The tightness in my throat could be dust but is
something more. Bernie is working on weather for the military. The room is cold and I am cold, but I am suddenly
colder. I clutch the stubby little pencil until my hand hurts.
I read his proposal to make clouds where none have appeared. He writes, "Skillful exploitation of this tool" will
be of "significant military use."

Themis grows from a dream of LBJ's. The president
wanted to spread research money to second-string regional
institutions and away from elite universities. The funding
is equally part of the Cold War and his dislike of Harvard
and Yale. He orders federal agencies "to strengthen

academic capability for science." So the Department of Defense launches Project Themis, named for the Greek goddess of law and justice. One of the Oracles of Delphi, she embodies such abstract ideas as divine order, tradition, and natural law. Sometimes she wields a sword to cut fact from fiction.

Stare down at me from above, from maybe a spot in a ceiling tile, and what does shock look like in this room with no windows and a cart of file boxes next to me? It is a sense of something chilling, and the chill shudders through me. It's not just the air conditioning even in autumn, but seeing Bernie's name over and over. Rain is being made in Vietnam, and Vince is studying pollution. The country is in an escalating war. Bernie is working for the Pentagon, and in the war I know they have moved from seeding clouds with silver to lead. Vince is doing all this research into lead exhaust's effects on the environment, and his hire is talking about clouds as weapons. This all bleeds together, and I am numb, and the room buzzes, and an election looms, and there is a landscape of sand and dust outside.

I flick through folders and find initiatives Themis funds at other schools. They read like science fiction: "digital automata," "human behavior in isolation," "cryogenic engineering," "automatic image reading." The Pentagon describes this as "image interpreting technologies at extremely high speed." (This is the sort of thing drones deploy now so algorithms read images and people never see them. It's AI.) There's also technology that the Defense Department says will allow: "Data filed in one computer [to] be accessible to any other computer in a network by means of a query transmission."

That is the internet, or as it is known then, Darpanet. And, the ASRC get clouds and mist, fog and rain.

The research here includes studying bubbles caused by breaking waves to examine their impact on aerosols and viruses, and Bernie is going to create clouds in the clear blue sky. His previous cloud seeding has always required existing cirrus clouds to function. Now he wants to develop "clear-air seeding." This is what he calls the clouds he'll make from nothing. He hopes to deploy them to "control the flux of solar radiation to large areas of the Earth's surface." He wants to manipulate temperatures, he writes, "both in sunlight and darkness." In case that doesn't sound like enough of a weapon, he stipulates, "It should [. . .] produce a screening layer of cloud cover that can prevent observation from high-flying aircraft or satellites."

In his proposal he suggests large-scale seeding from "rockets," and in one long letter he says they plan to seed silver iodide at 35,000 feet in the air. Bernie asks for U2 planes and air force help in securing the aircraft that can fly high enough but also for "equipment by which we may introduce the silver iodide particles into the supersaturated regions at such high altitudes." That's far higher than any previous experiments sending the smoky insoluble silver iodide into the atmosphere.

—

And, Vince flies at 35,000 feet talking about how clear and pure the air is at the height.

—

I stand outside the library above the podium and watch bodies swaddled in jackets rush across. It's drizzling and cold. Below is the plaza with its grid and the stairs that seem to fly. The white ground is stained with people. They hug the colonnades to stay dry. It feels like the sand here has been heated to such an enormous temperature the grains have transformed into glass—and I am on one side of it. On the other is this grand vision before me, a dream of something universal, education and war—even LBJ who has this idea for education as part of war.

I think of us, together, the we—you and I—these pronouns of collectivity, the second-person plural *you* and first-person plural *us*. I look out on this campus and its strict rationalism, with its order and lines. They simply fall apart the further I write into them.

Gazing at the students, I try to summon this plurality. Clarifying who that *we* contains—me, my father, you, the reader, Vince, these students and then beyond—how far out can I hold us all in my mind at once? Can this *us* reach to the weeds and woods and plants, or even the boxwoods clipped and contained here in their geometric beds? The modifiers—the nouns, the actual bodies and beings and people I am considering—fragment. The *us* is too big to hold together, and there is all I know of universalizing and its failures, and who inevitably gets left out of that dream of a public. There is Gary and the reservoir. And I read in the archives that there are "no more than twenty" Black students at the university here in 1967, at a school supposed to be a path to inclusion. And yet I do not want to give up on some transcendent *us* held together in the air and breath and our atoms and stars and this moment here.

I drive to the sands and protected preserve where I met Neil the biologist earlier. On the trail, my sneakers soak through in the rain. Twenty feet away, traffic rushes by on the interstate, and the dunes here roll fifty feet high. The day Neil took me to the glacier, he showed me the black locust trees people started planting here in the nineteenth century because they grow fast. They spread and change the sands, fix the nitrogen, build soil, and start killing off the pines, destroying the ecosystem that developed around the sand. We stood in a suburb and one locust towered over me. He shook his head. The tree was on a private lawn that bordered the preserve.

In the shadow of the dump with the Febreze in the air, he told me it is likely impossible to save the Karner blue in the long run. You can't save one species, he says, but need all the species, with their interdependence. When people focus on this one butterfly, they miss the story. That day the goldenrod was in bloom and bees circled it drunkenly. He repeats, It's about interdependence.

Now everything is wet, autumn's brown upon brown, sepia and amber. The traffic sounds like waves and wind. A scarred section of the forest Neil and his team burned the season before is fenced off. Piles of brush are gathered together that they haven't burned this year because it's been too dry. I think of my ghost plant—the one that is the color of no color, pale and translucent, sharing nutrients, sharing the world. An eighteen-wheeler speeds by. On the trailer I can make out the name Mayflower and the outline of a ship. The dead grasses wave in the truck's wake. I think, too, how amazing that this space is left here between the interstate and landfill, that this even exists despite everything, that somewhere here are the butterflies' eggs.

Chapter 18

AT GE VINCE AND BERNIE both work for Irving Langmuir. He is the one who preaches the idea of pure science, he calls it, as joy with no responsibility or accountability, just curiosity and following your interests. It is not tied to a bottom line or shareholders or results. At the company, in the lab with the bridge in the air, he is a hero—a god. In photos Langmuir wears high starched collars, round glasses, and a pendulous expression that looks like it comes from an earlier era. He is a chemist and a physicist, and is claimed by several other disciplines too, including math and biology.

Many scientific developments are named for him. There are Langmuir waves (electron density waves), a Langmuir probe, and a Langmuir-Taylor detector, Langmuir streaks and Langmuir vortices in the clouds, even the Langmuir circulation on the Sargasso Sea. Not to mention his Nobel Prize for work on surface films. In 1932 he is the first commercial scientist in the United States to receive this honor. He doubles the efficiency of the incandescent bulbs upon which GE's fortunes are built and develops the vacuum tube necessary for radio broadcasts. He is also the one who plucks Vince from the machinists' shop. He asks the young man, just turned twenty-six, to be his lab assistant right after he returns from delivering his Nobel lecture in Stockholm. The man becomes a father figure for Vince.

Langmuir is also a hiker and mountaineer and im-
parts to Vince the same advice his own father gave him
about what to pack and how to plan for wilderness outings.
1) Always have a lunch.
2) Get an early start.
3) Never climb longer than half the time between
   departure and darkness.
4) Wear warm clothes in layers.

Together in those years the two fly in a tiny prop plane
over the Catskills. They're scouting for ski trails, ones that
don't yet exist. No trees have been cleared or lifts built.
There is no skiing as such in these mountains yet, so any
dream of schussing down a slope requires hiking up with
their gear and descending through forests and old farm
fields. In midair, Langmuir hands his assistant the controls. The two of them are at 5,000 feet. Vince banks a
turn. They climb higher. Langmuir teaches him to recover
from a stall. Later, Vince writes of these years as Langmuir
University. They will climb Mount Washington to visit the
weather station there, the highest and coldest place in the
Northeast. They ski down afterward. And, I see the view
from the plane—the green swell of mountains.

———

In a file of my dad's I find one fat envelope folded double
with "wallet materials" written in red pencil. The letters
slant with the aggressive lean of his handwriting. Inside are
his draft card, a radio license, and a ship's pass for Mobile,
Alabama. Another is for an unidentified port with in-
structions on the back. One number warns of "Venereal
Disease" "[BE CAREFULL!]" Number (5) lists what can be

taken ashore: "2 packs of cigarettes, 2 candy bars, NO WHIS-KEY." Several cards have stripes like the bars you'd affix to a military uniform. One card is for service in the Atlantic War Zone, another the Mediterranean–Middle East War Zone and a third for the Pacific. I have no idea he served in all of these. When I pressed him to talk about the war, he brushed me off. Once he mentions what it sounded like hearing bombs fall around you. They might hit the ship in front of yours or behind and your ship is unarmed. All the ships he is on are unarmed. He says, the one in front or behind or two ships back is hit, and you cannot even see it. It goes down and you are guarding fuel, long convoys, and there are U-boats, and you are the target and there is nothing you can do, nothing. He shakes his head; he says, the sound, just the sound.

Other cards in the envelope are for membership in left-leaning political groups, the SDA (Students for Democratic Action) and PCA (Progressive Citizens of America). The SDA card proclaims: "In our crusade for an expanding democracy and against Fascism and reaction, we welcome as members of SDA only those whose devotion to the principles of political freedom is unqualified." The SDA decries communism; the other, the PCA, includes communists, but they share this "devotion" in their language. He signs both cards.

Inside, too, are photos of other women, women before my mother. "To Bob, all my love, Liz." She wears pearls. Another woman with a heart-shaped face leans on a tree. The last of them looks young, like a teenager. She wears a checked blazer, the shoulders a bit too big, and lipstick. Hers is the smallest of all the photos. I stare at it and take a photo with my phone so I can enlarge it on my screen. I frown at her and see her eyes in mine.

That morning I bring coffee to David in bed. Do you think this is my mom?

He squints. He's barely awake. He lifts his glasses to examine the photo I'd presented on my palm. Sure, I don't know. Maybe?

———

I find, too, letters he writes on planes.

> Luv,
> Just had to write a few lines to tell you what a happy anniversary I had. It was beautiful, perhaps the most beautiful in all these years. As I fly above the clouds I think about how lovely you looked last night at dinner and at the Kennedy Center. You were radiant.
>
> All my love, Bob

Another time stamped "Sunday Evening" begins *Dearest Sandy,*

> Dearest Sandy, The plane is full . . .

> Dearest Sandy, We just passed over Los Angeles—couldn't see it because of the smog. I miss all of you very much.

> Dearest Sandy
> The flight was rough—just like being on a ship in

a rough sea. It brought back memories of the war.
Sun is now rising, and it is very pretty as I look
out over the expanse of the Pacific . . .

Dearest Sandy . . . Dear . . . my darling . . .

—

I tape these words next to a snowflake. His endearments
hold a love I never witnessed.

—

Kurt Vonnegut hates Irving Langmuir. In the plot of *Cat's
Cradle*, he is the villain. So too, is ice:

> The theoretical villain, however, was [. . .] "a seed."
> [. . .] A tiny grain of the undesired crystal pat-
> tern. The seed, which had come from God-only-
> knows-where taught the atoms the novel way in
> which to stack and lock, to crystallize, to freeze.

In the novel the narrator, Jonah, finds ice-nine, that "seed,"
that "tiny grain" from which ice will spread across the
world. Jonah has set out to discover what people were doing
the day the bomb was dropped. He's looking for Dr. Felix
Hoenikker—a thinly veiled Langmuir who in the book
worked on the Manhattan Project and was an employee of
one General Forge in Ilium, NY—GE and Schenectady by
any other names. Hoenikker is Langmuir, and here he is a
man hated even by his kids, a stand-in for Kurt Vonnegut's
own loathing. I think of Jonah's search and my own drives
through Schenectady, going through my father's papers,
his cards, the oaths, and my mom. In the novel, Jonah

travels there one winter day. "Sleet was falling through a motionless blanket of smog," and there's "a glacier of automobiles." So much ice and snow and smoke.

In the novel Hoenikker is dead. Instead Jonah visits Dr. Breed, his putative boss in the research lab (the name is the same). Breed says, Supervise him? "The man was a force of nature no mortal could possibly control." Can you oversee the tides, the birds? Hoenikker was only interested in his own curiosity and following it. That was a crucial value of this research lab.

What Jonah finds in Ilium is Hoenikker's next and final project: ice-nine. It comes from a tiny seed like the quadrillion particles, or, as Langmuir puts it to *The New York Times*, two hundred pounds could cover everything on earth.

———

Vonnegut's book comes out in June 1963. Two months later, the military first experiments with weather manipulation in Indochina. A few years afterward, Vince and Bernie return together to the sands on the outskirts of Albany. The ASRC publishes its research into spiderwebs and dew with its ice and carbon black. In the report I read: "Before the sunset, we note, some evenings, smoke layers, come from manufacturing or burning brushwoods. [. . .] These layers disperse and turn into clouds: the clouds assume the shape of the layers." With all the commas, like breaths, the pacing feels like a poem.

To make snow, you need smoke. There is plenty of it in Ilium, that smog Kurt Vonnegut described, but also so much exhaust and pollution from cars, factories, and planes. The environmental historian Stephen Pyne says we live in the pyrocene, with everything burning. This is our current era, and in the 1960s it already starts to weigh upon Vince Schaefer. It becomes his sole focus.

———

The spring of 1966 my dad flies to Nicaragua for the opening of the country's first electric co-operative. The day my sister turns ten he writes in a memo: "We probably have a generation to try to satisfy some of the needs of the miserably poor masses of Latin America. [. . .] In Nicaragua there is a fairy strong Communist movement, and I am sure they would rather not see rural electric co-operative development. But all over Latin America, time is running out."

I sit at my desk, and when he writes that, I am not alive, not even a zygote, but maybe I am a hope. My mother has had two, maybe three miscarriages at this point, and my father sits in a distant hotel room. I want to know what he is thinking, how he feels about the communists he mentions. I want to understand his politics in this moment, what he believes and how he understands the world. There are his cards, his wallet materials—one of those organizations includes communists. Why are these communists in the memo bad? What changed or did nothing change? Outside my window, a cloud shrouds the mountain. Mist presses into the trees, and I have a complex web of feelings I cannot fully identify. He works on co-ops whose histories tie to socialism, and he wants to change capitalism, and there are his oaths from the 1940s.

———

At the end of his life I ask questions, and I do not get enough answers or the right answers—or I am not paying the right kind of attention. When he tells me about his work, I want it to be important, so I only hear about the big, bold-faced names—the presidents. I want to know about the photographs I find of him with JFK and LBJ and Hubert Humphrey.

My father stands in a half circle around JFK. In another shot he is next to LBJ with three other men, all in ill-fitting suits in a pink room with a sheen on the upholstery in it. Everyone in the group surrounding Kennedy looks at the president except my dad. He stares at the camera: piercing gaze, skinny tie, one of the youngest men in the room. It is, I learn, the day after the Cuban Missile Crisis, and I'm sure dates are linked. He is in the White House because co-operatives are going to be part of the Cold War. One of the men, the president's advisor Fowler Hamilton, declares that co-operatives "will spread through the contagion of example [. . .] what these gentlemen and ladies [there are no women in the picture] are going to take down to Latin America in their heads is going to be a lot more important than what Government bureaucrats carry in their pockets."

———

In the slides I see my dad, too, in the years before I'm born: 1964 in Africa and 1966 in front of the co-operative in Nicaragua. Now he and I are at the dining room table, and he tells me about visiting the country when they energize the first co-operative. That is his word, "energize," not inaugurate or launch or open. It sounds like excitement, enchantment, buzzing through the crowd. In the photos most people watch the speeches. Flags fly, and the audience includes adults and children. An official holds a movie camera. A single boy stares straight at me through time. His face has the grave mien of an old man. My dad says, "These energizing ceremonies were often held at a school because education would benefit most from electricity."

That, too, is magic, what Senator Hubert Humphrey calls co-operatives in the early 1960s. Humphrey is the last left progressive in the Senate and will go on to be LBJ's vice president. In 1961 he travels with my father's boss, the head of the trade group for the co-operatives, across Latin America. He returns to the United States and thanks to his eponymous Humphrey Amendment, the co-ops are going to fight the Cold War. The idea is as impossible as snow and rain as a weapon.

> Cooperatives [. . .] serve as laboratories of
> democracy. [. . .]

Cooperatives are economic and social democracies. [. . .] A country covered with local cooperatives and their members [. . .] does not fear revolutions and military coups.

So, here is my dad with these presidents, and in another war, World War II, his co-ops are accused of being "fellow travelers" "teeming with communists." This man, this boy, has lost everything by the time he turns eight. He sleeps in an unheated attic, and capitalism has gone wrong for him in so many ways, and he is a socialist and signs cards with loyalty oaths. I could be shocked to discover the co-operatives are part of the Cold War, instead I am amazed. Or, I am both. My father has stood me outside Grange Halls and talked of rural America as the seat of socialism, and now my father's stories cross into the larger outlines of geopolitics. He is idealistic. His faith is naive and beautiful, and in this story I share his idealism if not those politics.

Then, there are all those shots from airplanes, always from the window: the view, the azure sky and an ocean or mountains covered in snow. I realize the photos are not saying goodbye but showing us what my father sees, so that we fly with him.

———

I like to read Kurt Vonnegut as autobiography. It's plain that he hates Hoenikker/ Langmuir and GE, and the story spins out from his experiences there. In his first pages, the first-person narrator Jonah declares, "The book was to be factual." I'm grateful that he takes the facts and threads them through with the ridiculousness and rage he finds. That seems truer to me.

I love the book's direct address and how the narrator starts off: "Call me Jonah," reprising *Moby Dick*, and then undercuts the reference, saying that his parents didn't actually call him that but John. Really what I love is Vonnegut's voice, the confiding tone, bringing us into this world. This is what gets me about the book, because the real world is so strange already. It is one where ice is war and war is cold. In *Cat's Cradle* Langmuir's fictional boss, Breed, has a son, who'd also worked at GE (or in this case GF, General Forge). The son quits because he cannot not stand to make more things for war.

When Kurt Vonnegut is working on *Slaughterhouse Five*, his novel about being firebombed in Dresden, someone tells him not to write an antiwar book. He should instead write an antiglacier one, because glaciers are as easy to stop as war.

Later, a friend sends me Kurt Vonnegut's prologue to his novel *Slapstick*, a book he says comes as close to autobiography as any he will write. He explains, too, that slapstick is "grotesque, situational poetry." Which sounds like a good description of all his writing, and he says that the book is "what life *feels* like to me."

When I first read Vonnegut in junior high, I found the world he created too weird, too cartoony and ludicrous— like it came from Looney Tunes, which makes sense knowing the comedy he describes and how he dedicates *Slapstick* to Laurel and Hardy. I also couldn't bear to watch them in the black-and-white reruns on TV in the afternoons. The show was too brutal, too violent. I didn't find any humor—and certainly no poetry. Now I love his novels.

In the prologue, Vonnegut recounts flying home with his brother for a family funeral. Bernie gets the window seat on the plane so he can watch the clouds, the weather. He carries a device, "a photoelectric cell connected to a small tape recorder," to detect storms. The gadget is so sensitive it detects lightning hundreds of miles away, and the two listen to it on a "tiny earphone" as if trying to pick up signals on a pocket transistor radio.

"The clouds have so much to say to him," Kurt says of his brother. He calls the moment "beautiful" as they listen to a storm as they fly. Both men sport the same mustache as their father, as if they, too, have grown into their dad. In *Slapstick* two siblings together fight the loneliness of the world.

Chapter 19

THE WINTER AFTERNOON I GO to the library in Margaretville, the librarian Doris stops me as I'm leaving. I stand at her desk. It's in a foyer with gray-carpeted floors. In the squeak of her voice and her ebullient curiosity, she asks what I've been looking for in the newspaper. I see her in her mask—the spun polymers, plastics extruded in such tiny filaments, at such high heat, they become fibers that cool and bond as fabric, each strand less than a micron. The material is dual layers, blue and white, and her hair is blond and gray and swept off her face. I tell her about the Rainmaker's Flood and how it's caused by a Cold War weapon.

A man is by the desk too, and before Doris can respond, he says, It's true.

He is burly, dressed in the same Carhartts I wear all winter. This afternoon we are still in a pandemic, and his mask is off, if he ever had one on, and I am nervous still about our breath and the air and aerosols. I do a calculus of assumptions about dress and demeanor, his beard and coveralls, politics and vaccination status, and he says, Yes, contrails.

I say, Exactly! And, I am pleased that someone else here knows—he knows—and that my judgments are wrong. The planes, the airplanes—I say—in 1950.

And China, he adds, is controlling it all.

I step back. I am flustered. I want, need, to tell the librarian, Doris, that it *is* true, just not *that* truth. It isn't China and not some fantasy. I am not a conspiracy theorist. I try to say how the exhaust from jet fuel makes contrails and that they are essentially cirrus clouds that are super-seeded. They have so much ice nuclei (I use the phrases *super-seeded* and *ice nuclei* that only specialists understand) it won't snow.

This is what Vince sees as he flies, the mirrors of ice that terrify him. He realizes that pollution isn't just making more rain. The pollution is preventing it. The iodide creates so many seeds for clouds that they become so full of moisture it won't rain at all. Instead there is just a "pervasive mist" Vince calls it, that lingers in the atmosphere, potentially poisoning us.

I stumble over my words and say something about the contrails and precipitation. One of the men discovers it, I manage to say, and our town has some part in it, in the process, in the flood, in the story. It touches us. I keep trying to explain, but in my mask, my glasses fog. Doris simply asks nicely if I put the volume back upstairs.

—

In the winter of 2020 at the height of the pandemic, when no one flies, we have more snow than usual, and I hear talk that this is because there is no air traffic. It's impossible to know if that is fluke or fact, or fate. I wish I could ask Vince.

—

Now my dad and I are in the dining room, the hub of our family life, when he tells me about Vietnam. A blue cloth covers the table. It is winter, and David is here too, sitting in his place at the end. Outside is dark. The walls of glass in my parents' house have turned to mirrors from floor to ceiling. They hold the world at bay. My father's cardigan drifts around his shoulders. One eye droops, and his lopsided smile pushes up at the side, and his voice dips too, to the register he still adopts for work.

I wish I could tell you exactly how it feels as he speaks. Here as a teenager I would argue with him about modernism, my hip thrust out. I'd go on about John Ruskin and how the Gothic age had more respect for the workers. Or, I'd tell him how modernism just imposes its values on people. I mean, look at public housing, I'd say.

This night he tells me about recruiting people from co-ops in the United States to go to Vietnam, and he says he has no idea what happens to the co-ops there after the war.

I must be stunned, but there are only three lines in my notes. He says, The Vietcong never attacked the co-ops. We never knew if the VC were on the boards.

All I can recall is a dull sense of amazement. I think part of what he is saying is that it wasn't important if the VC are on the boards, just that there are boards and members, and that people across the spectrum, average people, pay their membership dues and join and serve in the co-op, that it is about people coming together and being stronger together. But, here, too, is my father and Vietnam, and my parents oppose the war. They host SDS protesters, and my older sisters get tear-gassed at rallies. There is something in all this that's hard to untangle, the various beliefs and how they transmit down to me over the decades, even before I am alive.

—

The book with Sarah-as-Laura the hydrologist/cop veers toward her obsession with water, which is really my obsession with water. I wanted to write on things like stream piracy where one watercourse takes over another to carve a channel, but the phrase suggests to me lawless marauders over the landscape. Millennia ago in the Catskills, ice melts from the glaciers at the headwaters of one creek and migrates to another, creating Kaaterskill Falls, higher even than Niagara Falls. Or: there's the Twilight Park Conglomerate, which sounds like a mob syndicate but is rounded rubble from the Devonian age, when the continent's oldest mountains washed up in creeks. Now the rocks form a cliff of something like concrete, and like that, this book you are reading here, too, has been assembled from so many pieces—paper or rubble placed next to each other over a decade. The events happen in different years and eras but hang next to each other on the wall, so the meaning is proximate.

I cannot make these facts—my father and the war, the rocks and water, clouds and paper, the notes I tape up—serve a story or plot, and I want to know how do you relate things so enormous as the climate to a character and their development? On the wall behind me, index cards warp, and newspaper articles only three or five years old grow brittle and yellow.

—

It is winter again, and there have been so many Decembers of rain that it seems we have crossed some great divide. This month every Monday brings storms:

first three inches of rain upon which falls ten inches of snow. I am called out that morning—six a.m., eight a.m., wires down; someone crashes into a tree. I stand next to my chief on the scene, and his radio crackles with all the other disasters across the county. Falling limbs trap one department half an hour west of us after responding to a call. The next Monday: five inches of rain, and now it is almost Christmas.

Yesterday tornadoes ripped across the country. Today clouds drift. Fifty people are dead. Soon the number will climb to 100. One tornado touches down for 227 miles, a record. An Amazon warehouse is destroyed. Just before the holidays, it is staffed by contract workers. No one knows exactly how many, because they are contract workers, because no one has to know, because contract workers are there to save the company from knowing, from liability and lawsuits due to injuries. The news reports that clusters of tornadoes are now more intense and more common and tracking eastward. I think, too, of the track of capitalism. The "new normal," the head of FEMA says.

Here we have two thunderstorms in December; these storms usually come in May.

———

This Christmas morning there is an avalanche on a ski hill where seventy years before the rainmakers sent up their silver iodide. A slide like that is unheard of in the Catskills. The mountain's pitch is too shallow, but six inches of rain falls on three feet of snow and takes out the lodge. In my village I wake at three-thirty a.m. and pound on doors telling people to move their cars from a street that will soon flood. I bang too loudly. Behind one door in the apartment house, a child cries, and I feel useless. I'm not Santa. I don't bear gifts. As day breaks, I stand on the highway in a safety-yellow vest. I shift my weight and watch waters rise and tell people the roads are closed. "Don't drown, turn around."

———

David and I go for a hike on state land. The ground is sodden. Streams high. The local paper warns of hypothermia if you fall in. Trees are down on paths, root systems undermined and weakened. I show him three different species of club moss and regale him with things I love about them, how ancient they are; and the sex, I say, you cannot even imagine. The tiny, tiny spores, and of the billions that are produced, maybe one gets fertilized and makes a gamete and that alone lives underground, dependent on fungi, for seven years—all waiting for a phase that produces something like sperm with flagella that need water to fertilize what you might call an egg. Sperm swimming in droplets, rain, dew—.

Porny, he says, and hoists his pack. His beard is speckled red and gray and brown. He holds his trekking poles in one hand and grabs his jacket.

I tell him that's not all, club moss has multiple ways of reproducing. It takes so many years just to make spores, no wonder they send runners out to meet us. I wave at what look like thin green ropes trying to cross the trail, the club moss's stolons and sprigs. I look at him in the red knit hat and a cloud of breath. He catches me watching him and squeezes my hand.

What if we could sprout ourselves from a limb, an arm?

He says, Then the world would really have problems. Clonal humans?

We strip down to T-shirts because it so warm, then stuff our jackets in the pack. He tells me about time. His voice is gentle, a British accent that hums in the humid air. Archeologists declared January 1, 1950, to be the start of the present. Carbon dating was just discovered a couple weeks before in December, and so many nuclear tests had been undertaken with so much radiation, the earth would never be free from radiation, he says.

I tell him how the club moss's spores fueled the first internal combustion engine created by the Niépce brothers in 1807. The plants make up coal deposits, so they are still fueling our world.

He says part of this archeological present is because with all the radiation, earth will be in present time from now on. He looks at me and nearly steps on a long green runner reaching into the path.

Watch it, I say and use my poles to shield it.

You cannot protect them all, Jen. This isn't the fire department, and there are so many trying to grow into the trail.

But, I can from us at least.

Everything around us is brown and wet. Fragments of ice, clear as glass, edge the trail, where a spring runs through it because it is so sodden. I think about how the Rainmaker's Flood happens in November 1950, when all time becomes present tense.

———

This week I read poems by Jorie Graham, one on rain, the other the future:

is there a place to still be
out there
now, in the actual future, which came about
after all—because none of this
will survive, though from here see, so sun-dappled in
what we called hours,
long strings of human eagerness, & wonder curiosity
hope expectation belief—

And I find a line by the Lebanese poet and painter Etel Adnan: "I suspect that time no longer exists. The sky will follow."

Outside, the sky is gray upon gray. In the poem "Translation Rain," Graham writes "participation" but I read "precipitation." She describes how we have fractured ourselves into ever tinier fragments. These pieces are from our lives online dispersed on-screen and in the ether, in a social network—a spectral dream of collective public. And, the clouds are steel and ash, shadow and slate. It looks like someone tried to erase them and draw them back in, with smudges in repeating lines. These skies are stand-ins for what is inchoate, what I cannot say, for what happens when the clouds and smoke are portents.

—

In January 1967, a couple weeks after Schaefer's *Science* article with his lead-seeded snowflakes, in Washington, DC, it is a month of no snow and temperatures in the seventies.

A secret memo is sent to Secretary of State Dean Rusk. The military is seeding clouds to make rain in Vietnam. It's called Operation Popeye. How does a cartoon character who eats canned spinach that magically transforms his wobbly bicep into muscle give his name to a war with weather? Maybe it's that something as ephemeral as rain and clouds gets beefed up with mere seeds and becomes a weapon?

The first fifty test runs are only a few weeks before Schaefer stands in Mont Pleasant High, warning of lead and rain and cars.

Under "Background" Point 3 in the secret memo: "The results are viewed by DOD [the Department of Defense] as outstandingly successful." So much so that nine inches of rain fall on United States Special Forces in four hours, which is, to translate, no light shower. That kind of storm is a cataclysm, like the Rainmaker's Flood, like Irene, like the rain this month in Vermont and the Hudson Valley, destroying bridges and farms and taking lives.

9. Urgency. DOD wishes to inaugurate operations at once.

10. Impact in Target Areas. The target areas within North Vietnam are areas of relatively high population density.

Under number 12. *Consultation. There are thus legal, and perhaps moral or philosophical, aspects to the question.*

Is this "random chance" that Luna Leopold describes or something more like fate?

—

In *Cat's Cradle*, Dr. Breed, head of the research lab, likens ice-nine to stacked cannonballs. He's talking about how crystals freeze and "can stack and lock in an orderly, rigid way." He asks Jonah, the *I* who is also a stand-in for *us*, "to think of the several ways in which cannonballs might be stacked on a courthouse lawn." Kepler, in his essay on the six-sided snowflake—the gift from the man who has nothing to his friend and patron who probably has everything—also uses cannonballs in his bid to understand snow. Breed and Vonnegut don't mention Kepler, but I am sure his ghost is here. It turns out that Hoenikker had a hobby of taking pictures of cannonballs on courthouse lawns.

Kepler was trying to understand how ice crystals stack together and learns of the cannonballs from the Elizabethan mathematician Thomas Harriot, though the idea is known as Kepler's Conjecture. In the 1580s Harriot advises Sir Walter Raleigh on the most efficient way to stack cannonballs on the deck of his ship going to Roanoke Island, just off what we now call North Carolina. He realizes the best way to pack a sphere, whether cannonballs, oranges, or snowballs, is in a pyramid.

In 1606, Harriot writes about the cannonballs to Kepler. Eventually this stack of cannonballs will be called hexagonal close packing. Logical though it seems, the complex calculations needed to prove the theorem remain elusive until 368 years after Kepler's death. The solution is only published in 2017. Mathematician Thomas Hales discovers it in the late 1990s, and it takes another twelve mathematicians more than a decade to check for errors.

The reason for the cannonballs: colonization, domination, and plunder. Sir Walter Raleigh gets the charter to Virginia (named for the Virgin Queen, Elizabeth) for these "remote, heathen and barbarous lands, countries and territories, not actually possessed of any Christian Prince or inhabited by Christian People." In exchange he pledges to give her a fifth of all the riches his ships bring back.

———

At General Forge one of Hoenikker's cannonball photos hangs in his old office as if a hint. At GE (or GF) do they think about Kepler too? Are the cannonballs a nod to his ideas, all this snow, the nix and nichts that goes into Bernie and Vince's work and into war? What about colonialism and plunder?

———

In *Cat's Cradle*, ice-nine turns everything to ice, to glaciers, so the troops are no longer stuck in the mud. Rain, though, weather modification, has long been a dream of armies, mud being a weapon of war. Or, at least, a side effect that slows the advance of enemies. Greek historian and biographer Plutarch writes, "Extraordinary rains generally follow great battles," and well over a thousand years later, soldiers in the Civil War believe this as they slog through the muck and mud of battlefields, once so many farm fields. They attribute the rain to the explosions of battle. One soldier writes home of the "muddiest mud ever invented." It is, he says in his letter, "knee-deep" and "unctuous."

Dr. Breed tells Jonah, "The marines after almost two-hundred years of wallowing in mud, were sick of it." But, the snowmaking, which is rainmaking, is to make mud, but also floods to take out roads and bridges. A slogan used in Vietnam: Make Mud, Not War.

———

In my local paper soon after the Rainmaker's Flood, Langmuir is quoted as saying, "The effect of silver iodide under optimum conditions equals that of one atomic bomb." An army general declares in *The New York Times*, "The nation that first learns to plot the paths of air masses [. . .] and learns to control the time and place of precipitation will dominate the globe." The GE executive in charge of the research lab will tell Congress: "There are so many points of similarity between the release of atomic energy and weather energy." Meanwhile two months after the flood, a headline reports that the town calls a "Mass Meeting On Wednesday To Talk About Bombs."

———

What would Kepler think of cloud-seeding or snow as a weapon? Would he call it magic? Or science? The charges against his mother Katharina include becoming a cat, bringing on illness, and tripping a girl carrying bricks, paralyzing her hand. Over the years that he is back home defending her, he gets all the accusations dismissed. He is not even particularly fond of her, though; his childhood was hardly easy. In his *Harmonices Mundi*, published during that time, he looks at harmony in all geometrical forms and physical phenomenon. This harmony expresses God's pleasure and results from the tones made by the sounds of heavenly bodies. He also articulates in the study what becomes known as the third law of planetary motion.

I love that he finds joy—or harmony—in the world and that science combines with this heavenly singing, that the two are not distinct. This week I read, too, that the universe does sing.

> Every gravitational wave [. . .] is humming through the very constitution of the space you inhabit right now. Every proton and neutron in every

atom from the tip of your toes to the top of your head is shifting, shuttling, and vibrating in a collective purr within which the entire history of the universe is implicated. And if you put your hand down on a chair or table or anything else nearby, that object, too, is dancing that slow waltz.

The cosmos thrums in our bodies, land, soil, trees, homes, hair, buildings—everything. It is the background music of the universe that scientists find by studying pulsars—dead and dying stars. This music pervades everything, all of us together in synch with each other to a soundtrack we don't even hear but simply express. Scientists think, too, this might be the harmony of all time, the vibration from the Big Bang as if time reverberates through us all.

I attach the note to my wall with a gold star to mark it out. I want to hold this thought forever.

Chapter 20

FOR FIVE YEARS MY FATHER is a weight in the firmament, barely perceptible like a ripple in the water, or humidity in the air surrounding me. He's with me as I walk in the woods or swim across lakes. With each stroke, the presence of water marks a space, and that space is my dad. I see him crossing another mountain lake when I am little and feel the way he loves water.

———

One afternoon, maybe six years before he dies, I talk him into going for a walk. This is during my campaign for information, for something that might quantify his distance and my longing. We're in a park along the Potomac, and he takes slow, deliberate steps. His blood disorder makes him unstable. His blood can't carry enough oxygen. He's supposed to use a cane or a walker but refuses, and this outing is my suggestion. I think I can ask about his childhood and the things he won't discuss at home. We slowly walk over the paved paths. He says he can't tell me anything; he cannot remember. I say, Okay, I understand, but maybe telling me something, anything, it will come back to you. What about the house? Or your grandparents and Pittsburgh? Or your mother, what about her?

I've already learned some from my aunt, his older sister. His mouth is set. He focuses on where he will place his foot. Silence spreads between us, but I cannot leave it alone. See the trail curving toward the water, the river's muddy shores. There's the grass, the path, the smell of low tide, a puddle and a purple earthworm struggling toward it. I ask again. He says no. I try another approach, a different question. I say that Dorothy, his sister, has said—. I don't finish my sentence.

Can you stop, Jenny. Stop. Just stop. His voice is peevish, and he slips into using my name from childhood which I hate. No! he says, Stop pushing me.

I stare at the worm. The sun beats down overhead. The worm struggles to reach some place of safety. I grow defensive—my chest hardens, tightens against my guilt, which is to say I am mad, because I am hurt, because I hurt him.

———

The secret memo to Dean Rusk says, "People still blame nuclear explosions for freakish weather." And in the nineteenth century people are so sure storms follow war that after the Civil War the US military tries for decades to make rain by setting off dynamite and explosions. On my wall the 1953 voice-of-god *New York Times* narrator compares Schaefer's rains to those caused by nuclear bombs and finds them unconnected. I still wonder if Doris thinks I am crazy with the planes and weather and clouds. Maybe I am. There's the way I see all these moments connected and have to keep searching in archives, as if there I will find my father too. As if some greater answer I need awaits. I hear my father's voice that day on the path, how he sounded like a little boy—petulant and terrified. I pushed him to talk about something he'd hidden since childhood. I realize he'd kept those years secret to protect himself and us—to shield us all from his pain.

It is summer now. I drive to Ilium, to Schenectady, the Electric City. I pull up to the airfield where the ASRC lab is originally housed in an abandoned hangar. "Air Museum" is emblazoned on the side, and the place isn't a museum for the air or atmosphere but vintage planes. The parking lot is nearly empty. When *The New York Times* comes in 1968, the reporter describes rows of machines sucking in air from the outside to test for pollution. Under the sub-head "Building a 'Fog Channel'" the journalist mentions they are constructing a 140-foot chamber. It is paid for, I know, by Project Themis.

Vince and Bernie work here together. One for war, the other the environment. In a report to the military Vonnegut writes that in this fog channel they manage to "suspend large drops of water in the atmosphere for appreciable periods of time. Including chemical agents for a variety of purposes, for example, insecticides."

I kick at the crumbling tarmac. Queen Anne's lace grows into the cracks, so does knapweed with its purple feathered flowers, and a plant achingly named heartleaf four o'clock. Its buds look like lanterns limned with rose. The name, though, is literal—the leaves have the shape of hearts, and it blooms in the late afternoon. I think of Kepler and his nix and nothing. There is Agent Orange and all the rainbow herbicides, White, Blue, Purple, Pink, Green, plus Super Orange—an even more toxic version of the original—dropped on Vietnam, and there are all the ways, too, Vince and Bernie's work bleeds into each other, as if a Venn diagram with the Pentagon and Popeye at the middle. *The New York Times* says the chamber will also be used to study thunderstorms.

A beetle crawls on the heartleaf. In Latin the plant is called *mirabilis*—marvelous. It spreads to "disturbed" earth, and both wild carrot and heartleaf have long taproots. I think of all the ways plants can spread and be, and what is hidden under the soil here far from my gaze beneath the broken concrete and tarmac. There are chemicals and microbes, some of which are calming to humans. Knapweed creates its own herbicide, a compound it exerts on other plants, yet still these are all together here. I think about lingering an hour or two until the heartleaf opens with its dangling magenta blooms. Knapweed's name comes from Chiron, the wounded healer, and I wonder if the weeds with their taproots and wind pollination could offer a different language for how to be and write.

I wait and wait for the shade of the afternoon. I walk to the side of the building and back and study the buds. I doubt Vince knows what the Pentagon is doing. Bernie probably doesn't either. Or, at least his brother doesn't think so. Years later in an interview with *The Nation* Kurt Vonnegut says his brother "was deeply chagrined to find out that the Air Force had been spewing silver iodide all over Vietnam." I'm not sure what to believe. I hold the heartleaf flower and will it to open. The beetle has fled, and finally I decide to leave.

In the same interview Vonnegut talks about Langmuir's fantasy of pure science: "Langmuir was absolutely indifferent to the uses that might be made of the truths he dug out of the rock and handed out to whomever was around. But any truth he found was beautiful in its own right, and he didn't give a damn who got it next."

That is pure science, not giving a damn.

On the modernist campus I look for the two men's offices. In one photo I find, Bernie talks on the phone in his office. It has narrow windows and a view onto two towering buildings. I wander the paths and stare up, trying to match the picture with what I see. I have a picture of the picture on my phone, and I am sure his office faces one of the school's high-rise quads where students live in dorms named for the Haudenosaunee nations. Another complex bears names of famous white colonizers, Livingston, Paine, and Delancey, and one of the buildings in the Dutch Quad honors the wealthy landlord Van Rensselaer who until the 1840s keeps his tenants in perpetual peonage. The late afternoon sun casts a golden light on the slender white columns. They grow from vaulted ceilings. Vaguely Moorish/futuristic, the ceilings are topped by clear domes. Overhead giant amphorae dangle like UFOs.

On the plaza the fountain springs to life, and the clock tower strikes five. The school is a copy of a complex just outside Islamabad, the Pakistan Institute of Nuclear Science and Technology (PINSTECH), paid for by the United States' Atoms for Peace Program where we helped our allies invest in an atomic future. It hails from the same era's dreams of fission and fusion, the twinned beliefs in progress and prowess that trumpet faith in future technologies to fix everything. It now houses the country's nuclear weapons program. Like Kurt Vonnegut writes, I find in the doubling some strange situational poetry.

SUNY Albany and PINSTECH share the same architect, Edward Durell Stone. He has a penchant for doubles. The Kennedy Center in Washington, DC, mirrors his design for the US Embassy in Delhi, and the school he lifts from his office's plans for that other campus, as if haunted by it. There a dome covers the reactor shield. Here the fountain stands in its place. Both have reflecting pools. The tower that holds the reactor's exhaust stack is now the clock tower. The university is supposed to be a place of firsts, where people who haven't had the opportunity for higher education get it, and that is to lead to a ladder of success— progress—this unstoppable path to better futures.

A scientist who works with Vince and Bernie tells me that Bernie's office is long and narrow with a single window at the end. In the photo there are three though. Inside is chaos, he says. Every surface is covered with something— unfinished projects, piles of paper, and publications. There are glass bottles and Popsicle sticks to which he's pasted circuits. In the photo the wall is lined with a filing cabinet, and the window ledge is stacked with books, boxes, and gold cartons of Kodak film. One spindly snake plant struggles for space. Bernie jokes about the havoc. "You think this is bad," Bernie will say, "you should see my brain."

Kurt Vonnegut tells nearly the same story about his brother's brain in the prologue to *Slapstick*. "His laboratory was a sensational mess [. . .] where a clumsy stranger could die in a thousand different ways, depending on where he stumbled." Some official at GE complains, and Bernie points to his head, "You should see what it's like in here."

Another coworker says Bernie had a dry, midwestern sense of humor, but I think it's more like rage. In the 1950s he quits GE after the confrontation over his messy office. The work is also no longer about the joy of following your curiosity but is to be results driven, tied to corporate goals and shareholders. Later, at SUNY at Albany he won't speak to his secretary for more than a week when she makes the mistake of tidying his space. He'll fight with her, too, about language, apparently. They'll argue for days over a phrase in a paper, and I imagine standoffs over gerund agreement or dangling participles. The researcher who recounts this comes to the ASRC as a grad student in 1967 and gets roped into Bernie's attempts at clear-air seeding, trying to make clouds where none exist in the sky. Every morning at dawn he has to let balloons off the top of the building with a chunk of dry ice. It sounds tedious. Even more than fifty years later, after he is retired, he still sounds drained from it. He says, It works maybe five times. The science is there, but the conditions—his voice trails. At least it gets him a deferral from Vietnam.

I find the letters written on his behalf also in the archive.

——

In the photo at his desk Bernie looks hesitant, like he's been caught off guard or caught doing something wrong. At his feet: a single crumpled sheet of paper.

——

Sometime in the late sixties in Vietnam the military starts seeding warm, unstable cumulus clouds—not the wispy cirrus that Vince and Bernie experiment on originally but ones like that Titian cloud I saw, the high cumulus of rising heat, moisture, and ice. They are unstable. They bring thunderstorms and sudden downpours in the summer heat. In the letter to his air force contact, Bernie writes of seeding clouds 35,000 feet up, and Vince describes cumulus clouds full of ice. There are silver clouds, silver hoops and seeds and smoke. *Cumulus* means "heap" in Latin. Luke Howard bestows the name in 1803 when he creates a taxonomy for the clouds. In his *Field Guide to the Atmosphere* Vince Schaefer writes about Howard. Goethe does too. He dedicates a cycle of poems to him and writes that cumulus clouds reveal "the soul's secret thoughts." They also "tremble" and "frown above," coming freighted with foreboding.

They come for me like Diaz's clouds, the ones on my wall. "What is America if not a clot of clouds—or blood?" They look like castles and carry imperialism and war, the buffalo that limps to Jesus, weeping blooms of white smoke. They come to destroy, to flood, to drown. They come for war.

———

Dearest Sandy,
Hope you get home from the airport okay and Jenny didn't lose her Lifesavers. I so appreciate the two of you going to the plane with me. It was nice to spend these few final minutes visiting together . . .

———

The New York Times reports on Popeye on July 3, 1972. The program ends two days later. None of the sources will say what the military is using to seed the clouds, just that, as one official explains, it manages to "foul up mechanical equipment—like radars, trucks and tanks." He adds that the chosen substance "wasn't originally in our planning." He calls the unnamed lead iodide "a refinement." The military, it seems, has taken Vince Schaefer's research. Two years later in secret hearings before Congress, the government finally admits they have been using lead iodide. In the hearing there are jokes, something about elephants and mice I don't understand, and they talk, too, of herbicides being sprayed and report, "They could find no lasting damage." They mention in passing Operation Rome Plow used to strip the green cover in the country. There are the names invoking Greece and Italy, Themis and Rome Plow, the jokes, the language, how the country goes from a dream of peace built from collectivity and co-ops to this. In two years.

In the Senate hearing, Dennis J. Doolin, deputy assistant secretary of defense, testifies about using the rain and floods instead of bomb: "Frankly, I view this in that context as really quite humane."

———

I watch Popeye cartoons silently on my screen so I don't disturb David across the office. I mute them, too, because I'm embarrassed to be caught watching. There is a love triangle between Bluto, hulking and brutal; skinny little Popeye, blind in one eye; and Olive Oyl with her Modigliani face, hair in a bun. The jokes are always on Popeye; something is switched so a swarm of bees chases him, or he falls, or is foiled. It's slapstick, that situational poetry, and its cruelties are hard to bear. I remember hating the show when I was little. Now I keep getting distracted by the setting. There's a picket fence, rolling hills, and a red barn. I freeze on a frame and want to take out the characters. What is left is the sparsest suggestion of a landscape, nearly abstract: wisps of clouds and an achingly beautiful blue. It takes my breath away.

—

At the end of her first dream of the atmosphere where she sees the silver hoops, Rebecca Cox Jackson envisions herself ministering to the people: "I comforted them with the words that was given to me for them. They were all colored people, and they heard me gladly [. . .] I, Rebecca Jackson, was two-score and eight years and twenty-six days old, when in 1843, I dreamed about my people."

In another vision she describes guns and violence. A Shaker brother comes to her door. She sees a river of ice, and three men upon the rocks . . . The shaking of the earth causes the river, the rocks, and the men to move up and down, and the men move their hands like a person shooting. Then they transform into "one transparent brightness—white as snow and bright as silver. [. . .] Rays of light [. . .] formed a beautiful circle."

I think of this as I stand by a pond at the original Shaker settlement across the road from the airport on a dead-end street. A single car is parked here. Rain careens off the gray ice. Overhead, jets take off. Signs warn of Lyme disease. There are the Shakers and their gift of seeing visions of the spirit world. I'm cold and wet and worried about what that lone car is doing on an isolated road in the rain. The weather carries this weight of violence. Nearby on former Shaker land, what once was a socialist utopia is now a jail and an ICE detention center and the homeland security building where David is interviewed to become a citizen.

Jackson sees herself as the second coming of Ann Lee, the Shakers' founder. Ann Lee sees herself as Jesus's Second Coming. Do I go on to describe Jackson's relationship with another woman also named Rebecca? Rebecca Perot. They join the community at Watervliet together. Later they live in Philadelphia, and Jackson does minister to the people. The Shakers call them the two Rebeccas. In one vision she tells Perot to lock their bedroom door with three forks against one of the Shaker brethren. The women are inseparable, inscrutable. They don't fit into our time, maybe not even into theirs. At Jackson's death, the other Rebecca takes her name.

Jackson, the first Jackson, writes, too, that the Shakers are too self-absorbed. "How will the world be saved if the Shakers are the only people of God on earth, and they seemed so busy in their own concerns?"

On an index card I highlight that question too. How will the world be saved?

Today the news reports that the Atlantic circulation—the current that includes the Gulf Stream, that circles the ocean and brings warm waters to Europe—will shut down in our century. The last time that happened, it was in a period of warming and then drastic cooling caused by the massive flood and flow of ice and water draining down what is now the Hudson River, that led to the sand sea outside Albany. That created the landscape where Jackson lived, and I read in her words the failures of heaven on earth. The SUNY system also doesn't build a meritocracy, and the Atoms for Peace program doesn't deliver on its promises either. I suppose one dream of clouds for war is that they are better than bombs, like Deputy Assistant Secretary Doolin says.

I see all of my failures—the beliefs I hold dear and often don't express. Or can't. I think of how I also see my father as a failure when I am young. As a child I take on my mother's criticisms of him and his failings, and then as a teenager I dismiss him. I call him a pragmatic Marxist, so not a real one, not one *truly* committed to his values. There is, though, how he talks of the public good. Those two words, "public" and "good," sound so substantial to me when I'm little, I am sure they are something you can reach out and touch. Here I am now with the ghost plant, the obligate parasite and its pale pink flesh and delicate hairs. I think of how it is dependent on those around it, on roots finer than thread, and think about what we have and what we share, of the man who gives up his home to make way for the reservoir and says for the news cameras filming the last days of his village that he can't stand in the way of progress, and I think of the public, the we—the you and I—of us, and what I want to hold, the ideas that seem to slip away the more I try to describe them.

———

On the drive home from Albany I think about Karl Marx and Friedrich Engels and their friendship. As Marx is dying, Engels writes him a letter to comfort him about their unrealized revolution, "Remember the Shakers!" He wants to remind Marx that it takes the group years to build their community. This is the last thing Engels says to him, *Remember . . .*

Soon Marx collapses at his desk. At the end all that

is left of the Shakers in Albany are the women, these sisters living together in kinship and going to the movies on
Thanksgiving.

The year after Marx dies, Engels writes a condemna-
tion of capitalism and marriage. It is a hundred years after
Ann Lee's death, and in *The Origin of the Family, Private
Property and the State* he describes how the family is a tool
of capitalism and women's oppression. The book is based
on one of the first studies of anthropology, written about
the Haudenosaunee, the people whose land I drive on right
now. This very interstate follows a route that has been
theirs for time immemorial, following the water west.

———

Today the clouds are cirrus; slender wisps rise in the air.
The name means "lock of hair." I think of my own dream
for a better world and that the co-ops are part of it, as well
as the Shakers and that historical moment in the 1840s
when Jackson joins them. Socialist uprisings shake the
world then. Chartists stage the first mass worker uprising
in the UK. My neighbors in the Catskills rise up and es-
pouse something that looks like socialist anarchism. People
build utopias and communes and try out different ways to
live. Capitalism doesn't seem preordained. There are other
experiments and possibilities. Many of them bloom across
New York State on land wrested from the Haudenosaunee,
including where my parents' co-op is based. The only thing
about building a utopia is that it often means not seeing
what is there already.

Chapter 21

AN EARLY WINTER DAY THREATENS icy rain. The sky presses down. Iris and I walk up an old logging road toward the woods where I first found my dad. Fat, heavy drops sting, and old snow collects in beads like glass. We push past trees dotted with lichen and talk about her plans now that her thesis is complete. She tells me how the work is going to turn her dissertation on Mary Norbert Korte and Diane di Prima into a book now that she's finished her PhD. We talked about the two women on Vroman's Nose and how Korte taught Iris about time and the redwoods and clouds. Iris points to a low-growing plant with oblong leaves that have one thin line up the center. What is it? Do you know?

Wintergreen, I say. My voice lifts. It tastes like mint, and it's here all season.

She draws the hood of David's old parka she's borrowing over her face. She says, When Mary Korte was a nun, she and di Prima would meet secretly and trade work. Their friendship went beyond writing. It became a sort of ethics, friendship as ethics as poetic affinity.

I take her to a goldthread patch. Iris tells me how the women's friendship persisted over decades. The plant has three leaves like clover, only frilled, dark, and glossy. Logging this land would kill them and they'd never return. I tell her the threads of its name are delicate rhizomes, gold roots good for canker sores. It's antibiotic and antiviral.

Like goldenseal?

Yeah and rare, I say. I never pick them, but I love them. Look, it's here still, so delicate and alive, even now. And that—I point excitedly—is shining club moss. We stand on the edge of a circle of little pine fronds.

You know, she says, Mary Korte heard messages from the universe, not like she was schizophrenic, but that's part of why she became a nun, because in that world hearing messages was okay. Then she left and went to nature, became this forest hermit.

I say, But the forest is so full of life, you're never alone.

She tells me about going to Joshua Tree years ago. Maybe I was twenty, she says, and I realized plants communicate with us, and mostly we have lost the ability, but some people still can.

In the brown world around us, the green that is left— the club moss and wintergreen and goldthread—radiates around us. Iris says that the poetics of that moment—in the Bay Area with di Prima and Korte and their friends— took in an entire life. What you did, your actions, was important—more so than writing a good poem. It was about the planet and ecology and how you might feed the unhoused, and being a spiritual seeker. She talks about these affinities and ethics, and I think what if they aren't just about human actions but something holding all of us all here together? Plants and people and these woods and the soil.

I imagine Vince and my father and their work at the same time and tell her that the club moss feels like it holds my journey in this book. My dad too, I almost say. She asks what I like in it.

I don't know—. I stumble to answer and whatever it is I would or could say about the plants and us and ethics and relationships, I don't. Touch the fronds, I say. Feel how soft—.

You have it too, she says, to communicate with the plants.

I stare at the ground. Frost has heaved from it, sending up daggers of ice, crystals that force their way up from the mud. I want to ask what she means, what she sees in me. In our friendship she has been a conduit to connection— to interconnection—between us, between her and me, and also the plants and the world and my writing. The cold air draws out the earth's moisture, and it freezes. With each step of ours, there is the crunch of leaves underfoot, and how bright this shining green is amid all the dead and dying other plants, the blueberry bushes and grasses, and we stand on the edge of forest where I found my father.

———

In March 1970 Vince addresses the Senate's new Subcommittee on Air and Water Pollution. "I'm an optimist," he says. He is sixty-four, hair white, brush cut and bristling up. See his dark suit and dark tie, pens in his chest pocket, a glass of water by the mic as he talks to the senators. He tells them if he had to do it over again, he wouldn't experiment with cloud seeding because of its polluting the atmosphere. He talks of his work at Vroman's Nose to make a fog, and his "dismay" at pollution's pervasive blue haze. He is here to talk of the dangers of leaded fuel and clouds. He describes smoke and blue haze and the size of molecules—five thousandths of a micron. He tells the committee that we must ban leaded fuel in cars and talks about

SSTs—supersonic jets traveling at the speed of sound. Congress has been planning to fund them; so, too, is Europe and the Soviet Union. The jets will fly too high in the atmosphere, he says. There are no clouds at that height and no rain, nothing to clear the pollution the planes will create, and no way to know the dangers this might unleash. The risks are too great. It is just over a month before the first Earth Day and six months before the founding of the EPA, which will be born from the urgency of testimony like his.

"If we can put a man on the moon, we can solve our pollution problem. At the same time we must rethink our sense of values [. . . and] seek goals that are addressed to our community well-being in every sense of the word." The committee chair, Senator Ed Muskie, asks him for solutions. Vince suggests smaller cars with smaller engines, mass transit, outlawing automobiles in cities, reducing the use of electricity. "We must begin to reorder our values. I, for one, am willing to do without some things that I now consider to be something I am entitled to."

His "our" with its commitment to a collective future breaks my heart. I hear in him my dad too. Vince talks about "community" and "hope," and "absolutely and especially the young people. We have a fantastic reservoir in our youth. I consider this our greatest natural resource."

The United States still hasn't done most of the things Schaefer suggested. Our cars are not smaller; our electrical usage grows exponentially with the internet. But back in the seventies, Congress responds, at least in part. They ban SSTs, thanks to Vince Schaefer, and in 1973 the EPA begins to phase out leaded fuel.

The thing that haunts me most in his testimony is

what he says in closing: "The time is passing when the American community will tolerate arrogance, hypocrisy or cynicism on the part of anyone or any group whose activity will further degrade the quality of the environment. This is not a fad. Anyone who believes it is does so at their peril."

I add this, too, to my wall. I tape it next to my dad's testimony in Albany, with his resounding thoughts of the public, of us.

———

It is a spring of fire and smoke. New words and language are developed for this weather. We check statistics hourly. There is a sky that never resolves into elements I recognize. At dawn the sun glows like a pink moon, like a planet, like Mars. Photos of it feature on the news, on feeds, in images on my screen, and on my phone I take pictures of this glowing orb. There are new letters I learn that day: AQI, air quality index. It rises from 114, to 180, 228, 259. Someone tells me later that it tops 400. I cannot go outside with my asthma but stare at the eerie light. A friend reports seeing bats take to the air that afternoon. It is a dark day full of smoke, and there is George Washington describing the "Dark & at the same time a bright and reddish kind of light." Others find "the very beginning of sorrow." This is smoke from forest fires eight hundred miles away but still on the East Coast, a place not supposed to burn in June. The air feels heavy, grainy in my throat. I close the windows. The air feels like rain.

I search congressional records to see if my father ever testified there too, sure there must be something. After all, he was a lobbyist for a few years. There he is: a slim young man with an earnest expression. In a photo he stands in three-quarters view, wearing a striped tie and serious demeanor.

It is June 1954 and he tells a congressional committee that because the government is developing nuclear power plants—and paying for them, that this, too, is a "public good and in the public domain, and should benefit all instead of a few large private industrial companies." His statement, which is read into the record, is called "Transforming the Atom."

There is this white space, but it is not big enough to indicate all the feelings I have. I could tell you about a moment in Vermont when I am little. Something hangs in the air in the car that I don't understand. We leave a farm stand. A humidity surrounds our three bodies, my mom, dad, and me. Her voice lowers, and she says, *Well.* The word contains both humor and rebuke. My dad brushes his unruly hair under his khaki hat and says, "Oh, Vermonters. They just can't get behind the rural electric co-ops because of that nuclear issue."

What you could intuit now from this is that we are

in the mid-1970s, and I am little, and there is everything that people have learned about atomic energy, and my father still supports it. Or, we could jump ahead a few more years, and I pick a fight because, of course, I pick fights with him, because I am almost a teen, and this one happens to be about nuclear power. My dad and I stand in the kitchen facing each other. He has on a shirt and tie, loosened as he gets a glass of water. There is the windowsill with plant cuttings, and overhead is the clock he buys that chirps with birdcalls on the hour, and it nears chickadee o'clock. I say he's gambling with my generation's future. The bird cheeps *chicka-dee-dee-deee*, and he says, Jenny you just don't understand. I yell back that it is stupid, criminal.

Or, there is the moment after he dies and I ask my mom about their phone's being tapped before I was born. I'd heard—absorbed—this information somehow as a child. She looks at me confused.

Tapped? she says.

Yeah, in the 1950s, you know McCarthy and all? This is part of the heroic story I tell of my parents and their politics, that my dad had been investigated during the communist witch hunts.

No, she laughs, our phones definitely weren't. She asks where I got that idea.

Well, I always just thought—.

Friends from Oberlin were accused of being communists, but your dad had the highest civilian clearance, a Q clearance, because of the co-ops and nuclear power. You should have seen his office with the most ridiculous array of alarms jerry-rigged across the place.

Or, we could just stay with the white space as I try to decipher my dad's words, the dense language, the sentences printed so tightly in the *Congressional Record* that my eyes glaze. Or, there is this way I want the white space to hold all of that.

———

I do not know what to say about nuclear power either. Pollution kills between five and ten million people a year. Compared to COVID or anything else that has endangered us recently, the number is staggering. Climate change is making parts of the world uninhabitable before our eyes. So, nuclear power. We don't seem to have the will to consume less, and I'm not even sure what "we" I mean—myself, Americans, the world? Can the white space hold that? Right now as I write, the world is blurred with smoke, and I sit in a room with a houseplant my father tripped over and nearly died. He almost fell through the plate glass windows on the modern house and had to be airlifted to hospital.

———

Putting a man on the moon, transforming the atom, nuclear power, rain as a weapon, these ideas share a belief in engineering—faith in science and better futures that can be created. If there's a problem, throw enough resources at it, and we can fix it. There is Vince's *I am an optimist.* I want to be, but this dream of progress seems impossible, but also it allows—excuses—violence.

Walter Benjamin wrote about progress and violence in his last essay, his "Theses on the Philosophy of History." It is early 1940, and soon he will commit suicide on the French border, when he is sure he is about to be turned in

to the Nazis. He carries with him an unfinished manuscript, and in it is a tiny line of writing about the weather.
("Architecture, fashions, yes, even the weather are in the
interior of the collective [. . .] They persist in unconscious
and amorphous dream-form [. . .] just as much natural
processes as the digestive processes, respiration, etc. They
stand in the cycle of the ever-identical until the collective
gets its hands on them politically, and history emerges.")

His *Theses* come in fragments. Everything is so cata-
clysmic and chaotic, linear writing is impossible. The most
famous lines are about a Paul Klee drawing of an angel. Benjamin imagines what it sees, which is really what
Benjamin sees. "One single catastrophe [. . .] a storm is
blowing in from Paradise. [. . .] This storm is what we call
progress."

I read Vince's lines and my dad's and see Klee's sketch
of his angel with its big terrified eyes and bird wings held
out, begging someone not to shoot. The modernists and
communists, capitalists and Nazis—technologists all—
believe in progress, whatever teleology or endpoint or es-
chatology that is. For them progress itself is ahistoric, a
condition of the world, which means whatever they do is
ordained. But, that would mean the disasters unfurling at
that moment Benjamin writes are inevitable. He cannot
accept that, so in the essay he carefully separates history
from the notion of progress. The idea, though, doesn't exist
in a vacuum, it just requires one to exist.

A few sections below the angel and the storms, he calls
progress "boundless," and "irresistible." It is this unstoppable
figment and fiction that happens in "homogenous empty
time," that allows this faith in the "infinite perfectibility of
mankind [. . . where] progress was regarded as irresistible."

I am raised in this belief, and I struggle to see outside of it, even as I recognize what it has sundered. I grew up in a home where we managed to believe our architecture could change the world, and where we dreamed of a better world to come. Modernism allowed us, the us that is my family, but perhaps, too, the *us* that is more than simply my family but that is hard to pin down here and identify, to believe in a greater good. That belief has not served all, not every one of us. It also allowed the human, the public—our social relationships—to be abstracted, as if they could be supplanted by architecture. What happens afterward if we don't believe better worlds can be built? What is on the other side?

Now maybe we are in the era of weather and the collective. Maybe politics and history emerge.

The crime novel comes bearing the boundless fiction of progress. Solutions always come, stability is restored, and there is something comforting in that. I do not want to take away pleasure. My mom loved murder mysteries and would read them more than once even though she knew what would happen. As she was dying, it was all Agatha Christie, old crumbling paperbacks, over and over again. The glue on the spine was gone and the pages floated free.

—

Soon after his lead iodide discovery, Vince writes about the breathing trees and how they create the blue of distance. I love that image. These conifers exhaling nearly invisible particles, so tiny they scatter light only at the blue end of the spectrum. "Sometimes," he writes about the hemlocks and pines, "the blueish cast is almost florescent." Each time I read the words, I pause, struck by their beauty, by what he observes in the world around him. Then, there are all the other blues he describes—the sky, the haze, fog, and smoke. From the observation about trees, he goes on to develop a simple test for ozone in the air. Around the same time, Bernie writes to Donald Rumsfeld complaining about cuts in defense research funding. It is 1976, and Rumsfeld, the man who will come to be famous for his "known knowns and unknowns" in another war as pointless as Vietnam, is the secretary of defense in the Ford administration.

That year Kurt Vonnegut's *Slapstick* is published, with its siblings who are so close that they defend each other at all costs from the rest of the world. Together they campaign to fight loneliness by creating extended families that remind me of the Shakers. In the book, oil is running out, and in the country we are at the far edge of a gas crisis. It is the Bicentennial; people wave flags and swear allegiance. My father takes a picture of our house. I'm superimposed overtop in a double exposure with a flag and a bike with streamers. A solar flare cuts down the middle, and I'm dressed in some colonial costume, floating like a specter. My hometown talks of George Washington but not the people he enslaves. A farmer is elected president. The ERA is still a possibility; women have the right to abortion. In my family no one talks about how remarkable we are as a family—my cousins, aunt and uncle and us, white, Black, Jewish, Christian, and atheist, all of our parents growing up poor and all of them serving in the War, which is at this point a war with a capital *W*, meaning World War II. We do not discuss race, yet we see our family as a marker of how far we have come: civil rights and women's rights, all these rights that we feel we have won. I am not even a decade old but stand outside a high school and tell people to vote for Jimmy Carter, a man who installs solar panels in the White House and pleads with people to turn down their thermostats. Put a farmer in the White House, I say. I wear a gold peanut on my lapel.

And if I tell you of this, can you see my childhood? Mrs. Schmidt's class in Hollin Meadows Elementary. There is the hallway with its celery-green tiles and the folded paper cutouts of snowflakes, a row of twenty-seven Santa faces we made of construction paper and cotton balls we have been instructed to bring from home for his beard. There is snow in the DC suburbs, and now it is February, and I run candles across the runners of my Flexible Flyer and sled down Mason Hill. Older kids, those who are ten or eleven, comment on how fast I go. I feel proud. My sisters have just left home, and in my classroom, I will study my desk, the seat and how it pulls out, the steel painted a dusty pink.

Could I hide beneath it? Would it protect me? We practice our handwriting but never drills for atomic bombs. There is no ducking and covering at Hollin Meadows. So, I examine the desk and plot routes to escape.

Seen from overhead, the school is a set of rectangles; there is its breezeway and ball fields and the woods behind. I will run down the shortcut that goes through them, through the brush and scrub where I once got poison ivy, then sprint up one road and another to my parents' glass house on a hill. Will I make it fast enough for my mom to drive us away? How fast can she drive? How fast can I run? How far can we get? How much time do we have? It sounds remote and fantastic, this fear of the world ending. I try to picture in my mind roads all the way to West Virginia, where my aunt and uncle have a cabin.

One day I admit this to my mom. She is in the kitchen at the sink. She turns to me. Her hair is bobbed; she wears lipstick and old jeans. Her purse is slung over a stool at the counter near where I stand. See the long galley kitchen that grows longer and narrower as if narrowed to a single point of light as time spreads out in the pause waiting for her response.

Oh honey, she laughs. Never.

There is something like a smile that is not a smile.

We are too close to the Pentagon and Washington, and there won't be any time. You—you don't want to survive, not that.

—

In Bernie's papers, I find a file titled "SDI Research Protests." It contains clippings from the school paper on campus rallies against Reagan's Star Wars. "Books not bombs," students chant. "Money for tuition not ammunition." A student group, Peace Project, hands out sheets of aluminum foil because SDI, the Strategic Defense Initiative that promises to blow up nuclear missiles with lasers, is as ridiculous as using tinfoil for protection. Hand-drawn bombs scroll across a poster that reminds me of ones from when I was a teen and going to punk shows and protesting Star Wars in DC. Above one article someone writes, "<u>Bernie</u> for your collection? I tried to reach you on the phone." In the archive I take a photo on my phone and look at it now. I am reading a page from the *Schenectady Gazette*. Just above a report on the campus protests, whoever writes the note to Bernie puts a big X next to: *Bernard Vonnegut, a professor of atmospheric sciences, has a four-year $350,000 SDI contract.*

What to say? In the archive there is that hollow feeling again, where the room is too small and the information too big, and the words unspool before me. Here on my phone on this smoke day, the fan on the HVAC system filtering the air kicks on. The world outside is red and hazed. The sun doesn't rise but the sky changes color. And Bernie, of course, Bernie. He is still focused on his clear-air seeding from his Themis years. He hasn't quit the idea. He writes about it in 1981, how creating clouds from thin air, or the blue sky, can be used to control temperatures in Fairbanks, Alaska. Then, he starts research on the atmosphere's highest clouds, which will have applications for Star Wars.

He is seventy-four, seventy-five, older and shrunken. His eyes seem too small for his head. His grin is wry and crooked, cocked to the side. He wears a bright-pink striped shirt that was stylish a decade earlier with a striped tie and plaid jacket. The way they all clash is almost charming. He still has that mustache he and his brother share with their father. He is a "distinguished research professor," meaning not teaching—not that anyone at the ASRC really taught—a colleague tells me. In classes he was always distracted, like he was bored or the students bored him, the colleague who is his-once-student says. Even with grad students he was disinterested. Soon Bernie will become emeritus, and yet he is working—still on war—still on clouds, either because he loves them, or believes he has the right, or believes this is right.

I remember finding the Themis files and how long it took me to put together the country's war, and Bernie's funding, and Vince's research on lead exhaust. I studied the lists of projects the Defense Department was sponsoring, and even though I knew about the Pentagon's rainmaking in Vietnam, I couldn't quite connect it to the school. I couldn't believe it. It was too strange, and I was sure a coincidence, but there was the shiver of recognition. And Bernie was the link.

The *Schenectady Gazette* reports his research will help "design weapons and observation systems capable of penetrating clouds."

Right before my eyes he's turning into one of his brother's characters with this doubling, this mirroring, as if each other's opposite but both looking like their father, and both loving the other deeply.

———

In President Reagan's plan for SDI the lasers will blow up Soviet warheads in space. Some lasers will be mounted on satellites, others based in large arrays with giant mirrors in Alaska. One government official talks to Congress about "fighting mirrors" and "striking at the speed of light." He calls it "magic." The government's own researchers, though, including the inventors of the laser and Nobel laureates, insist the technology is decades away from working—if ever.

Thousands of scientists across the United States pledge not to take any Star Wars research money. The *Washington Post* runs a cartoon with "Laboratory Experiment" written over a maze. A bureaucrat bearing bags of dollars rings a bell and nervous scientists enter a trap labeled "YES, I BELIEVE IN STAR WARS." For this, Bernie is going to burn holes in clouds with lasers.

I comb through papers and reports. There's a hand-drawn map for a meeting in DC a block from NASA's headquarters, an itinerary, his flights on US Air, where he stays in Washington, a meeting agenda stamped with an eagle and its talons clutching arrows. The symbol originally comes from the Haudenosaunee to represent their nations uniting in peace, and here it represents our country and war. The words US Navy Office of Naval Research circles the bird.

The front of a paper Bernie submits is stamped SE-LECTED. "This document has been approved for public release. Its distribution is unlimited." I find agendas and programs, lists of papers delivered by scientists from NOAA and NASA, other universities and research centers. It's hard to understand what SDI means for the clouds and sky. I hear that moment my mom says, "Oh honey."

Bernie is studying noctilucent clouds. The name means "night shining" in Latin. They are the highest in the sky, fifty miles up, and they are new. They fall outside Luke Howard's taxonomy. They didn't exist when he set out to catalogue the sky; there wasn't enough pollution. Most clouds form at four miles up in the atmosphere. These, though, rise fifty miles high in the mesosphere. They are first identified in the 1880s, and for years people aren't even convinced they are real.

To aim a laser you must see through the clouds all the way up to space, through even the highest clouds that might exist.

Bernie writes of them: "It is not known whether the ice crystals comprising them are of cubic habit, as has been suggested, or whether they are hexagonal, as in tropospheric clouds. [. . .] Also unknown the nuclei present so high up." He asks, is it temperature or humidity that causes the clouds to form?

Vince calls them "evanescent" in his field guide. Other scientists describe them as "shining with silvery blue light." They are caused, scientists now realize, by climate change. The mesosphere is extraordinarily cold, and as our climate warms, it has apparently gotten even colder. Methane condenses there with dust, maybe space dust. Who knows? But Bernie is going to study the ice nucleation, glassy structures, and crystal lattices.

In the northernmost latitudes just after sunset, just below the horizon, the sun's sinking rays reflect off these clouds in the mesosphere. They sound to me like the way Rebecca Jackson writes of the atmosphere: "Nothing can live above it. [. . .] It is always calm and serene between its face and the starry heaven. The sight, to me was beautiful." As I put all these pieces together, the very, very high clouds caused by climate change, our warming and their cooling, and the terror of their shimmering beauty, plus Vince's warnings about the sky and air, I am shocked that Bernie is studying them. For war.

Vince writes in his guide, "The authors hope the reader will be privileged to see them."

———

Bernie attends another conference in Washington on May 10, 1989, hosted by the Navy. The subject of the meeting is aerosols from the sea level up. For SDI the problem is clouds and condensation. In the meeting's report, WHY AEROSOLS is in all caps. There are presentations on "Aerosol Generation at Sea Surface White Capping, Source of Nuclei for Clouds." Under a column titled "NEED" the Navy says: "Characterization of Sea Surface for Surveillance."

Discussing the very high mesospheric clouds, the "Scientific Rationale" lists: "Cloud Characteristic Unknown, Scattering Characteristics Raising Fundamental Clouds Physics Questions." Another column in the spreadsheet touts: "Discovery That Polar Regions Covered Most Summer," and a few pages down under "Accomplishments" is "Quantitative Measurement Made of Extinction and Optical Depth of 'Invisible' Cloud That Could Obstruct Weapons."

Reading this now with all the stiff diction of the military, I wonder if that language with its implied proximity to power makes Bernie feel important?

———

It is a smoke day—yet another—as I type this, after so many this summer that in all the catastrophes, floods, deaths, migrants dying at sea, battles over borders, the smoke no longer rates much news coverage.

—

A few weeks before the meeting, the Navy official hosting it writes Bernie and asks him to "prepare comments on what it takes to bore a hole in a cloud (even thin cirrus) with a laser." Could he "generate a viewgraph or two?"

"We are planning a small dinner party the evening of 9 May."

In Bernie's notes preparing for the conference the type is large, maybe so it is easier to read from the dais. **THOUGHTS ON BORING HOLE IN CLOUD WITH LASER.** The font has the pixilated look of an early dot matrix printer.

The host continues that the party's "exact time and place have not been established." *Looking forward to seeing you.*

—

Bernie writes equations on the front of a letter from the Department of Navy. *v=1/2 100 X 1 over 160.* There are pages of formulas with the schematic of a cloud in the shape of a rectangle and little dots inside. I assume they represent condensation or ice or rain. "Hole of radius, r. z=Z Cloud z =0." "Power needed to vaporize cloud particles is volume dV. Raise its temperature by [triangle shape] T degrees and maintain the cavity below. [. . .]"

A meter-wide hole in a cirrus cloud will refill in a thirtieth of a second, and a new cloud will form of smaller displaced particles. This, too, will need to be penetrated by a laser, so the Navy can then fire another laser accurately at a nuclear missile in space. It happens in time frame so small and precise I cannot even register it in a breath. How would it be possible to aim a laser or a missile? Does it happen in the time it takes me to imagine running home?

———

In Schenectady in 1989, Vince is writing his final book, the one on Vroman's Nose, Onistagrawa. In his technical report, Bernie writes that the particles in a noctilucent cloud are only a fraction of a micron, "less than or equivalent a wavelength of visible light," essentially invisible.

In the report, too, I find Bernie is also researching ice and spiderwebs. "Ice crystals grown on a 20 μm diameter wire instead of the spider webb [sic] used in earlier work." There were those spiderwebs with the dew and the carbon black, that I find so beautiful.

———

I have read Jorie Graham on the future, Etel Adnan about the sky that no longer exists. There is the language I cannot escape: Generate a viewgraph or two, a small dinner party. REPRODUCED AT GOVERNMENT EXPENSE is printed across the top of all the pages. There are the microns, the cubic habit, glassy lattices, the spiderwebs, the dew, and the ice. I see Bernie and his brother as twins, and the campus and its twin in Pakistan—a hallucination of nuclear peace, and my dad transforming the atom.

That night I dream of formulae. There is d=, and the d is David. I see the bore holes and dot matrix type. Lasers beam light, and I find moss too. It appears in emerald patterns—geometries, fractals, and diamonds. They come together and break apart, and I want to grasp onto the moss.

I know what it is, though it does not look like moss I see in the woods. It is the saturated green of moss when wet, because it is permeable with water. There is a question in my dream of history and time, and the answer is this moss.

———

Online I read about how moss, too, leads a catastrophe even before the ice age or the Devonian sea. One hundred million years before the first trees, mosses cool the earth. They break apart rocks, and the rocks lower global temperatures. Carbon dioxide was nearly twenty times today's levels. The mosses and rocks lead to an ice age. Now scientists want to shatter rocks again.

———

One evening when the smoke has cleared, David and I go to a mountain where Mabel raises her children. It is the season of wild strawberries, and Mabel is with us in this moment, missing the wild berries. The mountain hunkers over the damned valley, where Betty lives, and she is here too. We sit on the hood of the car at the base of a ski lift. It's a resort the state runs. The parking lot has a view of the sky to the north. In the archive I learn Vince helps convince the governor the ski area should be publicly owned. It is where Wallace Howell seeds rain in the floods. David hands me a thermos of tea. I see Vince fly and bank his turns with Langmuir. Science is pure; the hills are green. There is Bernie with his equations; his brother says in an interview "I am a pacifist, I am an anarchist, I am a planetary citizen, and so on." The sun sets. There is no moon.

———

One summer night when I am little, I sit on the deck with my dad staring at the sky. My mom is inside. Maybe they are fighting; maybe it is some standoff over attention, but I am here with him, and he identifies the stars for me. See that—he waves at distant pricks of light whose name I have now forgotten.

I realize he knew them from his time in the Merchant Marine, about which I understood nothing. Look, it's _____, he says. And, I cannot see the constellation, cannot even recall its name, whether it is Orion or the Dipper or Pleiades. There are too many mosquitos. I am too cold. I go inside.

———

Do you see that, there? I say to David. I point at something high in the air, shimmering. That's it, right? See?

He says maybe. I convince myself I've seen them, this silver sheen in the sky lit by the sunset.

———

I read about Soviet cloud seeding after the Chernobyl nuclear disaster to try and stop the fallout floating over Moscow. Silver iodide bonds with the radioactive dust. Military pilots are sent out to fly over the reactor and the clouds floating east. The rains fall all night and into the morning.

When the power plant melts down, one engineer goes outside. "From where I stood," he says, "I could see a huge beam of projected light flooding up into infinity from the reactor. It was like a laser light, caused by the ionization of the air. It was light-bluish, and it was very beautiful. I watched it for several seconds."

———

Friends send me photos of burning cities. Someone emails me to eat seaweed for the iodide because of the war in Ukraine. Russian soldiers dig trenches around Chernobyl. Surrounded by forest fires, towns in California and on the East Coast look like Mars, like night, like a forever-setting sun. In the seaweed I find clouds, just like Vince and Bernie make. Kelp, brown algae, releases iodide from its tissues when exposed to sun and ozone. The iodide detox-ifies the ozone and produces iodine, which seeds clouds. All these doubles and mirrors swirl around me. There is the testimony about *putting a man on the moon* and *trans-forming the atom*, Vince and my father, a school in Albany and its double in Pakistan. There are the space mirrors, the undersuns and ice crystals, fighting mirrors, and moss that once ruptures rocks that scientists now want to pulverize to save us. Engineers also want throw iron into the oceans and produce seaweed farms to absorb carbon dioxide.

Bernie's clouds are also now a fix for climate change. His dream of clear-air seeding, aerosols sprayed high in the atmosphere to create cloud cover, could cool the planet. In some applications, sea salt has been pro-posed to reflect back the sun's heat, and countries like the Gulf States that are drier and drier and hotter and hotter are using cloud-seeding for rain. Wallace Howell said, We will never make the desert bloom. In 1981, Bernie writes that the clouds he hopes to create "in the upper troposphere might have the effect of decreasing daytime maximum air temperature near the ground by up to 1 degree Celsius and raising the nighttime mini-mum air temperatures by more than 3 degrees Celsius."

Imagine the haze this morning, the grainy light, grainy air in my throat.

And, in a stray line of congressional testimony I have read countless times, in this summer of smoke, I find Luna Leopold. He is Dr. Leopold. "Dr. Langmuir of our group has made a careful study of the reports prepared by Dr. Leopold—." I had imagined conversations between him and Vince and Bernie, but here they all are. I find Leopold's experiments online and hang the pages up too. There is no space left on the wall. It's covered in blue tape and these sheets that blow across the room whenever there is a breeze.

Déjà vu hovers around me in all the coincidences and doubles. They have tracked me through this book with a shadow of recognition or premonition. Leopold, the hydrologist whose paths of water led me here, makes clouds and rain too.

> An onshore breeze is generally present. [. . .] The third and not the least interesting type of data was a series of rapid motion movies in color. [. . .] Ice formed on planes while seeding. [. . .] Clouds in vicinity [. . .] Rain was falling from cloud [. . .] Showers over seeded area. [. . .] Heavy rain observed [. . .] Cloud built rapidly [. . .] Cloud top dropped 500 feet [. . .] Small showers. [. . .]

Is this his random chance? He writes of these rains and clouds in 1948 as he finishes edits on his father's book. And, I think the book of my father is the one I am always writing.

———

Crime novels come with cliff-hangers driving the story forward. In my world we reach new cliffs every day that feel like a marker of this time. I dream of kelp and its clouds in my season of fire and smoke. All the photos wreathed in haze that friends post are too pretty by half. iPhones are not calibrated for cataclysm.

———

I visit Sarah Miller in her father's sap house. The air smells of burning sugar and caramel. Her skin flushes from the heat when she opens the stove. She has on old jeans and work gloves, the elastic fraying at her wrists. She's back to help her father tapping trees. It is early February, a month sooner than maple season came when I moved here and first met her father as he collected sap buckets.

Outside the sun blazes, and it feels like spring. Before I come over, she warns to dress warmly. The stove is so well insulated, the shed where we stand is colder than outdoors. She hands me chai made from sap. For years we have joked about how people here should market the sap like our own version of coconut water. They could become rich on water, we say, wouldn't even have to boil it down. I clutch my paper cup, and Sarah's boyfriend tidies the woodpile next to us.

She says, I came back because who knows how much longer we'll be able to do this?

Well, your dad is in his eighties—.

No, the trees, the season, who knows how much longer it will last—or they will.

She's has been living in the Southwest, has worked for the Army Corps, and is finishing her PhD on streams and flooding. Her boyfriend opens the stove to pile in log after log of wood until the firebox can't fit anymore, and we crowd close for the warmth. He jokes that when she finishes her degree, they're buying property in Saskatchewan so they can still make maple syrup.

I say something about this year with no snow and how there are all the animals that need it for insulation, like the Karner blue—.

Even the maple roots are frozen, she says. Her musical, melodious voice is flattened and quiet. Her father comes bearing a bag of cookies Jane has made. He urges them on me. Sarah says just being here, the number of cookies . . . I say, Okay, one, and he says, Eat two, three. Take some home for David.

Steam rises from the long stainless steel pans where sap evaporates. It boils down, moving from one tray to the next, reducing and getting darker. A thermometer is stuck in the final pan. The aerosols—the particles—float, and the clouds condense on a strip of corrugated metal overhead. We tilt our faces into the steam and breathe in the sweet smell. We joke about maple facials. I tell her about Vince and the seeding and how I just figured out that Luna Leopold was experimenting with it before anyone else, almost in real time as the technology was developed. Before even the flood here. She says, Of course he was. He was trying that out in Hawaii. She's known all along.

—

In the fire department we get our first brush fire in the end of February. Now it is spring, and we have dozens of fires. They are also caused by globalization, by the fact that our power company, NYSEG, has been offshored. It's the utility my father mentioned and my parents hated. Not a co-operative but a multinational based now in Spain, it refuses to pay to cut back boughs and brush near power lines. Instead, the wires arc and burn on these hot, dry days when the last of fall's foliage has yet to green up. This day it is a record 90 degrees in April. There are ozone warnings. Those warnings say that I should not leave the house, with my asthma. I leave the house. Of course, I do. There is a blaze. The fire department is called out.

I stand on the road directing traffic. Kelp's Latin name is *Laminaria digitata*, for its long fingers. I stop cars, wave them down, so we can get a pumper truck up a narrow dirt road to get as close to the flames as possible. I read that the ozone level can be dangerously high in rural areas for reasons scientists don't understand.

I wear a florescent-yellow tearaway vest. My colleagues in their heavy turnout gear race up a hill bearing shovels and rakes and heavy packs of water. At low tide, waves pound kelp fingers against the rocks. Someone in a Porsche yells at me. The driver demands to get on the other side of the fire line, past our trucks. This could be comic or a cliché. He is young. He has a tan, a collared shirt. A friend in the passenger seat stares at me out the window. The sea is low and the sun high, beating down its radiation, and the fingers wave. The seaweed releases iodide from its tissues into the atmosphere. Because it's not a vascular plant, the iodide seeps into the air.

I ask the driver to turn around. He refuses. I tell him we need the road clear, we need to get in another department's trucks and an ambulance. The man with his tan and shirt says, We'll just wait here until they come. I say no. His friend says, We're not doing anything. His friend declares that I have no authority to tell them what to do. I tell them I do. I tell them he must move. He refuses to move. He says, Are you going to make me move? He looks me up and down.

Sirens screech, wailing toward us. I yell, Go now. Get out of the way. My throat hurts with the screaming and heat and dust. The Porsche driver demands my name to report me to my chief. He claims to be friends with my chief.

The algae detoxify the ozone and oxidants, and the kelp creates clouds, and I imagine rocky shores coated in the seaweed's calming mist; clouds growing over kelp forests.

Chapter 22

One afternoon, I park outside a narrow tract house that's supposed to be Bernie's. I find the address in the archive. The grass has gone brown, and the street and sidewalks are empty. I'm hoping for the gift, for some understanding of another era.

How could Vince and Bernie be friends? I picture one man's humor, the other's self-seriousness. One experiments on clouds in space and the other says he'd never do it again. Friendship, like love, is a mystery to those on the outside. It contains so many things—nostalgia and time and untold qualities impossible for others to see. For years I wanted my parents to divorce. I couldn't understand how they stayed together.

A neighbor's door opens. A woman stands at the screen and scans the road. A tricycle sits on her stoop. I drive off before I can alarm her.

I head toward the butterflies and sands and modernist school and strip mall and think about the poetic ethics of friendship that Iris told me about and how writing wasn't separate from a poet's action in the world, from their lives and their intimacies. I think about our friendship, and the thrill I feel when we are together.

How to describe this moment? That it includes all those things in my heart, and the sound of Joni Mitchell on the car stereo. There is Sarah Miller too, and that scientists have identified some region of our brains, the amygdala, that holds this joy and the hormones that produce it, oxytocin and serotonin. I see them rise in our exhalations and breath. All of this is simultaneous with my questions of Vince and Bernie and my parents and their marriage and thinking of my chemotropic plants and Walt Whitman and his *leaves of joy* from a poem cycle about being enmeshed with others, everyone, around him, and the eroticism of that. Joni Mitchell sings of the hissing of summer lawns, and the car speakers are blown, and they vibrate, too, with the music of the universe and its soundtrack from dead and dying stars. There is the woman in the yard by Bernie's maybe-house and the warm steering wheel and its synthetic smell all together in this one moment.

———

On the phone I speak to another of Bernie's colleagues. We talk about the climate, and he says, "You look at the data and see some warming, and it's not the end of the world. You don't know how much is natural and how much is man-made. It's okay to be skeptical."

My mouth goes numb. I feel myself grin uncomfortably, even though he can't see. He says he shouldn't talk to me like this, which is what someone says when they want their listener to give them permission to keep going, to normalize a conversation that is not okay. I do tell him it's okay. I feel trapped.

His voice lowers almost to a whisper, as if imparting a secret. "All species, 99.9 percent of species that ever existed, have gone extinct, and every species is invasive at some point."

Now I drive over the Devonian Sea and its floodplains. I follow my father's route. The sea maps to the oil-rich Marcellus Shale like its ghost. I think of the colleague's comments, and my chest tightens. This is the largest natural gas reserve in the United States, and one of the hardest to access. It takes splitting apart rock, fracturing it—fracking, which sounds so much like *fucking*—with chemicals and water. The residue poisons soil and wells, not to mention the pollution from burning the gas or the methane released in drilling for it.

I pass a roadcut, a massive cliff face, and in my mind my dad stops here and we are now in the middle of the Devonian age. There are corals and sharks; seas come, seas go. Millions of years pass, but it is still to us one age in geological time. This sea now is 390 million years ago, and he crosses it too—the continent is Pangea. The mountains here rise from the rubble deposited in a delta, the floodplains where the trees appear. I live on the shore of that sea, and the Acadian orogeny—the *oro* as in mountains—they are lifting, and the past is held in this place like time itself.

The extinction here is called the Age of the Fishes. I think it should be the Age of the Tree—or the fern or the club moss. The oxygen is 75 percent of ours. It is six degrees warmer, with eight times the carbon dioxide; and plants, which are then mostly in the fern family, lead a cataclysm. The oxygen levels change and increase. The atmosphere goes from warm to cool, cool to killing. Now we dig up that history and burn it.

This sea, that is a floodplain, has held all kinds of life and plants and disasters. I read about the Karner blue written in 1992. "The butterfly originally occurred as [. . .]

metapopulations across a vast fire-swept landscape covering thousands of acres." Sixty-six schoolchildren write letters to protect the butterfly, but according to the federal government's report, one person "questioned the Karner blue butterfly's contribution to society."

Over millennia species do appear and die out, but in Bernie's colleague's version, our meddling with the environment is abstracted, turned into some kind of biological determinism. I think, too, that we are nature, not outside of it. Everything—all our actions—our cars, computers, homes, synthetic materials, and cell phones, our clouds in the air for data, all of it, is nature. I don't believe in some prelapsarian moment, an Eden before the fall, before humankind. Or rather, I think, yes, we are all the fall, but in the colleague's version we don't have to do anything but accept this. There is no accountability and also no reciprocity or relationship between us and other species on earth.

———

In my dad's papers I find a speech about individualism. It's the eighties, the age of the yuppie and Wall Street bankers. He says all this focus on the self is a problem, all this I I I—"the age of self-fulfillment," my father calls it. "Many individuals, too many, are asking questions like How can I satisfy all my needs and desires; how much commitment should I make when I have other things I want to do even more? What does personal success really mean in terms of what one must sacrifice?"

What does he want instead? Co-ops, where we join together for the common good; co-ops, which he sees as a possibility outside of capitalism where we share resources and profits. I remember fighting about this, too, as a teen.

He was helping co-ops in the Philippines, and I said he was working for dictators, thieves. He told me co-operatives give people a voice, a vote, and then told me again—yet again—of the Rochdale Pioneers, twenty-four poor weavers outside Manchester, who built the first co-op and won the vote for the working class in the UK.

In this speech about selfishness, I find something else at the very end. He quotes a letter I write home from summer camp. I'm talking about just sitting in the woods and being quiet and listening. I write to him that I am grateful for all he has given me. I have no idea what I say matters to him, not until I find it in his files. I am twelve.

———

Today in the paper it is hottest year ever, yet again. We are always crossing that line; the winters that no longer snow, the glaciers that disappear, the horizon we thought might be decades away only to find it is now, today, this day.

A headline reports that exhaust from billionaires' space launches is destroying the stratosphere. It is just one layer above the mesosphere, a place so remote that for years scientists couldn't even track clouds in it. Yet, these rockets might also cool the earth. Their exhaust could block the sun's rays. The plumes of rocket fuel are also destroying the ozone, a thin layer in the stratosphere, while these men, whose wealth is of a magnitude so much greater than anyone else's, seek salvation—eternity and escape, rocketing off earth as if fleeing our realm is the only way to survive. Vince testifies that we should never pollute the stratosphere. He says that we should join together, talks of community and young people. Now the billionaires also build bunkers to isolate themselves from calamities and chaos on earth.

—

It is summer and I visit a hemlock forest that grows down the hill from New York City's ridgeline where my father first appeared. It's a mile and a half from the house with the gingerbread and turret. I part a fringed bough like passing through a gate from the old farm fields. The stream Bull Run marks an edge. Light filters through the trees and vibrates up verdant brilliance from a patch of jewelweed.

I look at the scintillating light and think about the plants curling at my feet and all of the life around me. What I want to tell Iris is that I feel cared for and warm, and maybe other words, too, I don't even know. The sensation is a yellow-green glow. I brush it away. Writing here, I take the idea back, stop and start that sentence, delete it and begin again. Just the notion of plants caring for me is too crazy. It is outside my worldview, so utterly unproveable by science or Western medicine that there is no logic in the idea. Or, rather it doesn't translate to my logic, so I cut myself off.

For the seconds I let myself feel it though; looking up at the canopy and around at the mosses and fungi, tiny waxy purple mushrooms growing on the ground, I am convinced that this sense of care doesn't come from my paying attention to the forest and its life, but that they produce it. Then I stop myself again. I think about the modernism I was raised in and the abstract principles, and how my father was away so much he felt abstract to me too, and for him the very idea of family seemed distant, another abstraction. There is modernism and the strangeness of modern science that keeps me from thinking I could have some relationship with the world around me.

All of these characters, Sister Lucy Bowers, my father, Vince, and Bernie, were also flying in planes. Sister Lucy came to the Shakers as a little girl maybe an orphan, maybe abandoned by her family, and my father who loses his mom and then his dad and his home. There is Bernie who loses his mother to suicide but also nearly his brother, too, and then holds his brother tight afterward; and Vince whose family is nearly made bankrupt by an illness and who takes to planes to stare at clouds, all of them take to the skies, to the air.

Neil Gifford, the biologist in the Pine Bush, talked about interdependence of species. You cannot love just one, not save one, but all. In the shade of the hemlocks, the air tastes sweet and pungent, as if something happens inside the air itself.

———

Iris sends a card with a Mary Korte poem that ends:

> The woods at work
> is a huge Person singing
> all over the place

Maybe this is what writing is for, to feel into a different world, one where the woods sing and breathe.

Paul, the historian, tells me the Mohawk word for hemlock is *Ohneta honwe*, meaning "original pine" or "true pine," with the sense that they were the first or most significant conifers around. Eastern hemlocks, *Tsuga canadensis*, once account for much of the woodlands here in the Northeast, and the trees live five hundred years or more.

They are our redwoods, holding time, long time, and creating this place. The hemlocks absorb water and exhale it. Their transpiration supports the mosses and ferns, the chanterelles and the reishi, mycelia and mycorrhizal networks I don't even know.

———

Over the years I bring friends to this forest. I bring Anna, and I bring Iris. I bring Sarah. I bring Jenny and Chris. I bring Laura, I bring Amy, and Diana and her daughter Meadow, who live in London. This is the first meadow she visits. I bring Adrian, and I bring my sisters.

———

There is Iris's ethics of friendship, and I think about our friendship and this idea that there could be something in the air between my friends and me. Blooming nearby is a ghost pipe with its luminescent white stalks, fleshy little fingers, and tiny pale bloom, at the center a hint of yellow. Many think it's a fungus, but it's a flower that depends on mycelia that pair with the hemlocks. My ghost flower by the reservoir is chemotropic, and maybe we are too? Maybe there are chemicals like oxytocin and serotonin, something that happens between the plants and us?

———

The redwoods make clouds, Iris learned, and Vince found in pines and hemlocks the blue of distance and his test for ozone. I read that plastics now seed clouds, and there are Bernie's clouds—his clear-air seeding—to cool the climate. I am an alien in this world with the trees. I dream of a public that includes all of this, these woods and mosses, mushrooms and goldthread. There is the dream of science that has kept us separate from what we study, as if better, different, superior, and removed. Meanwhile, the eastern hemlock, this first tree, is dying from an insect the size of an aphid brought to the United States. This grove will not probably live another decade, then it will release all the carbon it has stored. There is Iris's question about what I like in the club moss. I decide my answer is time outside my human scale but also survival. In the tiny green fronds at my feet, I can picture species surviving our era.

Chapter 23

DUST SCRATCHES FLICKER ACROSS THE celluloid on my computer screen. I watch silent film footage from my dad's childhood. Nearly a century away, it's the Fourth of July. It's mute and menacing. I don't recognize anyone. Men wear admirals' hats too small for heads, making them look ridiculous. There are women in white dresses and kids on a playground, legs soaring in the air from a swing set. The American flag is hoisted, and the stars and stripes fill the screen. A man with a fleshy face clenches a cigar between his teeth and leers; other men in suits—white men, upright men, the upstanding leaders of this town, with their high, tight white collars—give speeches I cannot hear. Their lips move, and I imagine what they say. I witness a disaster unfurling that I can see from this distance, but whoever holds the camera has no idea what is coming.

Soon, in his store my grandfather will accept payment in potatoes and cooked dinners. His creditors won't take potatoes and cooked dinners. Then, his neighbors burn a cross on the lawn.

—

In the fire hall after the brush fire, my friend Lissa, a single mom who writes on the environment, leans against the wall. She has pink hair and brilliant blue eyes. Her cheeks are flushed from the heat of the blaze. She tells me she has to take time off from journalism because she's so overwhelmed trying to report on the climate, with people's refusal to do anything. She says, I can't. I just cannot, not anymore.

She is going to start bartending instead. We drink Coors Lite. She lifts her silver can to me, and we stand under a framed crocheted American flag. She says she's angry, so angry. Then we laugh because she says, Well, people still always drink, particularly in an apocalypse. Remember Irene?

—

Now it is winter, an earlier time in the first Obama administration, which feels so much more innocent though it is not even that long ago. It seems distant because there is snow in Virginia. It is January. I am back in my parents' home. My father is sleeping often. His head droops at the table, and he'll shuffle off to bed denying he needs any help. His memory is going too, so his conversations are stilted and repeated, something he apologizes for too. This afternoon he heads to bed for a nap, and I follow, ostensibly carrying a glass of water and turning on the heater he likes to have run.

Can I nap with you, I ask, if it's okay?

He nods. I lie next to him trying not to shift my weight so he can sleep. Outside I look at the bare trees and dusting of snow, grass poking through the layer of white. Photos from my childhood adorn his bureau. A whistle sits on the bedside table so he can call my mother if he needs to get up in the middle of the night. (He will not call, not when he needs it most.) A dark shadow marks the spot on the floor occupied until recently by a rug. Now it is rolled up in the closet so he won't trip on it.

He wakes, startled to find me there, and apologizes for sleeping. So many apologies now. I tell him it's nice lying here. He takes my hand, and I don't know how we get on the subject of my childhood. Maybe he says something about being proud of me, which he often says, as if it is one of the few things he remembers. It never stops feeling special, and however we get to talking about it, I apologize for being an awful teenager, how I argued all the time with him and had to be right, about art and politics and architecture, about the world, about the music I listened to and the volume I played it at. It must have been exhausting, I say.

He tells me he doesn't remember that at all. He tells me he loves me.

He dies a month later.

—

Now I write from a room with a picture of his bedroom in it. A photo of his dresser hangs on my wall, like a portrait of him. On his bureau I smile a gap-toothed grin. A snapshot of my mom in jeans and T-shirt, four-wheeling with friends, is tucked into the frame. There's another of her the day she starts chemo. My nephew stumbles in a picture taken just as he's learning to walk, and there's an ugly clay mushroom I make in Mrs. Schmidt's class. I can't believe he keeps it. In the mirror over the bureau, you can see a batik bedspread from one of his trips overseas. Also reflected are the windows' slender mullions holding up the walls of glass, as if the house is porous to the world.

—

I talk on the phone to Tom Porter, with his soft, burnished voice. I've seen him in pictures; the images are regal. He wears a shirt bordered with ribbons, ceremonial feathers on his head. I explain that I've been searching for information about the region because I'm writing about Vince Schaefer and floods and how he made a technology that floods where I live, but that I wanted to talk to Tom because so much of this happens on Mohawk land.

He says, Oh yes, I know your scientist, Vincent Schaefer. Of course.

The air pricks in a blister, and outside it's summer. An iridescent hummingbird lands on a feeder, and I cannot believe what I am hearing. The wires between us vibrate alive with the coincidence, and it sounds like the hummingbird's whirring. Tom says, Yes, it was 1993, and he wrote to us. He saw an article in the paper that we were looking for a home in the Mohawk Valley.

At the time Tom lived two hundred miles north on the Akwesasne Reserve, straddling the US/Canadian border. He tells me that Vince said, "I know just the place." In his letter he says, too, that he was friends with a Seneca chief, meaning Arthur C. Parker, whom Vince wrote to as a teenager and hiked with decades later. Vince goes on to describe the county home in Fonda, three hundred acres. The town was selling it off, and he says, Here's a really good place to look at. This place has been for sale for years, with a beautiful creek flowing through there, and this stream on the hill and really pure water, flowing into the polluted Mohawk River, but the stream is pure.

He offers to come with us to see it. He said this was where a Mohawk village had been.

I look outside, and the headphones are in my ears, but I can hear the birdsong and the buzzing of hummingbirds chasing each other, fighting over sugar water, and Tom

Porter with his soft voice where all the words sound like they've been washed by a stream for centuries. He says, We won it at auction the week he dies.

I nearly drop my pen. The clouds are cirrus; the outlines of hemlock are jagged against the sky. I sit in a room with the plant that nearly killed my dad. Again there is that bristle of repetition, of déjà vu, of circles and mirrors, and the air molecules rearranging over distances. I can smell the sweet clover through the screen door, and my hand rests on the yellow legal pad. Outside are clumps of weeds and wildflowers I cannot bear to mow. There is ragged robin and daisies, yarrow and campion. A tiny blue butterfly—not the Karner blue, but the eastern tailed-blue that looks like it and is not endangered—basks on a clover. Its wings flit, tiny flakes of snow.

Tom says, I visited Vince in the hospital. He took my hand and said now I can die in peace, and he did. He died a few days later.

The last year of his life, the last week, the last thing he does, Vince Schaefer helps the Mohawk community return to its traditional lands.

———

Bernard Vonnegut dies four years later in 1997. He works up until the end. In bed, in the hospital, he composes edits to a paper on convective energy in cumulus clouds, something he's been obsessed with since the 1950s. I see the narrow bed, the metal rails at the side, and papers covering his blankets. At the very last, as he is consumed by cancer, he is still with the clouds and lightning.

I find in his files testimonies of the weather. For

decades he tracks phenomena that sound like Rebecca Cox Jackson's descriptions. There is research from military U-2 planes into lightning atop thunderclouds, and letters written to Bernie in response to ads he puts in local newspapers.

Mrs. Marcella Benson of Toledo, Ohio, writes, "We thought we saw searchlights but there were no light beams shooting up. The lights were bluish in color." Mrs. Philip Anderson, also of Toledo, reports in 1966, "Then a great wall of white came. There was hard wind and all white." A clipping from the *Birmingham News* of Alabama describes a tornado, "Cracked with jagged streaks of fire resembling lightning." Mrs. Benedict D. Aiken of Coconut Grove, Florida, sees, "Glowing bluish-green light." Joseph and Yvonne Bolduc from upstate New York write in February 1977, "The color was just like lighted matches. It crossed Phillips Road and illuminated it. Like electrical thread. There was no odor. No noise. There were hundred unknown objects."

—

On my screen a picture of a plume from a billionaire's rocket blossoms purple and white, like a billowing flower of light.

—

In Margaretville I have my second flood of the year in the fire department, another high water event. I stand under the streetlight. A trout flops across the road. Its body is silver and gleaming. Don't drown, turn around, I think.

—

The summer before my mother dies, I visit a couple who live catty-corner from my mom. The woman, Margaret, has also just been discharged from the hospital—something to do with her heart, she says. We sit in the kitchen. The table has a bowl of fruit and on top sandwich bags full of vitamins and pills. She is dressed in white, her hair a puff of white. Her posture is erect and long. My mother is stooped with age, and Margaret's husband Arnold, who is also with us at the table, is tall. His voice sounds erect too, like New England, like John Updike. He explains that I'm looking to understand the neighborhood and modernism. She says in a faraway voice, The trees were so small. I knew your father and know your mother.

The thoughts seem disconnected. Her voice drifts, and she says, There was a whole group here who believed in gardening and co-ops and politics. Like your father, he says. He was part of that with the co-operatives.

Arnold shows me a chair designed by someone in Denmark with graceful teak arms. Those designs, he tells me, really represented a view on the world, the best designs of the times.

I just came from the doctor, she repeats. He wants to fix my valve. Her voice is thin. She says she does not know. I tell her my mom has had this surgery. She says, I think we're going to repair it. I'm not ready to die. Your father's memorial was beautiful. He was such a good man.

—

Afterward, I hear her words like a benediction. Somehow I understand that the gardens, the co-ops, politics, even the trees might be part of my father, or the public good, or whatever I needed to find. These neighbors articulate it for me, and it was in the architecture too, in the homes.

Now I live in a house that looks like my parents'—modernism as parent, that third parent—built in a field that borders New York City's land. Here the snow and rain, Bull Run, beaver ponds, and ridgeline are all protected for the water. Like Steve Miller I inhabit a recreation of my parents' lives.

Geologists see time in rocks. They make it solid, literal. It's also held in our breath and stars and snow. I examine those cards in my dad's wallet for years, wondering about his memberships in these organizations and what they mean. I pull the papers out, turn them over, and feel their rough weave in my hands. Each time, I extract a slightly different meaning, as if they could transmit something to me. I find typed dissertations on the League for Industrial America, and its student group, the SLID, the Student League for Industrial Democracy, of which my dad is a member too. It favors public ownership of utilities, natural resources, and banking and credit facilities and monopolies, as well as expanding social security and national health insurance and co-operative housing.

The PCA, Progressive Citizens of America, demands swearing allegiance to the Constitution. At first this confounds me. We live in a moment where we recognize the Constitution enshrined rights over other people, to own other people, and to protect and sanctify this inequality. Later though, I think, that in these radical, left-progressive groups is faith that the United States is worth saving. For my dad, patriotism includes communists and socialists and a belief in *us*, which is also a country.

My father and his siblings join a global war where he is

not even armed, and in the branch with the greatest losses of life. His brother loses his leg to a shark in this same war, and his sister, an army nurse—a young Jewish woman barely out of her teens—is at Normandy just after D-Day and the Liberation of Paris and at concentration camps. She says to me, The things I've seen, the horrors . . . but never specifies what those horrors are, at least not to me, because they are too horrible. I don't see anything in those experiences that bodes well for optimism in humankind, but my dad does, and that's what I think is in these cards. That's what I hang on to. The PCA are communists yet support the Constitution.

The card lies in my palm; the frayed edges are bent. The paper is dirty with wear maybe from his pocket, or maybe he studies it and the optimistic robin's-egg blue in which it's printed. The group's members include Frank Sinatra, Paul Robeson, and Lena Horne, and I read their oath "with faith in the common sense of the American people." It talks of "common purposes" and "participation."

What can faith and optimism and patriotism be, though, in the tragedy of this time with weather and murder, where the unimpeded progress of capitalism is destroying us? On the card, the final sentence ends on: "with equal freedom for all."

—

I return to the hemlock forest, and it is calming just to be in the shade and inhale the tannins in the air. In this great burning catastrophe I am desperate for an *us*, no matter how impossible that idea feels. I read about escalating weapons in the arctic and fires that once raged on Antarctica. The snow there contains stardust. Out West, wildfires are so big they create their own weather—storm systems and lightning. In their *Field Guide* Vince and his co-author write of firestorms—"so violent as to fell trees, tear burning limbs from them, and scatter embers from the upper levels."

Someone sends an article during a forest fire outside San Francisco. "I'm numb," the caption reports. I read another, "A Rip in the Fabric of Interstellar Dreams," and add that to my wall. Here we are on the cliff edge of the pyrocene, and the Karner blue needs fire and snow to survive, snow that the winters no longer provide. We, you and I, follow a deer path. We stand beneath the trees: moss and hemlock needles, the ground soft and cushioned. I think of Iris. I scroll a conversation between two writers, friends, who talk about a "socialism for all things," and I read under another headline: "Your consciousness can connect with the whole universe, scientists say," and I tape that up too.

Small patches of club moss and goldthread, with their elegant leaves and delicate orange rhizomes, surround us. The hemlocks create this place, humid and damp, and I think of the trees and their gifts. All of this is made in their image, I read. My father has been held in them too, these first trees—the original pine.

Their saplings can wait centuries for a moment when a disturbance gives them enough light and space to join the canopy. They regulate water and the temperature so it's warmer in winter, cooler in summer, and they protect the brook. They filter out chlorine and copper from the stream and keep it cool, stable, and oxygenated. The hemlock builds this ecosystem in its shadow, around itself, and the trees can grow two hundred feet high.

I read a novel by Canadian writer Sheila Heti, a great

blazing book on grief. In it a woman turns into a leaf to be with her dad. In the afterlife he is contained in a tree. She writes of his death; the room grows mauve. She reports from this afterlife with her father that the plants and trees "are the grateful recipients of all consciousness." She is also grieving a world that is dying where "Seasons had become postmodern."

What I felt wasn't my father in the hemlocks but the trees themselves, that the trees comfort me. When I wrote to him from summer camp, I was grateful to him for the opportunity to be in the woods, and I am in them when I discover this man, my father, in his mauve turtleneck as he catches me in a stream in another hemlock forest in the mountains of my youth.

Now you and David and Iris are with me, and we dangle our feet in the water from a downed trunk that crosses the stream. In the pool it creates, we watch for crayfish to play hide and seek. The creek flows over rounded river rocks worn by time, and Luna Leopold dedicates pages to how the water moves them. That is his "transporting machine."

Uphill is a bog and here, too, is time, running along-side it. Horsetails grow by the swamp. They are the living relatives of those giant ferns that were the first trees. Shin-high, they look now like a low-growing pine that's been conjured by Dr. Seuss. They're skinny, knotted, and awk-ward, like a green bottlebrush. The water seeps down from them to the bog, the bog to the stream, and the stream to the trout and crayfish and insects, and then to the city in sixty days.

The horsetails once cover the earth, I read, "thick as forests and had relatives as big as trees." These are the very plants that lead to the mass extinction ending the Age of the Fishes. Now only fifteen species remain. I find articles detailing how they are weeds and instructing me in a multitude of ways to kill them. Instead, what might they teach us?

I want to articulate the language of *us*, for it to be big and include all of this, even though I know everything that gets erased when we—I—try to make something universal or universalizing. Light glows chartreuse on the edge of the forest and carries me, us, back to the Triassic period two-hundred-and-some-million years ago with the first dinosaurs and earliest mammals, and in our time now horsetails can only live in a narrow band between forty and sixty degrees latitude north. They require the worst conditions—anoxic soil, metallic and saline, in roadsides and ditches, places no one cares about. Or, here. These few that are left in our era survive another mass extinction 66 million years ago, probably caused by a meteorite that also killed the dinosaurs. What if these plants are the public too?

They thrive at the edge of a bog that runs through these woods, where the diffuse light is dappled.

—

Aldo Leopold, Luna's father, wrote in his *Sand County Almanac* about being lonely. "One of the penalties of an ecological education is that one lives alone in a world of wounds." In it he talks, too, about "enlarging the boundaries of the community to include soils, waters, plants, and animals, or collectively: the land." To breathe is to be tree, fern, and horsetail, with the ancient plants that once built oxygen on earth and changed the world. We take in the oxygen that plants and moss create, their air and respiration, as if we are all one.

—

In his book on rivers and hydrology Luna Leopold ecstatically describes our planet and water. "Our Grand Circle," he calls it, which could be the globe or the hydrological cycle or both. He writes about flooding, and it sounds like we have trespassed on the river, on the river's land and its sovereignty, as if the body of the river is a body, a being. "We encroach," he says, "on area that the river must at times cover with water." The river has rights to that space. Now people are suing for the rights of rivers.

—

This morning I stand on the deck of the house in a meadow, the recreation of my parents' home. My friend Rudd is here. We look out at the great gleaming green of the world around us. A pair of phoebes has nested next to the heat pump on the house. The birds once nested in ledges and cliffs and have come to associate with humans and our homes. The birds flit in and out, carrying insects for their brood.

Rudd has on a pair of worn trousers with countless pockets and a shirt woven with narrow pinstripes like a railroad conductor should wear. His is patched and frayed at the cuffs and collar. I tell him about this book, the flood, the lives, and he has been through all my floods too, and more. He says, My pa told me about the hunters stranded there up Dry Brook in the Rainmaker's Flood. There's a sign up still from that flood just past one of the covered bridges. He gives me directions to it and then texts me a photo. I ride my bike up and down the road. He says, It's high up now. The tree's grown and the sign is no longer eye level.

Nearly sixty-five years have come and have gone, and here in the Dry Brook Valley, the damn valley, I reach the end of the road, thirteen miles from my house, past where the fire department has responded to a structure fire and a barn fire, past where the road peters out into a hiking trail. I turn around and cycle back, and there I find the last vestige of the Rainmaker's Flood. It's covered in Virginia creeper. The edges are worn and weathered and starting to splinter, but the orange paint still reads:

CAUTION 5 MILES

DAMAGED HIGHWAY

BY FLOOD

DRIVE SLOWLY

And here is Luna Leopold extoling the river's body, whose land this is as well.

I read the Russian American poet Eugene Ostashevksy's "Farewell Poem" that ends on these lines: "It is said there is water everywhere and that we, too, are water or rather / *water*—in cursive—and that the reflections upon its face are / not things that exist."

I can hear Sarah talk about her grandfather and how heroic he was, seeing others' need for water over his own home. Water is everywhere, and we, too, are water, and I follow the currents that I can see in the reservoir from the river hidden within it. In my book as the character Laura, she watches currents in oceans from airplanes and as she stands over a bridge crossing the Hudson River. She sees her dad and grandfather. My father takes pictures of meanders from river deltas. I feel him in me like a current, as I follow his path, as if one body is contained in the other, the river, the reservoir, the stream and currents, hewing to its path.

—

Today the clouds are castles. Lead and silver skim the edges. They rip apart, revealing stratus lines—squiggles— miles high in the air. The sky is lapis, and I'm sure this could be the ceiling in a baroque church.

I lie outside on the ground, eyes closed. I can still see the clouds. They rush in lines across the sky, west to east against the azure, as if I could see to the outer atmosphere, the blue that would be black. I have the butterflies of snow, and this landscape in four times: floods, extinctions, fires, and this dream of weather.

At the end of his essay on snow, according to one translation, Kepler says, "As I write it has again begun to snow, and more thickly than a moment ago. I have been busily examining the little flakes."

My version ends:

Nothing follows

The End

Chapter 24

IT IS NOW A LATE summer day; the season is edging to autumn. I go to meet Tom Porter. He lives seventy miles from me in the Mohawk Valley, along the Mohawk River, formed in the glacial floods that lead to the inland sand sea. As I drive, I pass the creek Paul the historian tells me is named for the driftwood bridge, and past the cliff where Vince makes his fog for war and the U-pick farm. Every time I pass it, it holds the memories of strawberries and visiting the bluff with Iris.

Place, time, and history are held together here. Maybe this is part of what I have been looking for too, a language of place, like Paul talks about. In "One-Way Street," an essay about love, Walter Benjamin writes that a feeling lives in the place where we experience it. "We feel a window, a cloud, a tree not in our brain but in the place where we see them." He says the same is true with love, that in it "when we look at the loved one, we are likewise outside ourselves." Trying to find my father, I have been likewise outside myself. He has been held in trees and club moss. In the fire department, places are linked inextricably to the memories I have of them. They are often the sites of tragedies and sadness: a fence where a runaway truck crashes; an intersection where I stood alone one night and shut down the road during a structure fire miles away; the state highway where I stop traffic for a pumper truck to fill tankers from four departments trying to extinguish a fire that destroys a young couple's home. It was lost, but I find a moment of beauty watching a girl on a swing set across the road and clouds come and go over hours accompanied by sound of blue jays hidden in the trees. Or, another day uphill from a car accident where I listen to the fluting sound of wood thrush as dusk settles and we wait for tow trucks to arrive. Other places hold fatalities, the distant crossroads where I have to stop cars at 11 p.m. under a waning moon as we wait for a hearse. The location and the losses merge: a street corner waiting for an ambulance for a neighbor and his wife who die of COVID together; the burn scar in a road where two cars collide. There are other moments held in the landscape too—the horse that returns to its home, Gary sitting in his kitchen but nursing the memory of a place that is gone. I see my father and we are on a hike, and I am in New York and Vermont at the same time, and also in a place of ice and glaciers.

One year, a woman who farms by Vroman's Nose tells me that when the fields are plowed, you can see a fire ring from a campfire those centuries ago. Here the Munsee, on whose land I now live, are told to move by Sir William Johnson, the British administrator of Indigenous affairs and brother-in-law of the Mohawk warrior Joseph Brant. Here, too, the Skóhare Mohawks welcome all of these refugees from white colonization. The nation has a tradition of embracing outsiders, adopting them in. I am on my way to Tom Porter. I drive past these fields, their village, where they share land with the Palatine Germans, escaped slaves, and the Munsee and other Indigenous peoples. I continue north, up into the Mohawk Valley, though this could all be called the Mohawk Valley, because it is all Mohawk land.

Tom returns in 1993 to build a community, Kanatsiohareke (Ga-na-jo-ha-lay-gay, with an accent on "lay"), to
preserve language and traditions. The name means "place
of the clean pot." On the phone he says with a dash of humor, You white people want to call it Canajoharie. That's
a town about a dozen miles away and has no clean pots. It
can be tricky saying the Mohawk.

Here for thousands of years rocks and water have
eroded the creek bed, scouring the limestone into a
near-perfect circle. What would Luna Leopold say about
this transporting machine, this creek, this place? Porter's
uncle also leads a return nearby in the 1950s but only stays
for a couple years.

As I pull up there's a cerulean sky and purple flag flying. The land is set between two bluffs like Vroman's Nose,
speaking the language of glaciers. Paul has told me how
names are not mute but alive with meaning and memory,
and here we are, you and I, staring out at the fields and
river and railway tracks edging the property.

———

I see Vince young again in a red wool hunting shirt and
boots, the easy, open smile and his small circle of friends in
the wilderness. How well he knows this land, and knows
that it is Mohawk land. He is the boy at fifteen writing
the New York State archeologist and Seneca chief, and the
one at sixteen forced to quit school and become an apprentice, and then in 1929, the person who loves hiking and
trees but has to return to GE. That year he is twenty-three
and starts the Mohawk Valley Hiking Club. He will come
up with the idea of the Long Path, and that goes from
Manhattan to the Adirondack Mountains and cuts right

through here, through Schoharie and over Vroman's Nose and up this valley. The path is not blazed so you have to discover the route. It demands a hiker be curious about the landscape.

This exact location was the site of Mohawk villages for centuries, then a trading post owned by the Fonda family that is burned in 1780 two days after the Dark Day. Overhead, the purple flag has four rectangles and one triangle, the abstraction of a tree. The banner is from the wampum belt for the Great Law of Peace. Under it the original five nations of the Haudenosaunee join together. The rectangles are the Mohawks, Seneca, Oneida, and Cayuga, and the tree is the white pine where they all bury their weapons on Onondaga land, near Syracuse. Together in the twelfth century, they create the world's first participatory democracy—for peace.

I want to pause on that date. It is nearly a millennium ago, a time when Western Europe fights the Crusades, persecuting Muslims and Jews, and yet the Mohawks join with the other Haudenosaunee nations for peace, creating a consensus democracy. That promise of peace is alive. It is still in effect, the governing principle is here, right here, and across the Haudenosaunee nations. The very idea that a nation exists for peace, that is what I want to hold—and that it is alive where I stand now.

———

Tom leads me around the grounds. He looks impossibly like my dad in old age, same stiff, cautious gait and gray sweatpants and sneakers, and round face, round shoulders, round belly. Around us cornfields spread out. A railway shakes the ground as it passes. He tells me that the land here was actually his family's village, the Bear Clan's—his clan, his great-grandmother's clan.

In Mohawk his name, Sakokwenionkwas, means "he who wins." Tom says it's more like he who prevails and laughs. He talks with a warmth and humor that seems hard-won. He tells jokes about the Queen of England because David is with us and David is British. The joke involves her love of horses and an archbishop. Bernie would love it; the punch line revolves around farts.

There is also a story about holy water and actual water and going to Home Depot. In this story, a woman in the store is offended by Tom's joking about holy water, and Tom says, A god who isn't funny? The idea is shocking. He says to her, I hope your god is laughing. He shakes his head and tells me, Indian people, we are funny people, with music and dancing all part of religion, and the Catholics and Christians are so stern. They have music but no fun. I don't think Creator goes to ceremony to be somber.

That's when I realize his humor isn't hard-won, or maybe it is, yes; exercised in the face of adversity, but it is also deeply part of who he is—of his faith.

Tom waves now at the rows of corn. They grow a variety that the Mohawk people have cultivated for thousands of years. He's dedicated his life to keeping alive Mohawk history, teachings, and traditions. He's received numerous awards and an honorary doctorate for his work with Indigenous cultures and climate change. He leads me past red gladiolus planted for an elder who came each summer from Canada to help on the farm, and he waves at gardenias and geraniums. For the clan mothers, he says. The way he talks of the flowers, it doesn't sound like they are simply here to honor people, but as if those people are here themselves, which could simply be me and my way of thinking, with my dad in the tree. I'm convinced, too, that my mom is in the wax plant that survived my parents' move to Washington, DC, in the 1950s.

On the porch he sits on a glider. Next to us is the beadwork he's been doing. There is a turtle with a pine tree—the tree of peace—and other patterns stitched in tiny beads. His daughter comes out occasionally with water or his pills, and eyes me warily, worried he is too hot, worried about all the people who have come to hear him over the years, worried this again, one more time, will exhaust him. I am grateful he's willing to meet.

Like with the elders in my community, I want to hold onto everything he says, each word and syllable, every joke and story. He has been the Native American chaplain for prisons in New York State, and laughs, too, at the ridiculousness of this because he doesn't believe in the state itself, because he has also spent his life battling New York State, because the state stole land that it has yet to return. Still, the state calls and calls and asks him to serve, and he says no. Then Seneca and Tuscarora and other Haudenosaunee people call, and he agrees to do it for a year. One year turns into decades.

We talk of Akwesasne. He grows up poor on a farm. They have no car but a horse and wagon. He is raised by his grandmother. She only speaks Mohawk, and I hear its cadences in his voice. He says, "She was a clan mother and medicine person, and I had the privilege to listen and hear, even if people didn't see me because I was little. And, I was like an older person, because I was around these old people, and I had no friends my age.

I was old ahead of my time, but it's like university, that experience.

"Myself and others," he says, "we put our foot in the door for tradition. Whenever we got the opportunity we push the door open a little further to hold on and teach it. Mostly the dead help me to do it."

I want to ask how but do not. I don't want to stop him; I understand the idea of being with the dead and learning from them.

On the porch now, he waves around at the hills and corn and road in the distance and tells a story of 1754—a year from the Western calendar he hears over and over as a kid and doesn't understand. "My great-grandfather," he says, "would be talking in Mohawk and say 1754, this year, very clearly."

It's funny as Tom tells it. His great-grandfather piping up *1754!* this one word which Tom delivers as a kind of comic punctuation, and he tells Tom, My great-great-great-grandfather explained to Ben Franklin and Thomas Jefferson in Albany about democracy. This great-great-great-grandfather, he is the grandfather of Joseph Brandt.

Tom didn't believe the story. This notion of a Mohawk teaching a founding father seemed impossible to him as a child. It is now the late 1960s, and Tom is in Albany with the White Roots of Peace. The group travels from Akwesasne across the United States. They go to every reservation, state, and university, he tells me. They talk about Indigenous values and the Great Law of Peace and the Thanksgiving Address, a prayer given each day addressing, and honoring, all of creation. He doesn't say this, but I know the group also helps inspire the 1969 Alcatraz occupation.

I am just a kid, he says, a young man, and he's at SUNY Albany with the White Roots of Peace, and their host takes us into the education building. It is part of the old teacher's college downtown that is being replaced with the gleaming white buildings on the sands, where Bernie works on clouds and war, and Themis with her sword— the goddess of justice—and Vince studies pollution and breathing in exhaust. Though I know he is in a different part of Albany, I picture Tom, too, on the campus as he tells this story. I see the architecture, new and disorienting, and the sands blowing across the school, collecting on walkways and in doorways. He says, "They take our group of ten of us, and the host says, I'm going to break the rules and take you to the cellar, and there"—Tom stops; he shakes his head—"are the old wampums."

These are the beadwork panels that record history and treaties, like the Great Law of Peace. They are important sacred documents. He opens his hands. He sighs. "We grew up knowing they had been stolen, and we knew who stole them. There'd been fifty, sixty years of litigation to get them back. And then"—he shakes his head again—"they take us to the second or third floor. This big, big wall twelve feet high, with a painting from 1754, and right away I knew what it was—what I'm looking at: Ben Franklin and Thomas Jefferson and Indian chiefs and wampum on their arms explaining how our government works." The painting hangs today in one of the main halls of the New York State Museum.

———

That moment in Albany in 1754, Albany is not the capital of New York; it is a trading post in a British colony, and the colonies are only starting to foment for independence. It is when Franklin coins "Join or Die" based on the model of Haudenosaunee government, this idea that the colonies could join together for peace in the French and Indian War. In thirty years, the US Constitution will be modeled on the Great Law of Peace. Even our symbols like the eagle clutching thirteen arrows are copied from the Haudenosaunee. This is part, too, of why I want to come to Kanatsiohareke. Our country owes itself to that dream of peace created here in upstate New York. Our constitution, the one my father and aunt and uncle fight for, is a poor copy of the Great Law of Peace, a constitution to create peace and based on consensus rule. Ours is majority rule, and it's easy to see just how undemocratic that majority can be.

—

Now an entire half century has passed, and still the moment shadows Tom. He frowns and studies something at his foot. He says, "I don't know how to explain. It was, here is the truth and I cannot tell you now how it makes me feel. So sorry. I was so sorry not to trust my elders."

He glances aside and gestures at the lush hills beyond. "This valley here is the cradle of democracy, the doorway of democracy. This is also part of how they take your culture; you're raised and taught in school not to listen to what your elders say."

—

I ask about his starting a freedom school on Akwesasne. He does it with a group of others in the early nineties, and it's modeled, he tells me, on the Mississippi Freedom

Schools of the early sixties. He says something about in-fighting and how hard the process was. He says something, too, about a civil war, and a look crosses his face. He mentions the war as if I might know it or should know it, and I don't ask. I am nervous, and I don't want to stop him. He says, "You sabotage yourself. Your power is taken, stolen with your language and traditions and this way of battling each other. We sabotaged our own efforts, and one of the ways colonization succeeds is the self-destruction of our own thoughts. It's like they take everything: your language, your beliefs, your religion, and keep you alive."

—

He tells me, too, about his uncle Standing Arrow who leads another return, an earlier return to this valley. Edmund Wilson writes of him in *The New Yorker* in the late 1950s, and the article posits the attempt as a beautiful, failed gesture, and here is Tom with his beadwork, the bold colors—blues and pinks and greens, and he says, "I don't know what motivated him. I was a little boy, ten years old, but it was very courageous what he did."

—

We sit for hours. They sky changes; the sun moves, and he tells me oral histories. I ask about the pine barrens, the sands near Albany named for the other side of the pines, and he says it's not that important. The place that really matters is Cohoes Falls, east of there. This is where the Peacemaker brings the Great Law of Peace to the Mohawks. He tells the story of the tests the Mohawks put to the Peacemaker to prove who he is and how they join this consensus democracy. Tom speaks in the present tense as he tells me. In this story, time is outside my reckoning of it, outside chronology and written histories. As Tom talks, his yesterdays contain eons, not tracked to the Western calendar, where the past is over. Instead it is continuous. It is now. He leans in and says, "I say it is yesterday, and when we remember yesterday, it can be millions of years ago but also yesterday. And this was that kind of time—a thousand, two thousand years ago—that I'm talking about."

His daughter comes out. The sun casts a sharp angle across the porch as the day grows long. Tom squints and shifts his position. He tells me a story from the 1960s. Someone calls him at Akwesasne. He's in the office of a paper there, *Mohawk Notes*, integral to the White Roots of Peace, and asks for him. It's a schoolteacher from a little town called Middleburgh, he says.

This is the town that holds Onistagrawa and Vroman's Nose and the U-pick farm. The teacher invites Tom down to talk to the students. They all are wondering how there's a Mohawk Dry Cleaner and a Mohawk Movie Theater and Mohawk Carpets and everything with a Mohawk name and yet no Mohawks around here. The teacher says they're in the Mohawk Valley, and Tom has never been to this valley, not yet, so he comes and meets with the kids. He teaches the littlest ones songs and dances and is exhausted at the end of the day.

The teacher makes him tea and points out the window and says, See that knoll there? Tom nods but has no idea what a knoll is. It is not a word to him. The Mohawks never say knoll in our language, he explains. The teacher says, just below that hill was a Mohawk Bear Clan village. Listening to Tom tell this story, I know he's talking about the place that is now the strawberry farm. He says to the teacher, Can I ask you a question? He asks it in Mohawk as he learns it from his grandmother, but he never understands it as a child. He'd ask her and she didn't know either. It translates to: "There are these German people, and they have a fondness, an extra love for us because they are indebted to us."

He asks the teacher if this means anything to him? The teacher says yes! He tells him how the Palatine Germans were starving with no land, no food, no homes, and went west—west being toward where we are now and to near Vroman's Nose—and were welcomed into the longhouses and fed and doctored and told to live with them.

Tom shakes his head, recalling the story, and now he is here on the porch on the glider, in the late afternoon sun. As a child too, he says, we heard we should go home to where we originally came from.

He tells me, too, another prophecy he hears when is young. His elders said a time would arrive when white people would come and listen.

———

In his letter to Tom about the land Vince writes: "Perfect spot"—his *perfect* is underlined twice—"for your ideas."

The letter is included in a book Tom writes on Kanatsiohareke, but we never talk about Vince, not while I'm here, which I think is amazing. Vince isn't the important history, not in that moment with Tom on the porch.

Chapter 25

IT IS NOW THE NEXT morning, six a.m. Clouds speed across the sky. Vince writes that the atmosphere is the most unsettled when the sky is blue.

I am at my desk. I look up the Mohawk Civil War. The war starts in the late 1970s and flares again in the late eighties and early nineties. Akwesasne, the Mohawk nation land—"the land where the partridge drums," it's called—is rent by infighting. The reservation, sometimes in the US called Saint Regis, is more than thirty-five square miles and straddles the border along the Saint Lawrence River, including islands in the river.

It's formed from another community, Kahnawà:ke, that leaves the Mohawk Valley in the early eighteenth century for a French missionary village in Quebec. Forty years later a group moves upriver to create Akwesasne. They're led in part by two chiefs, who are brothers, who are white, who have been adopted in. After the Revolutionary War, the community secures the right to cross this new border freely. Now all this time, centuries into the future, there is poverty in Akwesasne. The men still often leave to work in construction as steelworkers, and residents have to navigate a strange set of boundaries—the various laws and lines and borders of the United States and Canada, as well as New York, Ontario, and Quebec, and even two tribal governments because of these borders.

In the civil war, there are factions. There are traditionalists like Tom, which does not mean conservative but in favor of preserving language and heritage and the Longhouse Religion, while the Mohawk Warrior Society wants more direct action against United States and Canadian oppression. The group comes to support casinos. A schism grows in the community around money, around capitalism, and how to live. The traditionalists oppose gambling. There are standoffs, threats, violence. Tom's house is burned down. This is the context in which Tom and others start the Freedom School.

In this time it is impossible, though, to make a living on Akwesasne. You can't farm or fish, or follow any of the traditional lifeways. The few options are often smuggling, cigarettes, and gambling. The land is ruined, the water poisoned, and the reason is the hydroelectric dam. That New York Power Authority dam. The dam and dream my father drives on his own time to support, to lobby for his belief in the public over the private, the resources that belong to all of us.

I stare at the screen and my face is numb. No amount of white space between these letters, words, and sentences can contain the feeling.

Tom has said how colonization takes your language but also your values, so there is infighting and feuds. That this is how the colonizers win.

And I picture my father.

———

Pause, beat, time passes. Clouds move. A goldfinch darts between heads of grass outside the window, and I cannot say anything, or nothing that is enough.

In the 1950s the Saint Lawrence Seaway and hydroelectric project steal land from Akwesasne. The seaway is dug down to create a corridor big enough for huge ships, disrupting fish and other life in the river, and the dam destroys even more. It is promoted like a new TVA, the Tennessee Valley Authority's dams that brought flood control and electricity along with promises of prosperity to the rural South. Lauded by the United States and Canada, the dam is supposed to be a boon and create an economic stimulus, but people lose farms and land and ways of life to the facility. Then ALCOA, the Aluminum Company of America—later Reynolds Aluminum—and companies like General Motors build factories upstream for access to the cheap hydropower. People are dragged into capitalism, whether they want it or not, because the old ways are forced out.

The factories pollute the air, water, and land with emissions and heavy metals, PCBs, mercury, and fluorides. It is not even a decade before people realize. They report trees and cattle dying. A Mohawk scientist and farmer tracks his and his neighbors' losses. Akwesasne hires a Seneca biologist to work on water issues. It isn't safe here to fish or farm or even breastfeed a baby.

Zoom out and here I am at my desk, seven a.m., dirty hair, old T-shirt, face lit by the glow of my screen. My email pings; an airplane flies in a distance. Outside I hear the distant taunts of chickadees.

Tom's uncle, Francis Johnson—Standing Arrow—returns to his ancestral lands in Schoharie in 1957 as a protest against the dam being built. He comes with two hundred others, and Edmund Wilson writes that the group moves to territory that the United States has guaranteed in a treaty, a narrow swathe sixty miles wide. It follows the course of the interstate nearly all the way from Albany to Buffalo. At the time, the highway is only just being built. Johnson is evicted and offered land near Vroman's Nose. He doesn't take it, and I do not know the reasons. Another group in the 1970s goes to the Adirondacks with a manifesto for co-operative ownership. It declares, "The people shall live off the land. The co-op system of economy shall prevail." (Like my dad, they are also accused of being communists.)

I look up my father again and search the "New York Power Authority" and his name. I want to know what he says, what he knows, what he believes. And, there he is. He appears before two Senate subcommittees. It's July 14, 1955. My oldest sister is six months old, my father in his twenties. He's young and skinny, his suit is gray and loose. He has a

sharp nose and a crease in his forehead. His voice drops an octave so he sounds more authoritative. Before the thirteen senators, including Albert Gore, the future vice president's father, and the white supremacist Strom Thurmond, as well as others I've never heard of from Connecticut, Oregon, and Ohio, he is saying that the dam is a public good.

He complains, too, about the New York Power Authority. They've signed a long-term lease with ALCOA, forty-three years, promising to sell the corporation a quarter of the dam's energy at a cheap rate. He's upset about this public resource being diverted to a private company on preferential terms. I pore over the testimony and find nothing from him or anyone else about the Mohawks and Akwesasne or Saint Regis Mohawk Reservation. There is nothing about protests, though there are protests; nothing about rage, though there is rage; nothing about people displaced or land stolen after so much land has been stolen; and nothing about the court cases brought, the court cases summarily dismissed. It's not just my father, either; no one mentions it to these senators, and no Mohawk witnesses are called.

—

On my screen, the cursor blinks. It is an open space I wish I could fill. It is impossible. The air stings my throat. The blinks flash between letters and the moment spreads out. Seconds pass. They slip into minutes, minutes an hour.

Behind me on the wall the cards encroach. They cover every surface in this claustrophobia of catastrophe. Walter Benjamin writes in his "Theses on the Philosophy of History," "There is no document of civilization which is not at the same time a document of barbarism. And just as a document is not free of barbarism, barbarism taints also the manner in which it was transmitted from one owner to another."

I have been trying to find connections, to search time and place and history to understand how to live in our world now. I've tried to link the modernism in which I was raised and dreams of a better world and the ways it's been engineered—the rains and floods, silver and clouds, and how the floods here track through millennia—through time beyond conception. The Mohawk people and their forebears have lived here, too, in time beyond conception. They are matrilineal, with shared land and property and a government whose foundation is women. Tom tells me on the phone that whatever men are chosen as spiritual or political leaders have to be nominated by women. And, if the men don't obey the laws, the women impeach them. Dehorn them, he calls it. Then, the United States demands that the Haudenosaunee follow US-style democracy, which is less democratic and at the time has no power for women.

There are all the ways the United States has tried to force its ways on the Haudenosaunee, making it less representative as the United States steals their land. And, there are all these white men and their technodeterminism and faith in fixed futures.

There, too, is my dad. I have been hoping he could give me some answers in this moment, in this place, in our age. This man for whom capitalism goes wrong in countless ways when he is still a little boy, when he loses everything. When he continues to have faith in our country.

The floods spiral in and out of time here and I am dizzy, trying to see all these things I've tried to follow over a decade, as if all were built on sand—where the landfill, the strip mall, suburbs, the Shakers, the university—these dreams of utopia flutter like those butterflies. They live for a couple days and die. There are these other collapses too, with the ferns and mosses and fish; floods and ice ages. I believe place holds its history, that time is alive, and in this time I have used all the magic I think I can get from my father. On the wall the cards, notes, and photos beckon and bloom.

He sits before the senators and talks about co-operatives. In his testimony he says they "are small and unimportant, but how small and unimportant are they when one considers [. . .]" My mouth goes numb, and I think of how expendable places are, that are small and unimportant, areas that get turned into dump sites or get sacrificed for highways, overpasses, and dams. And that these losses collect under the language of a greater good, and who is counted as *us*, who as *them*.

I finish his sentence, and he says, "But how small and unimportant are they—the co-operatives—when one considers that they offer one of the only forms of competition to the large private utilities." For him these unimportant co-ops are urgent in the fight against corporate power. Still, I don't understand the lines that get drawn between *them* and *us*, whichever communities are being ignored. Or, are allowed to be ignored. Or, maybe I do understand that line. I just don't comprehend it, because it is about whiteness.

My father goes on, and in his resounding faith, says that hydropower is "a great natural resource belonging to the people." Which people, though? Those in Akwesasne don't get an ownership stake even as it is their land. I want to ask what he is thinking—or not thinking, what he hears, what he ignores, how he justifies it. And, there is no answer. He isn't here with me now, and if he were, would any answer be enough?

He says to the senators, "The only question is who shall develop the remaining power at Niagara Falls?" For him that question is between public and private, between shared ownership and a corporation.

Is that the only choice?

———

I go for a bike ride, up to a cemetery high above the Pepacton Reservoir where unclaimed graves and bodies are moved from the ten flooded cemeteries. The graveyard has a lofty view down to the reservoir, and it feels like you also could reach up to the sky. High above Shavertown and Gary's submerged home, a handful of pine trees shade the headstones and mowed grass. Two benches face the graves, though I've never seen anyone else visit.

I wonder if the man who dies in the 1950 flooding, whose body is found after days, who isn't recognized, who is put in a pauper's field in another drowned cemetery is here? Through the trees in the distance, the silvered surface of the water shimmers below. From high above you can see the currents, the ghost river, still flowing underneath. My community is tied inextricably to Akwesasne. A dream of progress binds us together, and there's the accumulation of losses that dream conceals. They disappear in the waters, the floods, the dams. Gary talks of losing his home and the irony that his father is hired on the dam and that this is supposed to be good work. For a while he does earn good money too. The same thing happens at Akwesasne with the dam that brings jobs that are supposed to be good jobs but destroy community connection.

There is one other thing that links us too. Most of my county gets cheap power from the NYPA dams, from Akwesasne, because my county is served by a rural electric co-op.

—

When I visit, Tom talks of the Creator and recalls a story of his great-uncle. He was trying to explain the Creator to a professor visiting from Harvard or Yale. Tom's great-uncle says just answering the question would require two hundred, three hundred years, and you'd have to have a giant adding machine and calculate all life down to the tiniest creatures—how many deer in the world and how many humans and you can't forget the baby a minute old, and how many trees in the world and even the little one just sprouted, and how many stars in the sky at night. You add it up, that is the Creator—everything, everywhere in the universe.

This is not a human-centered god, not one who creates a world in our image for us to use, not a world where we are the pinnacle of existence.

Tom is also often called on to give the Thanksgiving Address. This is a prayer not meant for one day—a harvest holiday celebrating white perseverance over Indigenous people at that—but a prayer of thanks given each day. Tom calls it the foundation of everything, the foundation of why we're here on this earth and also the foundation of why Kanatsiohareke came into existence. Listening to him, in this thanking, the connection is between us all.

Everything is thanked: Mother Earth, the sun, the wind, thunder, animals, birds, plants, water, and rivers. Tom gets to them and he thanks "the rivers and the water that is in the wells and the streams and the rain, and when the Creator and the Mother Earth make the water, they put a spirit in the water so the water is living. That's why the water in the river is always moving; the water in the ocean always has waves and always has motion; the water in the creek, it is always moving; the rain, it is always moving, and when the water stops moving, it dies."

At the end of each section when the river or the sky or the birds have been thanked, he says, "Now our mind is one." I stop on this. What if our minds are united with the other animals, the moss, the water, and the hemlocks? This is the socialism for all beings. This is what I want, radical empathy between communities.

———

One summer day when I am home with my mother before she dies, she sits in the living room in her recliner—just like Mabel and the other neighbors I interview about the flood. It is dusk. She has been out of the hospital for a week now after having pneumonia. I bring her a glass of wine that she barely drinks, but to give up the idea that she does drink is too much for her, so it rests at her elbow. We talk about the neighbors I went to visit and what they said about faith in modernism and also co-ops and gardens.

My mom wears old jeans and a T-shirt my sister brought back from a Buddhist retreat. I try to explain this word they use. Belief, I say. She glances at me and I hand her the wine. She says, Your father believed people were always improving. I loved his optimism in people and progress.

In his letters to her he writes,

> I felt so close to you that last weekend—it was
> a beautiful weekend. I miss you and our beauti-
> ful outdoors. Give Jenny a big hug for me. All my
> love, Bob

I read it and hear him write his father, *Dear Daddy, When
are you leaving? Do you know where you are going? Please
write please. Bobby. A hundred more kisses.*

I find another note written on tissue-thin Air France
stationary. The top of each sheet is printed: en plein ciel,
In midair. I can feel the pen press through on the other
side of the sheet like braille. I am four, and I am now a
middle-aged woman reading my father's words:

> Dear all,
>
> Good flight. As we left San Francisco and headed
> over the Pacific we could see the California coast
> very clearly from 33,000 feet. Tell Jenny the
> dragon enclosed is for her.

The Dragon Is for Her.

I have no idea now what the dragon was. A toy I'd fold
together that's mailed flat in the envelope? The dragon
though is what I have. It's what I will grapple with for the
rest of my life. I live not far from where my parents spend
their early years. I believe in co-ops just like my dad, with
this faith in an ideal out there that I see so clearly as a possibility outside of capitalism I can nearly touch it. I live in

a model of their house on Munsee land, in a field near a hemlock forest, overflowing with abundance and love, and the clouds this day are fat cumulus. Their pewter undersides flatten in the sky and the tops glint in the sun. They cast a shadow across the ridge—the New York City land, the land for water.

———

Everything I have comes from my father, from that work of his, lobbying for those dams in the 1950s. He goes to DC, works for co-operatives, and my parents who want alternatives to capitalism buy a home and then move to another home. They have a mortgage and then another mortgage. In that way that mortgages work and mortgage tax breaks create wealth—white wealth—there is money for me to go to college, move here, and have a home.

The cursor blinks and time bleeds.

I go outside and lie in the grass. I stare at clouds. "This is what the inside of a cloud looks like," GE announces after Vince manufactures one in the lab. Looking inside it is like seeing a specter. There is the mist to coat the landscape and fight a war. What is the dream of progress, these dreams of a better world and their inevitable failures? To control the weather is to control the most ephemeral and, maybe, dangerous of the elements. It is to end drought and to stop war with rain, which itself is an amazing dream if it were that simple. It is to slow our warming planet, to make mud not war, but it is also to see these elusive hopes of engineering a better future in a world on fire. We have been shaping the land and burning it as far back as we have been human.

Overhead, I see bones. Particles in the air hold dust

from rocks, spiderwebs, seed heads, and pollution. There's also sea salt and sea spray and smoke. The smallest of these particles, Vince writes, "are formed by the condensation of vapors, the chemical combination of reacting molecules, the photochemical effects produced by the ultraviolet radiation from the sun, and the electrical and other ionizing forces that come from thunderstorms, cosmic rays, and radio-activity." There is the blue beam of light the engineer sees at Chernobyl, and how these particles that create vapor can stay in the air for years. I read about our breath and think about time. Vince stops time by capturing the snowflake. Stardust that has traveled so many light-years is found sometimes as the ice nucleus in snow around which a crystal grows. Our breath contains molecules from ancient times. We breathe in, breathe out. There is Cleopatra or Jesus or some person you have never known. Utter their name here. Rebecca Cox Jackson; or Tom's uncle, Standing Arrow (Francis Johnson), say. They are all part of you, of me, of us. All the microscopic dirts and dusts over other centuries and millennia around which water coheres in the sky.

The clouds scroll quickly. I close my eyes and still see them.

Epilogue

Now it is early summer, three years later. I do not have an answer for my father's actions. I don't expect one. I don't want closure, or maybe closure is too simple. It feels more important to live with my questions. In writing, sentences create a sense of progress—beginning, middle, and end, building to understanding and suffused with linear time. But I do not understand, and I do not want order here. Kurt Vonnegut and his grotesque situational poetry, I think, exist in this kind of realm.

I've laid all these elements side by side because I cannot create order from them, not from the news, not the weather and disasters, not the climate, and not my family—love my father as I do. To write against chronology is to hold these moments together and all at once so they are not over. They are unresolved and uncomfortable. There is no epiphany at the end.

—

It is June and Kanatsiohareke is having its first Strawberry Festival since the pandemic, and it is three years to the day since Iris and I climb the cliff and look at the names carved in rock and I tell her about Vince. Now the U-pick fruit farm is owned by a Mohawk community, and the farm has been renamed Iotsi'tsisons (Skywoman's) Forever Farm, in Schoharie/Skóhare, the place with the driftwood bridge where the floodwood washes up and crosses the river. It is upstream from the dam where the river runs north. This is the dam where the ancient horsetail trees are found, the dam the governor visits in my second flood and then he is stranded in my town during the flood with a woman's name, Irene.

Here at Kanatsiohareke in the same Mohawk home-lands between the two glacial hills with the clean pot carved from rocks in the river, where corn grows and a red barn rises, crowds circulate. Some wear ribbon-lined skirts, others jeans and sneakers. There are old hippies in T-shirts, long, lank gray hair under baseball caps; young families with kids in strollers and toddlers skipping ahead. I volunteer to help with parking. Before the event, I say in the email sent round that I'm good at traffic. It's what I do in the fire department, and I offer to bring extra reflective safety vests.

I staff an entrance with Ron Garrow, Tom's nephew. He wears a T-shirt emblazoned "Homeland Security Since 1492" with a photo of four Apache men, including Geronimo, all holding long guns. Ron tells me of getting the school system in Rochester, where he lives, to honor Indigenous People's Day, a task of so many conversations over so much time, I do not get to hear it all, but it ends, I know, in success.

Now all these people are arriving, so many there are nearly not enough spaces in the field mowed for the cars. They come from across Haudenosaunee lands and from the lands that should be Haudenosaunee still. There are near neighbors and people from Akwesasne and Kahnawà:ke and Buffalo, Syacuse, Ithaca, and the Catskills. A white woman tells Ron that she's house-sitting in the mountains for a friend and read about the festival and had to come. She stresses the word *had* and looks earnest in her T-shirt bearing a blue globe of the earth. Other people ask where they can buy strawberries and are confounded at first to hear none are for sale. There is a strawberry drink, Ron says, but it is a time to gather to tell stories and meet up like we would with the wild strawberry harvest to celebrate spring. These people then nod and say cool or okay. Two elderly Black sisters come from Albany, one with a walker. Tom sits on a porch and so many people approach him I am nervous to say hi.

The parking is down the hill from the day's events, and I don't see much of the dancers or hear the stories told. From under a pavilion, I witness a tiny bit of the Rabbit Dance where they call out for everyone to join its bobbing back and forth. An Amish buggy pulls in. Someone says, There's my Uber. I say something about being shocked to see the Amish, too, here among all these people—this great glorious combination of us, Black, brown, and white, young and old; men in pickups and Stetsons and college students in cutoffs and Doc Martens. Ron tells me the Amish are just neighbors too.

That afternoon I staff a folding table with Bonnie Jane Maracle, who is on the board and is director of the language program. Before us are fliers about the day's events and Mohawk language classes coming up and raffle tickets for sale. There's a beekeeper with an empty hive. It's filled with photos of bees to suggest actual bees inside. Bonnie Jane teaches language immersion and is finishing a PhD in the subject. She wears a blue flowered tunic with ribbon edging and pedal pushers. Her hair is gray and her voice quiet. She smiles; she nods as people stop by to say hello.

She stands to hug a friend she hasn't seen in years. It's been too long, the other woman says.

In the distance someone over the PA talks about the Two Row Wampum. I hear them say, Four hundred years ago.

The wampum belt has two parallel lines of beads representing two paths side by side. This is the treaty set out between the Haudenosaunee and the colonizers that they can coexist, that they do not need to intrude in the others' ways or affairs. It is this idea that we both have our own paths, and we can live with mutual respect.

The day before, I hear a talk in my town delivered with religious fervor about history and letting it be, that history is history. It is a fact, this person says. It has happened. The speaker drops a pencil to the ground. He says, That is history. (That, being a pencil on the ground.) It is there, he says and points to it. It is a fact; it does not change. History, he insists, we just need to leave it be.

Here though, the Two Row Wampum is not past, not over, but living and alive. It is being created right now as it is being discussed. It is still the basis of all Haudenosaunee treaties with various white settler governments and groups.

—

Bonnie Jane watches the scene before us. There are young farmers who talk earnestly of skill-sharing and tool-sharing, co-operatives and collectives; people from the Pine Bush— the place between the sands—and the new local librarian, dressed in skinny jeans and a ball cap. It has been threatening to rain all day, and the skies finally open. Kids leap from puddle to puddle. She is delighted with their exuberant joy. I remember doing that, too, as a child, she says.

We sit next to each other taking it all in. She says, It's the best Strawberry Festival ever. The beekeeper agrees. The beekeeper first comes here to take language classes and says, Then you never leave. A man long and lanky, wearing a Two Row Wampum T-shirt celebrating the treaty's four hundredth anniversary a decade earlier, comes up. He's a documentary maker and lacrosse coach visiting for a week from the Netherlands. He talks in his Dutch accent of hearing all the stories and how special this day is, that everyone here brings friendship. Even the rains, he says.

Bonnie Jane points out two young women in cropped T-shirts and army pants, low slung on their waists. They're selling tickets for the fifty-fifty raffle, and one of them, Bonnie says, is from Washington State; the other Massachusetts. They have this tight friendship that is maybe forged this day volunteering or maybe forever. And, maybe they are partners or maybe they have just met. There is Ox, a young farmer who grows up nearby, and his friends, all new farmers too. There is the joke about the Uber and the Amish buggy and Ron's talking of Indigenous People's Day. It is a story of communicating, of reaching out. It is also a story of perseverance and the costs of that work, the years and countless conversations Ron has to have. Here, in this moment, too, is this great swelling of love, even with the guy in the MAGA hat who studies the beehives and frowns, which might just be the look of concentration. Bonnie Jane says she's amazed at all the energy and all the different people, all the young people. I think how Mohawk communities have always welcomed in outsiders and others.

In her soft voice, she tells me, There is a teaching we have, a prophecy of two paths. I strain to hear her over the sound system. I listen and I don't quite understand. She says the right path brings ease. It just feels right, and the wrong one involves struggle like fighting upstream. Essentially we are at a crossroads; one path leads to chaos and the other to harmony with ourselves and others and nature. I don't want to interrupt to ask questions.

We look out at the crowd together, the two people dressed in Black and Trans Lives Matter T-shirts and the others, the upstart farmers and the librarian and the Indigenous families and even the Trump guy. Here for this one moment together, there feels like possibility—and love. Bonnie Jane says, The right path, it just feels easeful.

Notes

THE OPENING QUOTE IS FROM Walter Benjamin's "Theses on the Philosophy of History." He wrote it a few months before he died. It was 1940, and he was working in the cataclysm of fascism, borne of a belief in progress as an immutable truth. Thinking about his essay and how he approached history unites both *The Eighth Moon* and *Nightshining*. I was raised in the last gasp of this dream of progress, with modernism and technology and Western science held out as their own good, leading to an ever-better world.

History is not "causal," one translation of his "Theses" puts it. Instead, it is created "posthumously, as it were, through events that may be separated by thousands of years." The way the historian links events, "He records the constellation in which his own epoch comes into contact with that of an earlier one." I love that history doesn't transcend time but is a product of our own. How we see events and connect them can link across thousands of years so that the moments are alive. Now. Benjamin also wrote in fragments against the fiction of progress inherent in narrative.

Throughout his life, he sifted through his childhood and memory for what they might reveal of the world to make sense of his moment. He was obsessed with small details. Nothing was too insignificant for him. In her introduction to his essays in *Illuminations,* Hannah Arendt writes, "He was concerned with the correlation between a street scene, a speculation on the stock exchange, a poem, a thought." I still remember being twenty-one and reading a footnote about a salt ad he saw when he was little. This tiny stitch of memory was in his *Arcades Project,* the unfinished manuscript he carried in a briefcase to the Spanish border, where he committed suicide trying to escape the Nazis. That ad, he recalls as a grown-up, could hold the possibility of revelation. It held "the everydayness of utopia."

In his "Theses" he writes beautifully in the third fragment of "the chronicler, who recounts events without distinguishing between the great and small." This attention is both Marxist and mystical. For him nothing is reducible. Everything is important, every single second and moment is indivisible. In this passage with the great and small, he says, "Nothing which has ever happened is to be given as lost to history. [. . .] Each of [humanity's] lived moments becomes a citation, a l'ordre du jour (the order of the day) [which I read as "at the end of the day"]—whose day is precisely that of the Last Judgment." Even the most minute detail holds the possibility of redemption, salvation. Here, for a man soon to die, is hope, hope beyond hope.

I want it too.

As I was working on my edits, I was at the New York Historical Society on the Upper West Side, on the top floor in a crowded room full of people. We sit on folding chairs. Some of us are masked, some not. The air is humid with our breath. At the front are four historians here to talk about climate change and the New York City watershed. I skulked through this building as a college freshman looking at paintings of the place I now live. They come freighted with ideas about who belongs and not and what uses the land could be put to.

One of the historians convened the panel. To his left is one who's written on the precolonial history of the city, another who has written of water supplies in the progressive era, and the last one a historian who is now head of the city's Department of Environmental Protection, which controls the city's water and its water supply, regulating land and its usages in my community. The overhead lights gleam. There is talk of how water is taking back the land, old histories emerging in swamps and creeks, wetlands that only exist on old maps and are now part of the landscape again, at least in heavy rains and floods. One of the panelists broaches idea that sacrifices will need to be made for the city to weather the changes to come. The group talks about environmental justice and equity. Someone says they believe sacrifice is still possible. The historians all laugh nervously. What is held in that laughter is the gulf after Trump's 2020 loss, when not everyone can manage to agree who is president and a pandemic where even masking to protect others is politicized, so the possibility of coming together to make collective choices seems distant. I hold out still for Vince's *I for one am willing to sacrifice.* In neoliberal capitalism, though, the individual comes above all else. When social structures are dismissed, the collective is fiction. It is now simply self-interest above everything. I want to believe in an *us*, one that is bigger, broader, one where we can come together.

Notes on Sources

Ginger Strand has written an excellent biography of Kurt and Bernard Vonnegut and their time at GE, which I relied on for their story. She is also much more sensitive to Bernard than I. See: *The Brothers Vonnegut: Science and Fiction in the House of Magic.* I had the luck of working on a project with the SUNY at Albany Art Museum. I was in the university archives researching modernism and the sands, and there I found the weather.

Ben Lerner's *10:04*, his glittering novel of floods and Whitman and the public in New York City around Hurricane Sandy, was also inspiring as I wrote.

Above, I referred to two different translations of Benjamin's "Theses." (It is also called in some translations "On the Concept of History.") Some of the quotes are from "Theses on the Philosophy of History," *Illuminations*, trans. Harry Zohn (New York: Schocken, 1969), 253–64. Others come from "On the Concept of History," trans. Dennis Redmond, 2005, Marxists.org, http://www.efn.org/~dredmond/Theses_on_History.html.

The lines in the epigraph come from Fragment XIII in the Harry Zohn translation, 260–61. The Hannah Arendt quote is from her introduction to *Illuminations*, 11. The salt ad is referenced in a footnote in Susan Buck-Morss's *The Dialectics of Seeing: Walter Benjamin and the Arcades Project* (Cambridge: MIT Press, 1990), 462.

Chapter 1

6   *This summer* Kasha Patel, "Greenland Ice Sheet Experiences Record Loss to Calving of Glaciers and Ocean Melt over the Past Year," *Washington Post*,

November 23, 2021, https://www.washingtonpost.com
/weather/2021/11/23/greenland-ice-melt-2021-recap/.

Chapter 2

16   **I speak to someone named** Phone call with FEMA, July
10, 2006.

16   **The governor sends a trifold mailer** Governor George E.
Pataki, Mailer, "Floods of June 2006," n.d.

18   **On the back** Federal Emergency Management Agency
Application / Registration for Disaster Assistance,
FEMA Form 90–69, April 2000.

18   **His name is Randy** FEMA inspection, July 16, 2006.

20   **A question in the Hokusai manual** "Introduction to the
NFIP," undated photocopied brochure, 21–22, 15.

20   **A community must come together** "Introduction to the
NFIP," 2–3.

20   **I do not realize** Letter from FEMA National Processing
Service Center, Hyattsville, MD, July 17, 2006, Disaster
No. 1650. (There is no actual signature on it, but the
printed letter reads "Sincerely,
SUPER.")

Chapter 4

33   **The generosity creates** I learned in that disaster that
what really helps are cash cards, even if only the amount
you'd pay for postage or to drive your donation to a
collection site. People need money to replace the things
they have lost.

34   **In my mind, I've never** Andrew M. Cuomo, "Read the Full
Transcript of Gov. Andrew Cuomo's Resignation Speech,"
New York Times, August 10, 2021, https://www.nytimes
.com/2021/08/10/nyregion/cuomo-resignation-speech
-transcript.html.

34   *On my screen it is* Andrew Cuomo, "Hurricane Irene, August 28, 2011: Governor Cuomo Tours Flood Damage in Delaware County," Flickr photos and video, August 28, 2011, https://www.flickr.com/photos/governorandrewcuomo/6089320138.

35   *As I write, in Tennessee* Rick Rojas and Michael Levenson, "A Tidal Wave of Water and At Least 21 Deaths as Floodwaters Ravage Rural Tennessee," *New York Times*, August 22, 2021, https://www.nytimes.com/2021/08/22/us/tennessee-flash-flooding.html.

35   *It's a cutoff low* Jason Samenow, "How Weather Patterns Conspired for a Flooding Disaster in Germany," *Washington Post*, July 16, 2021, https://www.washingtonpost.com/weather/2021/07/16/weather-pattern-climate-germany-flooding. Linus Magnusson, Adrian Simmons, Shaun Harrigan, Florian Pappenberger, "Extreme Rain in Germany and Belgium in July 2021," *ECMWF Newsletter* 169, Autumn 2021, https://www.ecmwf.int/en/newsletter/169/news/extreme-rain-germany-and-belgium-july-2021.

35   *Later this summer at Summit* Kasha Patel, "Rain Falls at the Summit of Greenland Ice Sheet for First Time on Record," *Washington Post*, August 19, 2021, https://www.washingtonpost.com/weather/2021/08/19/greenland-melt-august-summit-rain/.

36   *I read a line* Walter Benjamin, "Theses on the Philosophy of History," *Illuminations*, trans. Harry Zohn (New York: Schocken, 1969), 263.

38   *experiments with ice* Henri Dessens, "On the Radiative Balance of Atmospheric Particles," typescript of paper given at Sixth International Conference on Condensation Nuclei, May 9–13, 1966, 1, Bernard Vonnegut Papers, M. E. Grenander Department of Special Collections and Archives, State University at Albany, series 10, box 2, folder 12.

Chapter 5

43   *As soon as the flats of Vroomansland*   Vincent J.
      Schaefer, *Serendipity in Science: Twenty Years at Langmuir
      University*, ed. Don Rittner (Schenectady: Square Circle,
      2013), 108–14.

44   *Not long before he dies*   Vincent J. Schaefer, *Vrooman's
      Nose: Sky Island of the Schoharie Valley* (Fleischmanns,
      NY: Purple Mountain, 1992).

44   *During his life he writes*   Vincent J. Schaefer, "Some
      Physical Relationships of Fine Particle Smoke,"
      *Proceedings of the 13th Annual Tall Timbers Fire Ecology
      Conference* (Tallahassee, FL: Tall Timbers Research
      Station, 1974), 283–94.

44   *Stationed in New Jersey*   George Washington, "May
      [1780]," *Founders Online*, National Archives website,
      https://founders.archives.gov/documents/Washington
      /01-03-02-0006-0006.

44   *Yale's president, theologian*   Thomas J. Campanella,
      "'Mark Well the Gloom': Shedding Light on the Great
      Dark Day of 1780," *Environmental History* 12, no. 1 (Jan.
      2007): 35–58.

45   *He called for their*   George Washington, "From George
      Washington to Major General John Sullivan, 31 May
      1779," *Founders Online*, National Archives, https://
      founders.archives.gov/documents/Washington/03-20-02
      -0661.

45   *Below me this river-flat land*   The Mohawks in the area
      all tried to remain neutral during the war but were still
      attacked in Sullivan's Campaign. The Mohawk Elder
      Tom Porter calls it genocide, and in a 2021 email to a
      local museum about their monument to Sullivan, the
      historian Paul Gorgen and Porter write, "At the end of
      the Sullivan campaign, troops returning to the Mohawk
      Valley rounded up all the neutral Mohawks living in the

lower village at Fort Hunter and threw all the men into jail in Albany. When the survivors were finally released the next spring, they went home to find other people had taken over their houses and farms. This even happened to the families of a few Mohawks who had been captured and imprisoned by the British at the time while serving with the American forces."

46 **Vince Schaefer wrote that** Vincent J. Schaefer and John A. Day, *A Field Guide to the Atmosphere*, 7th ed. (Boston: Houghton Mifflin, 1981), 155.

Chapter 6

54 **On page 762** Austin M. Knight, *Modern Seamanship*, 10th ed. (New York: D. Van Nostrand, 1937), 762.

Chapter 7

58 **He includes his height and age** Schaefer, *Serendipity in Science*, 335–36.

59 **He enrolls as an apprentice** Schaefer, *Serendipity in Science*, 29.

60 **The city is the biggest landowner** From a May 30, 2023, email with Diane Galusha, Middletown town historian and author of *Liquid Assets: A History of New York City's Water System*. And a June 3, 2023, email with Shelly J. Johnson-Bennett, director of the Delaware County Department of Planning and Watershed Affairs. Both of them stress that the numbers are always in flux, always increasing for the city because it is constantly acquiring more land.

Chapter 8

69   *The city believes* Charles G. Bennett, "US Forest Expert Aids City on Water," *New York Times*, April 6, 1950, 20.

69   *I read that at an auction* Diane Galusha, *Liquid Assets: A History of New York City's Water System*, expanded ed. (Fleischmanns, NY: Purple Mountain, 2016), 212.

72   *pore over articles like* Daniel E. Mecklenburg and Anand D. Jayakaran, "Dimensioning the Sine-Generated Curve Meander Geometry," *Journal of the American Water Resources Association* (JAWRA) 48, no. 3: 63–642, https://doi.org/10.1111/j.1752-1688.2012.00638.x.

73   *I read about Wallace Howell* "City Allays Fears on Rain-Making; Effects, if Any, Only in Catskills; Recent Bad Weather Is Called of Normal Origin—Water Storage Shows Decline," *New York Times*, May 18, 1950, 31.

73   *I read in Luna Leopold's book* Luna B. Leopold, *A View of the River* (Cambridge: Harvard University Press, 2006), 57.

74   *Someone shows a 16 mm film* George Hoag, "Beneath Pepacton Waters," shot between 1950 and 1954, eds. Alice and Bob Jacobsen, 1995.

Chapter 9

82   *In her book* Lisa Robertson, "Tuesday," *the weather* (Vancouver: New Star, 2014), 18.

82   *In the next poem* Robertson, "Residence at C_____," 24.

85   *There's a Goethe poem* Johann Wolfgang von Goethe, "In Honour of Mr. Howard," 1821, Tottenham Clouds, https://www.tottenhamclouds.org.uk/goethe-in-honour -of-mr-howard.html.

85   *Howard is in the* Schaefer and Day, *Field Guide*, 45–46.

85   **In a 1953 New York Times** *article* "Bombs and Weather; Clouds of an Atomic Explosion Are Not Thunder Clouds," *New York Times*, May 3, 1953, section E, page 9. And Natalie Diaz, "They Don't Love You Like I Love You," *Postcolonial Love Poem* (Minneapolis: Graywolf, 2020), 19.

85   *Another poem of hers from* Natalie Diaz, "The Clouds Are Buffalo Limping Toward Jesus," *When My Brother Was an Aztec* (Port Townsend: Copper Canyon, 2012), 39.

87   *Her dead brother later appears* Rebecca Cox Jackson, *Gifts of Power: The Writings of Rebecca Jackson, Black Visionary, Shaker Eldress*, ed. Jean McMahon Humez (Cambridge: University of Massachusetts Press, 1981), 227.

87   *The GE press release* "Rain by Fire," General Electric News Bureau, General Electric Company, October 28, 1948. In Schaefer, *Serendipity in Science*, 381.

87   *The eldress testifies about* Jackson, *Gifts of Power*, 220.

88   *There is no evidence* "Bombs and Weather," *New York Times*, May 3, 1953.

88   *A headline this week* John Schwartz, "How Much Will the Planet Warm if Carbon Dioxide Levels Double?" *New York Times*, August 9, 2021, https://www.nytimes.com/2020/07/22/climate/global-warming-temperature-range.html.

88   *A survivor of Hiroshima says* Grace Lee, "In Japan, Young People Rush to Document Hiroshima Survivors' Memories," *Newshour*, PBS, August 6, 2020, https://www.pbs.org/newshour/show/in-japan-young-people-rush-to-document-hiroshima-survivors-memories.

88   *The picture runs on the cover* Vince Schaefer photograph, *Science* 154, no. 3756 (December 23, 1966).

90   *I read in a geology textbook* Y. W. Isachsen, E. Landing, J. M. Lauber, L. V. Rickard, W. B. Rogers, eds., *Geology of New York: A Simplified Account*, 2nd ed. (Albany: New York State Museum, 2000), 129.

Chapter 10

95   *There's a picture of the two men* Schaefer, *Serendipity in Science*, frontispiece.

97   *"I thought," he says of the snow* Schaefer, *Serendipity in Science*, 105.

97   *He writes a slim* Cecil Schneer, "Kepler's New Year's Gift of a Snowflake," *Isis* 51, no. 4 (December 1960): 531–45, http://www.jstor.org/stable/228611.

97   *Somewhere between poetry and philosophy* Owen Gingerich, "The Delights of a Roving Mind." And Guillermo Bleichmar, "On *The Six-Cornered Snowflake*," in Johannes Kepler, *The Six-Cornered Snowflake: A New Year's Gift* (Philadelphia: Paul Dry, 2010), loc. 108, Kindle.

97   *Here was something smaller* Kepler, *The Six-Cornered Snowflake*, loc. 256, Kindle.

98   *From this almost Nothing* Kepler, *The Six-Cornered Snowflake*, loc. 186, Kindle.

98   *A Victorian nature writer* John Burroughs, "The Snow Walkers," *The Atlantic Monthly*, March 1866, 303.

Chapter 11

101   *He is both imperious and goofy* Ginger Strand, *The Brothers Vonnegut: Science and Fiction in the House of Magic* (New York: Farrar, Straus and Giroux, 2015), 70.

102   *What is snow, Kepler asks* Other translations of Kepler's essay have this passage quoted as above. See Cullen Murphy, "In Praise of Snow," *The Atlantic*, January 1995, https://www.theatlantic.com/magazine/archive/1995/01/in-praise-of-snow/305654/. In the translation I'm using, the quote reads: "Since it always happens, when it begins to snow, that the first particles of snow adopt the shape of small, six-cornered stars,

there must be a particular cause." Kepler, *The Six-Cornered Snowflake*, loc. 270, Kindle. References to dust in the essay, loc. 227, 229, 252, Kindle.

104   *The freezer is so cold*   Vincent J. Schaefer, "Observation, Serendipity, and Climate Change," *Journal of College Science Teaching* 4, no. 1 (September 1974): 19–22.

104   *THIS IS WHAT INSIDE OF A CLOUD*   GE filing no. 8851, November 29, 1946, Vincent J. Schaefer Papers, 1891–1993, M. E. Grenander Department of Special Collections and Archives, State University at Albany, series 2, box 6, folder 15.

106   *I looked toward the sun*   Schaefer, *Serendipity in Science*, 131.

106   **The New York Times** *reports*   "Three-Mile Cloud Made into Snow by Dry Ice Dropped from Plane; Scientist Produces Fall Above Bay State Peak With 6 Pounds of Pellets, Opening Vista of Moisture Control by Man," *New York Times*, November 15, 1946, 24.

106   *The plane passes*   Schaefer, *Serendipity in Science*, 132.

107   *The crystal fog follows*   Strand, *The Brothers Vonnegut*, 61, 89.

107   *He'll hold a balloon*   Ginger Strand brilliantly explains how the toy gun and soda bottle create crystals. "Compressing gasses increase their temperatures" so when released into a room, the temperature of the gas decreased, and "the air in the popgun expanded rapidly, cooling the air around it, and the cold nucleated the ice." Strand, *The Brothers Vonnegut*, 70–71.

107   **The New York Times** *calls*   "Three-Mile Cloud Made into Snow by Dry Ice Dropped from Plane," *New York Times*, November 15, 1946, 24.

107   **Time** *magazine reports*   "Thinking Outside the Cold Box: How a Nobel Prize Winner and Kurt Vonnegut's Brother Made White Christmas on Demand," GE

Reports (website), accessed March 6, 2015, http://www
.gereports.com/post/78010633546/thinking-outside
-the-cold-box-how-a-nobel-prize.

108   **The GE press release** "Rain by Fire," October 28, 1948,
in Tomas Kellner, "Cool Science: How Kurt Vonnegut's
Brother Tried to Break Up Hurricanes," GE website,
https://www.ge.com/news/reports/cool-science-vonnegut
-ge-research.

Chapter 12

110   **It is "broken up** Jesse Pound, "GE to Break Up into
3 Companies Focusing on Aviation, Health Care and
Energy," CNBC website, November 9, 2021, https://
www.cnbc.com/2021/11/09/ge-to-break-up-into-3
-companies-focusing-on-aviation-healthcare-and-energy
.html.

111   **In 1959 he writes** Vladimir Vladimirovich Nabokov,
*Nabokov's Butterflies: Unpublished and Uncollected
Writings*, eds. Robert Michael Pyle and Brian Boyd,
trans. Dmitri Nabokov (Boston: Beacon, 2000), 467,
530.

112   **His novel Pnin describes** Eric Naiman, *Nabokov,
Perversely* (Ithaca: Cornell University Press, 2010), 75.

114   **It is supposed to close** Steve Hughes, "Albany Rapp
Road Landfill Future Up for Discussion Monday,"
Albany Times Union, July 3, 2023, https://www
.timesunion.com/news/article/albany-rapp-road-landfill
-future-discussion-18175490.php.

114   **This is where the Black Shaker eldress** For more on the
life of Rebecca Cox Jackson, see Jean McMahon Humez's
introduction to *Gifts of Power*, 1–50.

114   **I put some in my bosom** Jackson, *Gifts of Power*, 179.

Chapter 13

117 **She writes of visiting kids** Lucy S. Bowers, Wanamaker Diary—1929 and WaterVliet South Family, January 11–November 28, 1929, Shaker Heritage Society, Albany, NY, https://memoirs.shakerpedia.com/shaver/pages/?set=south&grp=023&id=53&next=&pg=7.

118 **Painting the blue, beautiful hues** Joe Burke and Al Dubin, "Painting the Clouds with Sunshine," from the film *Gold Diggers of Broadway*, directed by Roy Del Ruth (Burbank, CA: Warner Bros., 1929).

118 **And in my heart** Jackson, *Gifts of Power*, 99.

118 **He begins in vapor** Edward K. Spann, *Brotherly Tomorrows: Movements for a Cooperative Society in America, 1820–1920* (New York: Columbia University Press, 1989), 23.

121 **In writing on rivers and streams** Leopold, *A View of the River*, ix.

Chapter 14

123 **On Thanksgiving weekend in 1950** "Deer Hunters Sprinkled with Silver Iodide Day of Flood," *Catskill Mountain News*, December 8, 1950, 1.

123 **Not even six months** Guy Suits's testimony, *Weather Control and Augmented Potable Water Supply: Extracts from Hearings Before Subcommittees of the Committees on Interior and Insular Affairs Interstate and Foreign Commerce and Agriculture and Forestry*, 82nd Congress, session 1, March 14–16, 19, and April 5, 1951 (Washington, DC: US Government Printing office, 1951), 52.

123 **Bernard Vonnegut tells the senators** Bernard Vonnegut's testimony, *Weather Control and Augmented Potable Water Supply*, 54.

124 **Before the city starts rainmaking** Wallace E. Howell, "The Precipitation Stimulation Project of the City of New York, 1950," *The Journal of Weather Modification* 13, no. 1 (1981): 89, https://doi.org/10.54782/jwm .v13i1.40. A footnote on the first page says: "Originally dated February 20, 1951, this report is published now for the first time in its 30th anniversary year as a matter of historical interest. Several appendixes, omitted for the sake of brevity, may be obtained from the author."

124 **GE won't take the job** Wallace E. Howell, "The Precipitation Stimulation Project," 89.

125 **Photos show him climbing** Charles G. Bennett, "US Forest Expert Aids City on Water," *New York Times*, April 6, 1950, 20.

125 **On April 8, The New Yorker** "Cloud Physicist," Talk of the Town, *New Yorker*, April 8, 1950, 26–27.

126 **They hike after him** Charles G. Bennett, "Rain Makers Fail in Quarters Hunt; In Search for Field Headquarters for Rain Making," *New York Times*, March 18, 1950, 15.

126 **Two days later** "Rain-Makers End Search for Site," *New York Times*, March 19, 1950, 42. Charles G. Bennett, "RAIN MAKERS SHIFT SEARCH FOR A SITE; Downsville Area, on West Rim of Watershed, to Be Focus of Headquarters Hunt EARLIER OFFERS REJECTED Police Planes Will Be Ready Today to Start Tests in Seeding of Clouds the Water Situation," *New York Times*, March 22, 1950, 3.

127 **Howell's first attempt is** Charles G. Bennett, "IS IT HIS OR NATURE'S?; 'Howell's Snow' Irks Some But City Calls It Fine Stuff AS UNEXPECTED SNOWSTORM HIT NEW YORK AND SUBURBS YESTERDAY OFFICIALS PLEASED BY 'HOWELL SNOW' Not Sure Howell Did It," *New York Times*, April 13, 1950, 1.

127 **And here, I read in the Catskill Mountain News** "Deer Hunters Sprinkled with Silver Iodide Day of Flood," *Catskill Mountain News*, December 8, 1950, 1.

128 **It is moved 1,000 feet** "Record Flood Greatly Damages Mountain Area" and "Flood in Fleischmanns Damages Homes, Businesses," *Catskill Mountain News*, December 1, 1950, 1.

129 **Arkville, I read** "Arkville Loss Includes 750 Chickens and Cabins," *Catskill Mountain News*, December 1, 1950, 12.

129 **Another headline on the front page** "Flood's Best Joke," *Catskill Mountain News*, December 1, 1950, 1.

129 **In one photo a farmhouse is tipped** "Flood-Wrecked Houses and Pocked-Marked Mountain Landscape Are Scene of Area's Worst Flood," *Catskill Mountain News*, December 1, 1950, 3.

136 **In the paper, there's a tiny notice** "Union Grove Registers Highest Water in History," *Catskill Mountain News*, December 1, 1950, 7. (The piece is uncredited, but Steve's mother, Agnes, was the correspondent for Union Grove.)

Chapter 15

139 **Reading them, I'm struck by** "Killed by Grandfather's Pills," *Catskill Mountain News*, December 15, 1950, 1. "Two Killed When Egg Truck Hits Roadside Trees: Steering Heel Strangled Driver, Helper Also Found Dead," *Catskill Mountain News*, January 19, 1951, 1. "Andes Fireman Cut Driver from Wrecked Truck," *Catskill Mountain News*, December 29, 1950, 1. "Fires Floods Almost Murder in Roxbury 1950," *Catskill Mountain News*, January 12, 1951, 2. "Hunter Finds Wrecked Plane on Slide Mountain," *Catskill Mountain News*, November 2, 1950, 1.

139   *The partially frozen, half-clad body* "Arkville Man Drowned in Flood of December Four," *Catskill Mountain News*, December 15, 1950, 1.

139   *There's also all the crime* "Forgery and Auto Accidents Take Attention of Police," *Catskill Mountain News*, December 15, 1950, 1. "Thief Steals Handsome Buck at Big Indian," *Catskill Mountain News*, November 24, 1950, 1. "Trooper Locates Hit-Run Driver," *Catskill Mountain News*, December 8, 1950, 1. "Hit-Run Driver in Bank Corner Crash," *Catskill Mountain News*, January 5, 1951, 1. "Home Burglarized Four Times," *Catskill Mountain News*, November 17, 1950, 7. Hunters are warned to watch out for drunken bears because of fermented apples in the column "Mountain Dew," *Catskill Mountain News*, November 17, 1950, 10.

140   *The local Chevy dealer* Advertisement, Dawson Chevrolet Co., in *Catskill Mountain News*, December 1, 1950, 6.

140   *That same week of the flood* "Valley Folks Gain Millions by Unprecedented Court Decisions," *Catskill Mountain News*, December 1, 1950, 12.

140   *I find, too, an editorial* "About the Value of Water as Such in This East Branch Valley," *Catskill Mountain News*, January 19, 1951, 1.

141   *Saturday morning Peter Eder* "Arkville Man Drowned in Flood of December Four," *Catskill Mountain News*, December 15, 1950, 1.

142   *Angry water surged* "Pine Hill Woman Describes Flood Which Hit Village," *Catskill Mountain News*, December 8, 1950, 1, 6.

142   *On the same front page* "New York Has Ample Water," *Catskill Mountain News*, December 15, 1950, 1.

143   *Of course you realize* Claude, "Of Course You Realize, Mr. Masters," illustration, *New Yorker*, April 8, 1950, 26.

145 ***Where the plant's erect spadix*** Walt Whitman, "For You O Democracy," from "Calamus" in *Leaves of Grass*, 1891–92 ed., Walt Whitman Archive (website), https:// whitmanarchive.org/published/LG/1891/poems/45.

147 ***One person records a honeybee*** "One-Flowered Broomrape *Orobanche uniflora* Broomrape family (Orobanchaceae)," Illinois Wildflowers (website), accessed May 20, 2024, http://www.illinoiswildflowers .info/woodland/plants/of_broomrape.htm.

148 ***I read about this*** Illinois Wildflowers (website), "One-Flowered Broomrape."

Chapter 16

157 ***There's a line*** M. Stephen Miller, *Inspired Innovations: A Celebration of Shaker Ingenuity* (Lebanon, NH: University Press of New England, 2010), 126.

158 ***I study an article that says*** Bryce Nelson, "Albany: New York State University Center On the Way Up," *Science*, n.s., 155, no. 3769 (March 24, 1967): 1521–25.

160 ***I read Vince's notes*** Vincent Schaefer, "Something in the Air," 1967, Vincent J. Schaefer Papers, series 6, box 24, folder 91.

161 ***Trace of dawn light*** Vincent Schaefer, "Time Lapse Film from a Jet Airliner," March 1, 1956, and "Record of Boeing 707 Flight: Moses Lake, Seattle, Washington, DC," October 16, 1955, Vincent J. Schaefer Papers, series 3, box 4, folder 6.

Chapter 17

163 ***The school sends out*** SUNY Albany Press Release, Public Information Office, H. David Van Dyck, mailed

November 14, 1966, dated November 15, 1966. Vincent J. Schaefer Papers, box 24, folder 78.

164   *A month and a half later*   *Science* magazine, like GE, was founded by Thomas Edison.

164   *She describes looking up*   Jackson, *Gifts of Power,* 209–10.

164   *In another dream*   Jackson, *Gifts of Power,* 179.

165   *It sounds beautiful, metaphysical*   Vincent J. Schaefer, "The Inadvertent Modification of the Atmosphere," *Bulletin of the American Meteorological Society* 50, no. 4 (April 1, 1969): 199–207. And "Auto Exhaust, Pollution and Weather Patterns," *Bulletin of Atomic Scientists* 26, no. 8 (October 1970): 31–33.

165   *Everywhere he goes*   Vincent J. Schaefer, "The Threat of the Unseen," *Saturday Review,* February 6, 1971, 56.

166   *Air is inhaled*   Schaefer, "Threat of the Unseen," 55–56.

168   *It is November 1968*   Reports, Project Themis, 1968–69, Bernard Vonnegut Papers, series 8, box 1, folder 21.

168   *He writes, "Skillful exploitation*   Bernard Vonnegut, "Research Proposal for Themis, 1967," Bernard Vonnegut Papers, series 8, box 4, folder 10: 12–13.

168   *Themis grows from a dream*   Vern D. Calloway Jr., "Project Themis," *United States Air Force JAG Law Review* 10, no. 2 (1968): 29–32.

169   *They read like science fiction*   Project Themis booklet, Department of Defense, November 1968, Office of the Director of Defense Research and Engineering, Washington, DC, Bernard Vonnegut Papers, series 8, box 4, folder 10.

170   *Now he wants to develop*   Bernard Vonnegut, "Research Proposal for Themis, 1967." The table of contents lists the areas of research the ASRC undertakes including "Tornadoes," "Bubble Studies," and "Large-Scale Weather Modification," Bernard Vonnegut Papers, series 8, box 4, folder 10: 12–13.

170 *In his proposal* Bernard Vonnegut, "Research Proposal
for Themis, 1967," 14.

170 *Bernie asks for U2 planes* Bernard Vonnegut letter
to Donald Fitzgerald, Air Force Cambridge Research
Laboratory, July 25, 1967, Bernard Vonnegut Papers,
series 8, box 1, folder 20: 3–5.

Chapter 18

173 *Langmuir streaks and Langmuir vortices* Schaefer and
Day, *Field Guide*, 276.

174 *Always have a lunch* Schaefer, *Serendipity in Science*, 34.

174 *Together in those years the two fly* Schaefer, *Serendipity
in Science*, 39.

177 *The theoretical villain* Kurt Vonnegut, *Cat's Cradle*
(New York: Dial, 2010), 45.

178 *Sleet was falling* Vonnegut, *Cat's Cradle*, 27, 30.

178 *Breed says, supervise* Vonnegut, *Cat's Cradle*, 21.

178 *In the report I read* Henri Dessens, "On the Radiative
Balance of Atmospheric Particles," Typescript of
Paper Given at Sixth International Conference on
Condensation Nuclei, May 9–13, 1966, Bernard
Vonnegut Papers, series 10, box 2, folder 12: 4.

179 *The environmental historian* Stephen J. Pyne, *The
Pyrocene: How We Created an Age of Fire, and What
Happens Next* (Berkeley: University of California Press,
2022).

180 *One of the men, the president's advisor* John F.
Kennedy, "Remarks at the Signing of a Contract to Aid
Electrification of Underdeveloped Countries," November
1, 1962, The American Presidency Project website, UC
Santa Barbara, https://www.presidency.ucsb.edu
/documents/remarks-the-signing-contract-aid-electrification
-underdeveloped-countries.

182   *Cooperatives are economic and social democracies*
Senator Hubert Humphrey, "Forward," *Implementation
of the Humphrey Amendment to the Foreign Assistance
Act of 1961* (Washington: Government Printing Office,
1964), iii.

182   *So, here is my dad* Ted Case, *Poles, Wires and War: The
Remarkable Untold Story of Rural Electrification and the
Vietnam War* (self-pub., 2017), 31.

183   *The son quits because he* Vonnegut, *Cat's Cradle*, 1, 27.

183   *When Kurt Vonnegut is working* David L. Ulin, "The
Reading Life: Kurt Vonnegut's 'Slaughterhouse-Five,'"
Los Angeles Times, September 9, 2010, https://www.
latimes.com/archives/la-xpm-2010-sep-09-la-et
-slaughterhouse-20100909-story.html.

183   *Later, a friend sends me* Kurt Vonnegut, *Slapstick, or
Lonesome No More!* (New York: Delacorte, 1976), 1–19.

Chapter 19

188   *Millennia ago in the Catskills* Stream piracy creates
Kaaterskill Falls, which millennia later becomes the
Catskills' first major tourist attraction for white settlers
which might be the true crime—the theft of this land.
The falls represent a romantic view of nature and its
awesome power, dwarfing humanity like Thomas Cole's
1826 painting *The Falls at Kaaterskill*, with its sole
Indigenous man miniature in this vast landscape, as if he
is nature himself.

192   *is there a place to still be* Jorie Graham "Before," *London
Review of Books* 45, no. 23 (November 30, 2023): 26.

192   *And I find a line by* Etel Adnan, *Time*, trans. Sarah
Riggs (New York: Nightboat, 2019), 96.

192   *A secret memo is sent* Document 274, Memorandum
from the Deputy Under Secretary of State for

Political Affairs (Kohler) to Secretary of State Rusk, "Weather Modification in North Vietnam and Laos (Project Popeye)," January 13, 1967, *Foreign Relations of the United States, 1964–1968*, Vol. XXVIII, Laos, https://history.state.gov/historicaldocuments /frus1964-68v28/d274.

193 *In* **Cat's Cradle, Dr. Breed** Vonnegut, *Cat's Cradle*, 45.

194 *Sir Walter Raleigh gets the charter* Harriot doesn't just advise on these voyages; he goes on at least one. Raleigh never does. Queen Elizabeth refuses to let him leave Britain. He simply lays out the money to pay for the excursions. While in Virginia, which is not actually what we call Virginia today but North Carolina, Harriot is in Roanoac, Algonquin-speaking territory, and learns to speak the language.

195 *One soldier writes home* Thomas H. Parker, *History of the 51st regiment of PA: From Its Organization, at Camp Curtin, Harrisburg, PA., in 1861, to Its Being Mustered Out of the United States Service in Alexandria Virginia July 27th, 1865* (Philadelphia: King & Baird, 1869), 99.

195 *Dr. Breed tells Jonah* Vonnegut, *Cat's Cradle*, 42.

195 *In my local paper soon after* "Mountain Dew," *Catskill Mountain News*, December 8, 1950, 14. (The quote appears in the anonymous column Mountain Dew and is quoting an interview with Langmuir in *The New York Times* after the flood.)

196 *An Army general declares* Frank L. Kluckhohn, "$28,000,000 Urged to Support MIT: Compton Tells Alumni of Need in New Era—Gen. Kenney Suggests Sound as Weapon," *New York Times*, June 15, 1947, 46.

196 *The GE executive in charge* Guy Suits testimony, "Weather Control and Augmented Potable Water Supply," 48–49.

196 **Meanwhile two months after** "Mass Meeting on Wednesday to Talk About Bombs," *Catskill Mountain News*, January 26, 1951, 1.

196 **He is not even particularly fond** Rocky Kolb, *Blind Watchers of the Sky: The People and Ideas That Shaped Our View of the Universe* (Oxford, UK: Oxford University Press, 1999): 44–45.

196 **Every gravitational wave** Adam Frank, "Scientists Found Ripples in Space and Time. And You Have to Buy Groceries," *The Atlantic*, June 29, 2023, https://www.theatlantic.com/science/archive/2023/06/universe-gravitational-waves-nanograv-discovery/674570/.

Chapter 20

200 **The secret memo to Dean Rusk** "Weather Modification in North Vietnam and Laos (Project Popeye)."

201 **When The New York Times comes** Walter Sullivan, "Supersonic Jets May Threaten Air: Scientist Says Pollutants Could Encircle Earth," *New York Times*, March 22, 1968, 94.

201 **In a report to the military** Bernard Vonnegut, Project Themis Proposal, Bernard Vonnegut Papers, series 8, box 4, folder 10: 2.

202 **Years later in an interview** Robert K. Musil, "There Must Be More to Love Than Death: A Conversation with Kurt Vonnegut," *Nation* 231, no. 4 (August 2, 1980): 128–132.

202 **In the same interview Vonnegut** Musil, "There Must Be More," 129.

203 **Vaguely Moorish/futuristic** In 1981 Jane Fonda starred in *Rollover* with Kris Kristofferson about financial manipulations and trading. The campus was to double as a sheik's palace.

204 **SUNY Albany and PINSTECH** Instead in most places, college has created a different way to drag us into capitalism. The promise of college is a better-paying job but first there's college debt, so much debt that you are forced into capitalism to work it off.

204 *His laboratory was a sensational mess* Vonnegut, *Slapstick*, 4.

205 *I find the letters written* Selective Service Exemption for G. Garland Lala, signed by Bernard Vonnegut, July 1, 1968, Bernard Vonnegut Papers, series 8, box 1, folder 21.

206 *In the letter to his air force contact* Bernard Vonnegut letter to Donald Fitzgerald, Air Force Cambridge Research Laboratory, July 25, 1967, Bernard Vonnegut Papers, series 8, box 1, folder 20.

206 *In his* **Field Guide to the Atmosphere** Schaefer and Day, *Field Guide*, 45–46.

206 *He dedicates a cycle of poems* Goethe, "In Honour of Mr. Howard."

206 **The New York Times** *reports* Seymour Hersh, "Rainmaking Is Used as Weapon by U.S.," *New York Times*, July 3, 1972, A1, A2.

207 *Two years later in secret hearings* "Weather Modification, March 20, 1974," United States Senate Subcommittee on Oceans and International Environment of the Committee of Foreign Relations, 93rd Congress, second session, made public May 19, 1974 (Washington, DC: US Government Printing Office, 1974), 122, 121.

207 *In the Senate hearing Dennis J. Doolin* "Weather Modification, March 20, 1974," 121.

208 *At the end of her first dream* Jackson, *Gifts of Power*, 179–180.

208 *A Shaker brother comes* Jackson, *Gifts of Power*, 210–11.

209 *How will the world be saved* Jackson, *Gifts of Power*, 29.

209 **Today the news reports** Raymond Zhong, "Warming Could Push the Atlantic Past a 'Tipping Point' This Century," *New York Times*, July 25, 2023, https://www .nytimes.com/2023/07/25/climate/atlantic-ocean-tipping -point.html.

210 **As Marx is dying** Robley Edward Whitson, "Introduction," *The Shakers: Two Centuries of Spiritual Reflection* (New York: Paulist, 1983), 23.

Chapter 21

215 **In March 1970 Vince addresses** Vincent M. Schaefer testimony, March 16, 1970, *Air Pollution—1969 Hearing Before the Subcommittee on Air and Water Pollution of the Committee on Public Works, United States Senate*, 91st Congress, Oct 27, 1969 (Washington, DC: US Government Printing Office), 89–102. Also, Schaefer, "Testimony to be presented to Joint Legislature Committee on the Environment—The Subcommittee on Air and Water Pollution," Vincent J. Schaefer Papers, series 6, box 23, folder 13.

218 **It is June 1954 and he tells** Robert I. Kabat Testimony, *Congressional Record—June 1, 1954*, 83rd Congress, 2nd Session, Vol. 100, Part 6, Bound Edition: 7409, https:// www.congress.gov/bound-congressional-record/1954 /06/01/senate-section.

220 **Pollution kills between** David Wallace-Wells, "Ten Million a Year," *London Review of Books* 43, no. 23 (December 2, 2021), https://www.lrb.co.uk/the-paper /v43/n23/david-wallace-wells/ten-million-a-year.

221 **Architecture, fashions** Susan Buck-Morss, "Benjamin's Passagen-Werk: Redeeming Mass Culture for the Revolution," *New German Critique* no. 29, The Origins of Mass Culture: The Case of Imperial Germany

(1871–1918), (Spring–Summer, 1983): 224, https://www.jstor.org/stable/487795.

223 **the blueish cast** Vincent Schaefer, "The Blue Haze of the Atmosphere," 1973, Vincent J. Schaefer Papers, series 6, box 9, folder 5. (See also Schaefer and Day, *Field Guide*, 7.)

223 **Bernie writes to Donald Rumsfeld** Bernard Vonnegut, letter to the Honorable Donald H. Rumsfeld, Secretary of Defense, February 19, 1976, Bernard Vonnegut Papers, box 1, folder 19.

226 **Just above a report** "Noted This Week: Quotes and Comments," *Schenectady Gazette*, n.d., 38, Bernard Vonnegut Papers, series 8, box 5, folder 7.

226 **He is still focused on his clear-air seeding** Bernard Vonnegut, "Clear-Air Seeding Proposal," submitted to the National Science Foundation, 1979, Bernard Vonnegut Papers, series 8, box 4, folder 8. Additional materials, series 7, box 8, folder 6.

226 **He is a "distinguished research professor** C. B. Moore and Haflidi H. Jonsson, "Biographical Sketch Bernard Vonnegut 1915–1997," Atmospheric Sciences, SUNY Albany website, https://www.atmos.albany.edu/daes/bvonn/bvonnegut.html.

228 **The Washington Post runs** Herblock, "Laboratory Experiment," *Washington Post*, May 14, 1986, A22.

228 **The front of a paper** Bernard Vonnegut, "Microphysical Studies of Noctilucent Clouds," January 1992, Bernard Vonnegut Papers, series 8, box 3, folder 7.

228 **I find agendas and programs** "Applied Research and Technology Environmental Program Review, December 15–16, 1987. At 2001 Wisconsin Avenue, Room 130 Washington D.C.," Strategic Defense Initiative Research Review, Bernard Vonnegut Papers, series 9, box 4, folders 3, 4.

229 **Bernie writes of them** Bernard Vonnegut, "Microphysical Studies of Noctilucent Clouds: Final

Technical Report," January 1992, 2, Bernard Vonnegut
Papers, series 8, box 3, folder 7. "Microphysical Studies
of Noctilucent Clouds Grant—ONR," n.d., series 8, box
3, folder 8.

229 *Vince calls them* Schaefer and Day, *Field Guide*, 136.

229 *Other scientists describe them* F. H. Ludlam,
"Noctilucent Clouds," *Tellus* IX, vol. 3 (1957): 341–64.

229 *They sound to me like the way* Jackson, *Gifts of Power*,
220.

230 *Vince writes in his guide* Schaefer and Day, *Field Guide*,
136.

230 *In the meeting's report* "Strategic Defense Initiative
Research Review," May 10, 1989, Bernard Vonnegut
Papers, series 9, box 4, folder 4.

231 *A few weeks before* Letter from Paul F. Twitchell to
Bernard Vonnegut, April 21, 1989, Bernard Vonnegut
Papers, series 9, box 4, folder 4.

231 *Bernie writes equations* "Strategic Defense Initiative
Research Review," May 10, 1989, Bernard Vonnegut
Papers, series 9, box 4, folder 4.

232 *Bernie writes that the particles* Bernard Vonnegut,
"Microphysical Studies of Noctilucent Clouds: Final
Technical Report," January 1992, Bernard Vonnegut
Papers, series 8, box 3, folder 7: 4.

232 *In the report, too* "Microphysical Studies of Noctilucent
Clouds," Contract No. N00014-85-K-0705. Co-
principal investigators: Bernard Vonnegut and
Aodhagan F. Roddy, Program manager Paul F.
Twitchell, 1987, Bernard Vonnegut Papers, series 9, box
4, folder 3.

233 *Online I read about how moss* The rocks release calcium
and magnesium as they weather. That combines in the
carbon dioxide and forms calcium carbonate, limestone
(drawing the carbon from the atmosphere and storing
it in limestone). Timothy M. Lenton, Michael Crouch,

Martin Johnson, Nuno Pires, and Liam Dolan, "First Plants Cooled the Ordovician," *Nature Geoscience* 5 (February 2012): 86–89; Oliver Jagoutz and Aaron Krol, "Enhanced Rock Weathering," MIT Climate Portal, https://climate.mit.edu/explainers/enhanced-rock -weathering.

233   *There is Bernie*   Phil Baker, "Kurt Vonnegut Obituary," *The Guardian*, April 13, 2007, https://www.theguardian .com/books/2007/apr/13/usa.kurtvonnegut.

234   *I read about Soviet cloud seeding*   Kate Brown, *Manual for Survival: An Environmental History of the Chernobyl Disaster* (New York: W. W. Norton, 2019), loc. 725–72, Kindle.

234   *When the power plant melts*   Michael Bond, "Cheating Chernobyl," interview with Alexander Yuvchenko, *New Scientist* 183, no. 2461 (August 21–27, 2004): 44–47.

235   *In 1981, Bernie writes*   Bernard Vonnegut, "Clear-Air Seeding," 1979, 1981, Bernard Vonnegut Papers, series 7, box 8, folder 6.

236   *in a stray line*   D. E. Chambers, Testimony, *Committee on Interstate and Foreign Commerce*, March 16, 1948, Vincent J. Schaefer Papers, series 1, box 5, folder 46.

236   *An onshore breeze*   Luna B. Leopold, "The Interaction of Trade Wind and Sea Breeze, Hawaii," *Journal of Meteorology* 6 (October 1949): 312–20; Luna B. Leopold and Wendell A. Mordy, "1948–1949 Trials of the Schaefer-Langmuir Cloud-Seeding Technique in Hawaii," *Tellus* 3, no. 1 (1951): 44–52, https://doi.org /10.3402/tellusa.v3i1.8610.

240   *The algae detoxify*   "Stressed Seaweed Contributes to Cloudy Coastal Skies, Study Suggests," ScienceDaily, May 7, 2008, www.sciencedaily.com/releases/2008/05 /080506103036.htm.

Chapter 22

243 *I read about the Karner* "Endangered and Threatened Wildlife and Plants: Determination of Endangered Status for the Karner Blue Butterfly: Final Rule," *Federal Register, Part III Department of Interior, Fish and Wildlife Service* 57, no. 240 (December 14, 1992): 59236–44.

245 *A headline reports that exhaust* Shannon Hall, "Filling Up a New Frontier," *New York Times*, January 9, 2024, D1.

248 *I read that plastics now seed clouds* Aliya Uteuova, "Microplastics Found in Clouds Could Affect Weather and Global Temperatures," *The Guardian*, November 16, 2023, https://www.theguardian.com/environment/2023 /nov/16/microplastic-pollution-changing-weather-climate.

Chapter 23

255 *He works up until* C. B. Moore and Haflidi H. Jonsson, "Bernard Vonnegut 1914–1997."

255 *I find in his files testimonies* Letter to Bernard Vonnegut from Mrs. Philip Anderson, February 4, 1966, Bernard Vonnegut Papers, https://archives.albany.edu /concern/daos/ww72bx05c. Letter from Mrs. Marcela Benson, February 27, 1966, Bernard Vonnegut Papers, https://archives.albany.edu/concern/daos/4b29bq09t. Observations: Birmingham Alabama News, April 22, 1956, NP; Bernard Vonnegut Papers, https://archives .albany.edu/concern/daos/d791t083v. Letter from Mrs. Benedict D. Aiken, June 26, 1959, Bernard Vonnegut Papers, https://archives.albany.edu/concern/daos /3b591v18b. Letter from Mr. and Mrs. Bolduc, February 17, 1977, Bernard Vonnegut Papers, https://archives .albany.edu/concern/daos/pz50hf27t.

259   *I read about escalating weapons* Minna Ålander, "High
       North, High Tension: The End of Arctic Illusions,"
       Foreign Policy Research Institute website, May 11, 2023,
       https://www.fpri.org/article/2023/05/high-north-high
       -tension-the-end-of-arctic-illusions/.
         Joseline Manfroi et al., "Antarctic on Fire: Paleo-
       Wildfire Events Associated with Volcanic Deposits in
       the Antarctic Peninsula During the Late Cretaceous,"
       Frontiers in Earth Science 11 (April 2023), https://doi.org
       /10.3389/feart.2023.1048754.

259   *The snow there* Marric Stephens, "Seeking Stardust in
       the Snow," *Physics* 12, s. 93, August 12, 2019, https://
       physics.aps.org/articles/v12/s93.

260   *In their* **Field Guide** Schaefer and Day, *Field Guide*,
       202.

260   *I'm numb* Thomas Fuller, "4 Years of Catastrophic Fires
       in California: 'I'm Numb,'" *New York Times*, August 24,
       2020, https://www.nytimes.com/2020/08/24/us
       /california-fires-wildfires.html.

260   *I read another* Dennis Overbye, "A Rip in the Fabric of
       Interstellar Dreams," *New York Times*, August 21, 2020,
       https://www.nytimes.com/2020/08/21/science/space
       -telescope-puerto-rico-arecibo.html.

260   *I scroll a conversation* "In Conversation: Patrik
       Svensson and Rebecca Tamás," *Granta* 167, online ed.,
       April 23, 2021, https://granta.com/in-conversation
       -svensson-tamas. Susan Lahey, "Your Very Own
       Consciousness Can Interact with the Whole Universe,
       Scientists Believe," *Popular Mechanics*, October 18, 2023,
       https://www.popularmechanics.com/science/a45574179
       /architecture-of-consciousness/.
         Dan Falk, "Is Consciousness Part of the Fabric of
       the Universe?" *Scientific American*, September 25, 2023,
       https://www.scientificamerican.com/article/is
       -consciousness-part-of-the-fabric-of-the-universe1/.

260 *The hemlocks create this place* "The Importance of Hemlocks," Hemlock Restoration Initiative website, North Carolina Department of Agriculture & Consumer Services and USDA-FS Forest Health Protection, https://savehemlocksnc.org/hemlocks-hwa /the-importance-of-hem.

260 *The hemlock builds* "The Importance of Hemlocks."

260 *I read a novel by Canadian writer* Sheila Heti, *Pure Colour* (New York: Farrar, Straus and Giroux, 2022), 98, 21.

261 *The horsetails once cover* Glenn Nice and Peter Sikkema, "The Ancient Horsetail" (pamphlet), Purdue Extension Weed Science, WS-29-W, Purdue University, May 22, 2007.

262 *These are the very plants* Kevin Vanneste, Lieven Sterck, Alexander Andrew Myburg, Yves Van de Peer, and Eshchar Mizrachi, "Horsetails Are Ancient Polyploids: Evidence from Equisetum Giganteum," *The Plant Cell* 27, no. 6 (June 2015): 1567–78.

262 *These few that are left* Vanneste et al., "Horsetails," 1574.

262 *Aldo Leopold, Luna's father* Aldo Leopold, *Sand County Almanac, with Essays on Conservation from Round River* (New York: Ballentine, 1970), 197, 239.

263 *Our Grand Circle* Leopold, *A View of the River*, 1, 113.

265 *It is said there is water* Eugene Ostashevksy, "Farewell Poem," *New York Review*, May 25, 2023, https://www .nybooks.com/issues/2023/05/25/.

266 *At the end of his essay* Philip Ball, "In Retrospect: On the Six-Cornered Snowflake," *Nature* 480, no. 455 (2011), https://doi.org/10.1038/480455a.

266 *My version ends* Kepler, *The Six-Cornered Snowflake*, loc. 631, Kindle.

Chapter 24

267   **Walter Benjamin writes** Walter Benjamin, "One-way Street," in *One-way Street and Other Writings*, trans. J. A. Underwood (New York: Penguin Classics, 2009), 54.

270   **This exact location** The Fonda family: Jane, Peter, and Robert originally hail from here.

278   **In his letter to Tom** Vincent Schaefer letter to Tom Porter, March 1, 1993, from Tom Porter's *Kanatsiohareke: Traditional Mohawk Indians Return to Their Ancestral Homeland* (Greenfield Center, NY: Bowman, 1989), 48–49.

Chapter 25

279   **The men still often leave** For more on resistance to the demands of false borders, see Audra Simpson, *Mohawk Interruptus: Political Life Across the Borders of Settler States* (Durham: Duke University Press, 2014).

280   **This is the context** Elizabeth Hoover, *The River Is in Us: Fighting Toxics in a Mohawk Community* (Minneapolis: University of Minnesota Press, 2017), 84. In this book and all her work, Hoover has claimed what are now known to be false Mohawk and Mi'kmaq ancestries. She writes of a "we" that does not include her. Her research does not stand contested and asks important questions. And I am surrounded by thefts and appropriations impossible to address in an endnote. See: Jay Caspian Kang, "A Professor Claimed to Be Native American. Did She Know She Wasn't?," *New Yorker*, February 26, 2024, https://www.newyorker.com/magazine/2024/03/04/a-professor-claimed-to-be-native-american-did-she-know-she-wasnt.

281 **Tom's uncle, Francis Johnson** Edmund Wilson, "Standing Arrow," in *Apologies to the Iroquois* (Syracuse: Syracuse University Press, 1992), 39–57.

282 **It declares, "The people** Samuel Wilson Rose, "Mohawk Histories and Futures: Traditionalism, Community Development, and Heritage in the Mohawk Valley" (PhD diss., State University of Buffalo, May 2017), 48, 65–75, 118. And Samuel W. Rose, "The Historical Political Ecological and Political Economic Context of Mohawk Efforts at Land Reclamation in the Mohawk Valley," *Journal of Historical Sociology* 31, no. 3 (2018): 258, https://doi.org/10.1111/johs.12182. And, Hoover, *The River Is in Us*, 48, 76.

283 **There is nothing about protests** The Tuscarora protested NYPA dams as well, suing the Federal Power Commission, a case that was ultimately heard by the Supreme Court. The court ruled against the Tuscarora, but in his dissent, Justice Black excoriated the litany of injustices by the federal government violating treaties. He added that this ruling was another broken promise. More recently a group of traditional Mohawks in 2024 occupied Barnhart Island, owned by the NYPA and site of dam. In 2022, a federal judge ruled that New York state illegally seized Mohawk lands in the early nineteenth century.

283 **Walter Benjamin writes** Benjamin, "Theses on the Philosophy of History," 256.

285 **My father goes on** "Statement of Robert I. Kabat, Legislative and Management Assistant, Nation Rural Electric Cooperative Association," *Niagara River Power Project: Hearings Before a Subcommittee of the Committee on Public Works, US Senate, Eighty-fourth Congress, July 13, 14, 15, 1955* (Washington: US Government Printing Office, 1955), 125–39.

288   *At the end of each section* Tom says to "gather our minds together and our thankfulness and our greetings and our love and our kindness," which I love too. Tom Porter's Thanksgiving Address in conversation with Ron Garrow, "Tom Porter Speaks on the Return to Mohawk Valley," Facebook panel, December 19, 2020, https://www.facebook.com/transer42/videos/10164655115345361/.

291   *The smallest of these particles* Schaefer and Day, *Field Guide*, 3.

Images

4   Photo of the author as a young girl taken atop Deer Leap in Killington, Vermont, by Robert Kabat.

22   Stills of Robert Kabat (Bobby) as a toddler from an undated family film.

29   Photo of the destruction from Hurricane Irene, August 2011, by David Rainbird.

30   Photo of the destruction from Hurricane Irene, August 2011, by David Rainbird.

47   Still from an undated Kabat family film in Somerset, Pennsylvania.

48   Still from an undated Kabat family film in Somerset, Pennsylvania.

75   Film stills of auctions in and around Shavertown, New York, just before New York City floods this village and several others. From *Beneath Pepacton Waters*, shot by George Hoag between 1950 and 1954; narrated by Alice Hoag Jacobson and edited by Alice and Robert Jacobson, 1995. Used with permission of Alice and Robert Jacobson.

76   Gary Atkin rides his bike as his brother Dale runs alongside him, in *Beneath Pepacton Waters*. Used with permission of Alice and Robert Jacobson.

77 The final building burns in Shavertown, New York, in *Beneath Pepacton Waters*. Used with permission of Alice and Robert Jacobson.

103 Entries in Robert Kabat's overtime logbook from May 1946 to September 1947 as he worked to secure ships and bring them back to the United States after World War II.

105 Vincent Schaefer breathing into an icebox, making snow with his breath and dry ice in the GE Research Lab as Irving Langmuir and Bernard Vonnegut look on. Image courtesy of Museum of Innovation and Science; Schenectady, New York; GE News Bureau Photograph Collection.

129 Gas tank picked up and moved by waters in the Rainmaker's Flood. Photo by Bob Wyer, originally published in the *Catskill Mountain News*, courtesy of Delaware County Historical Association.

135 The car that held Mabel West's friend Rosie in Emory Brook. Photo by Bob Wyer, courtesy of Delaware County Historical Association.

154 Undated photo of the author and her father in Roaring Brook, Plymouth, Vermont, by Sandy Kabat.

166 Slide of monkeys on car hoods from a trip across Africa visiting co-operatives in 1964. Photo by Robert Kabat.

167 Bernard Schaefer making "rain by fire," as GE calls it, in 1948. Image courtesy of Museum of Innovation and Science; Schenectady, New York; GE News Bureau Photograph Collection.

181 Energizing ceremony, inaugurating the first rural electric co-operative in Nicaragua, May 1966. Photo by Robert Kabat.

224 Photo of the author in the summer of 1976 in a double exposure shot by Robert Kabat.

264 The last remnants of the Rainmaker's Flood, are in one sign that has grown high above the road warning drivers:

"CAUTION 5 MILES DAMAGED HIGHWAY BY FLOOD DRIVE SLOWLY."

282   Robert Kabat in the mid-1950s, shortly after moving to Washington, DC. Photographer unknown.

Permission Credits

Lisa Robertson, "Residence at C____," *the weather* (Vancouver: New Star, 2001), quoted with the author's permission.

Natalie Diaz, "The Clouds Are Buffalo Limping Toward Jesus" from *When My Brother Was an Aztec*. Copyright © 2012 by Natalie Diaz. Reprinted with the permission of The Permissions Company, LLC, on behalf of Copper Canyon Press, coppercanyonpress.org.

Mary Norbert Korte's "Rooted in the Vernal Equinox" used with permission of the estate of Mary Norbert Korte.

Articles from the *Catskill Mountain News* quoted with the permission of Dick Sanford and the Sandford family who founded it.

Acknowledgments

I write from the borders of Mohawk and Munsee-Lenape land, much of which was never ceded. This book is borne of trying to understand the multiple meanings of this place in this moment. The mistakes are mine.

Writing for me is always about what is shared: ideas, friendships, community . . . None of this would be possible without the great generosity of so many, more than I could ever name or thank enough. My deepest gratitude for the friends who have been here throughout this process: Laura Marris, Iris Marble Cushing, Julius Taranto, Diana Evans, Paul Chaat Smith, Chris Kraus, Anna Moschovakis, Luke Neima, Corinna Ripps Schaming, and Steve and Jane Miller. For their shining example of how to live in this world, my gratitude to Kanatsiohareke and to the community around it, for dreaming of being "a Carlisle in reverse"— Tom Sakokwenionkwas Porter, Iehnhotonkwas Bonnie Jane Maracle, Ronald Garrow, Kay Ionataiewas Olan, and Paul Gorgen, who read these pages as I was writing and taught me the Mohawk word for hemlock, the original pine.

For their support, conversations, and insight: Rudd Hubbell, Adrian Shirk, Jennifer Krasinski, Jonathan Lethem, Niela Orr, Elvia Wilk, Kate Briggs, Jessica Lynne, Sarah Miller, Mike and Becky Porter, the Taylor family, the Margaretville Fire Department, Roz Foster, Claire Boyle, Daniel Gumbiner, Ania Szremski, Margaret Sundell,

Colleen Asper, Jody Kahn, Bronwyn Keenan, Marlene McCarty, Jodi Lynn Maracle, Pareesa Pourian, Kate Newby, Mina Takahashi, Michelle Grabner and Brad Killam and the Poor Farm, Dick Sanford, Marguerite Uhlmann-Bower, Lynne Tillman, Lissa Harris, Aaron Hicklin, Halimah Marcus, Sangamithra Iyer, David Godwin, Betty Baker (who died as I was finishing this), Mabel West, Len Utter, Gary and Barbara Atkin, Don Bramley, Robert and Alice Jacobson, Neil Gifford and the Albany Pine Bush Preserve, Matt Charles, Saul Anton, and Sabine Russ.

My gratitude to the historians: Diane Galusha, Town of Middletown Historical Society, the Delaware County Historical Association: Ray Lafever, Tim Duerden, and Angela Gaffney; the Andes Society for History and Culture: Joanne Kosuda-Warner and Linda Dunne; archivist Gregory Wiedeman and the staff at the M.E. Grenander Department of Special Collections & Archives, State University of New York, Albany. Thank you to my local public library, the Fairview Public Library and Doris Warner. A special thank you to all my students at NYU, the New School, and the School of Visual Arts who have over the years allowed themselves to be open and vulnerable, to think and write together. That process has held me in my own thinking and writing.

Thank you, Halley Parry and Jaclyn Gilbert. I am forever grateful to Joey McGarvey and Daniel Slager for your enthusiasm and care for twinned books exploring place and its reflected meaning, and for Daniel's generative and close reading of the ideas here. Thank you to the generosity of everyone at Milkweed Editions: Morgan LaRocca, Lauren Langston Klein, Mary Austin Speaker, Craig Popelars, Katie Hill, Zoey Gulden, and Sean Beckford. I cannot express my sheer luck and joy that I get to collaborate with you all. You are shining lights in the world of publishing. To Erika Stevens for everything, for your care for these words. It has been my great joy to work together.

Thank you to my family, my sisters Ellen Kabat and Gale Kabat, and to our father who saw the trees and hemlocks—who identified them as a teenager, who, I think, found the forest a home after he had lost so much. My great gratitude as well to my cousins Sara Ani, Fred Pollack, Gwen Pollack, Mark Kirby, and Ina Herlitzka. Thank you ever and always to David Rainbird for everything—for reading, for listening, for going to the hemlock forest with me, for also showing me the trees and their lives.

I had the privilege of launching *The Eighth Moon* in Joan Nelson's Portland gallery, Adams and Ollman, while her "Untitled, 2023"—the cover for *Nightshining*—hung behind me. The moment was thrilling (a launch!) and psychedelic (the excitement!) but even more so for the realm Joan creates here. With *The Eighth Moon*'s cover, it felt like she was transmitting the Catskills' scrubbed-down mountains and all their histories. Here, on the cover of *Nightshining*, her painting builds a landscape that says we are no longer earthbound, or perhaps not bound to the logic of the planet as we know it right now. Spangled bubbles emerge like clouds, fog, glistening mist . . . as if she had intuited the world I was writing, a world that bends into the place we both live, a place that has been used to create smoke, fog, and floods for war, for dreams of controlling the climate. Her glitter is as seductive as *Nightshining*'s dreams, Vince Schaefer's ice crystals and mirrors, and Rebecca Cox Jackson's sparks like silver. Thank you, Joan and Amy Adams.

Crucial support was provided by the State University of New York at Albany, a residency at Headlands, a grant from The Robert B. Silvers Foundation. *Nightshining* is made possible by a Delaware County Arts Grant and an Individual Artist Grant from the New York State Council on the Arts with the support of the Office of the Governor and the New York State Legislature and sponsorship by the Roxbury Arts Group.

Parts of the book were published previously by *BOMB* and *The Best American Essays* (as "Rain Like Cotton") and in *Harper's* and Notting Hill Editions Essay Prize as "The Rainmaker's Flood." Chapter 15 began as a short essay "River Disturbance" in the chapbook *Disturbances* that Laura Marris and I published in 2022 with Bushel, an arts collective in Delhi, New York, to coincide with its show on water. My gratitude to all the editors who have thought about and considered my writing. Your insights and ideas are here throughout.

JENNIFER KABAT was a finalist for the Notting Hill Editions' essay prize and has been published in *BOMB* and *The Best American Essays*. The author of *The Eighth Moon*, her writing has also appeared in *Frieze*, *Harper's*, *McSweeney's*, and *The Believer*. She's received an Andy Warhol Foundation Arts Writers Grant for her criticism and teaches at the School of Visual Arts and the New School. An apprentice herbalist, she lives in rural upstate New York and serves on her volunteer fire department.

milkweed
EDITIONS

Founded as a nonprofit organization in 1980, Milkweed
Editions is an independent publisher. Our mission is to
identify, nurture, and publish transformative literature,
and build an engaged community around it.

We are based in Bdé Óta Othúŋwe (Minneapolis)
in Mní Sota Makhóče (Minnesota), the traditional
homeland of the Dakhóta and Anishinaabe (Ojibwe)
people and current home to many thousands of Dakhóta,
Ojibwe, and other Indigenous people, including four
federally recognized Dakhóta nations and seven federally
recognized Ojibwe nations.

We believe all flourishing is mutual, and we envision a
future in which all can thrive. Realizing such a vision
requires reflection on historical legacies and engagement
with current realities. We humbly encourage readers to
do the same.

milkweed.org

Milkweed Editions, an independent nonprofit literary publisher, gratefully acknowledges sustaining support from our board of directors, the McKnight Foundation, the National Endowment for the Arts, and many generous contributions from foundations, corporations, and thousands of individuals—our readers. This activity is made possible by the voters of Minnesota through a Minnesota State Arts Board Operating Support grant, thanks to a legislative appropriation from the Arts and Cultural Heritage Fund.

Interior design by Mary Austin Speaker
Typeset in Adobe Jenson Pro

Adobe Jenson was designed by Robert Slimbach for
Adobe and released in 1996. Slimbach based Jenson's
roman styles on a text face cut by fifteenth-century type
designer Nicolas Jenson, and its italics are based on type
created by Ludovico Vicentino degli Arrighi,
a late fifteenth-century papal scribe
and type designer.